MkLinux

Microkernel Linux for the Power Macintosh™

Apple Computer's Reference Release
of MkLinux for the Power Macintosh

Rich Morin, Editor

Published by Prime Time Freeware

Sponsored by Apple Computer, Inc.

MkLinux: Microkernel Linux for the Power Macintosh

(Apple Computer Reference Release of MkLinux for the Power Macintosh)

Rich Morin, Editor
Prime Time Freeware
ISBN 1-881957-24-1

CD-ROM packaging by Univenture, +1 800 992-9662.

Prime Time Freeware   info@ptf.com
370 Altair Way, #150   www.ptf.com
Sunnyvale, CA   +1 408 433-9662
94086 USA   +1 408 433-0727 (fax)

9 8 7 6 5 4

Contents

Part I - Tutorial Introduction

Part II - Software Reference

Part III - Hardware Reference

Dedication

To absent companions . . .

Foreword

This Foreword is adapted from an article that is scheduled for publication in the Linux Journal in early Spring of 1997. PTF thanks both the author and the magazine for permission to include this material.

Linux? On the Macintosh? With Mach?

Victoria L. Brown
Apple Computer, Inc.

Although MkLinux has been under development for a few years, it has only been available to the general public for a short while. Apple's first public announcement concerning MkLinux was made at the Free Software Foundation's First Conference on Freely Redistributable Software (February 1996).

Apple announced that it was supporting a project with the Open Software Foundation (OSF; now merged with X/Open to form The Open Group) to port Linux to a Mach base and to port Mach to a variety of Power Macintosh products. The project was initiated, sponsored, and funded by Apple Computer.

OSF provided the Mach 3.0 microkernel (developed by Carnegie Mellon University and the OSF Research Institute) and the engineering team to do the ports. (An OSF paper on MkLinux – *Linux on the OSF Mach 3 Microkernel* – was presented at the conference and is reproduced in the Mach Overview chapter.)

Apple's February announcement predicted that the first port of MkLinux would become available in the Summer of 1996. Exceeding expectations, the first general release of MkLinux (Developer Release 1) became available in May. MkLinux DR1 was followed by DR2, released in September 1996. DR3 is currently scheduled for release in Spring of 1997.

MkLinux releases tend to incorporate large numbers of changes. Hundreds of megabytes of new or changed material must be acquired, whether by FTP or CD-ROM. A complete re-installation is typically necessary. Consequently, full MkLinux releases are made on a relatively infrequent basis (only when warranted by a sufficiently large or fundamental set of changes).

Between releases, Apple issues minor updates via FTP. Some provide bug fixes; others introduce new, experimental features. In either case, they are meant to be used in conjunction with a specific MkLinux release.

What Is MkLinux?

At this point, you may be wondering exactly what MkLinux is. Does it run the Mac OS Finder? Does it run X11? Are all the commands I know and love available? For that matter, how is the name itself pronounced?

First things first: MkLinux is officially pronounced M K (em-kay) Linux, but is often pronounced McLinux. This is in line with Linux tradition, which permits Linux itself to be pronounced in any of several ways. (Li-nooks, Lie-nooks, and even Lee-nooks are quite commonly heard.)

In any event, MkLinux is a complete port of Linux, with a full set of GNU tools and accessories, including X11R6, running on top of the Mach micro-kernel. Hence, Mk (microkernel) Linux. Because MkLinux is really just Linux, it doesn't run the Finder (yet :-). On the other hand, it does run just about any Linux command you could imagine. (Commands which require Intel-based hardware are, of course, non-functional.)

A Mach Primer

The Mach microkernel provides an abstract layer onto which other operating systems can be ported. It also provides multiprocessor support, kernel-level thread support, distributed and cluster computing, and other interesting features. By porting Mach to the Power Macintosh, Apple has cleared the way for a variety of research and even commercial operating systems to run on the platform.

The Mach 3 microkernel was developed at Carnegie Mellon University. Since then, it has been enhanced extensively by the Open Software Foundation (OSF) Research Institute. MkLinux currently uses MK7.2, a variant of the Mach 3.0 microkernel, but there are prospects for inclusion of a more advanced microkernel.

The Mach microkernel performs only a small set of functions. It handles inter-process communication, low-level I/O (e.g., access to SCSI and other busses), memory management, and scheduling. Higher-level functions (file systems, networking, etc.) are performed by one or more "servers".

Mach servers are user-mode processes that provide all or part of an operating system's "personality". They do not talk directly to the underlying hardware; in general, no Mach process does that. Instead, they communicate with the Mach microkernel by means of "messages".

Thus, when **cat** performs a **write** system call, the interrupt is caught by the Mach microkernel. The relevant information is then packaged into a message and passed to the appropriate server. Some number of actions, interrupts, and messages then take place, involving only the microkernel and the relevant server(s). Only when the **write** has been accomplished (or fails), does the microkernel restart the **cat** process.

In MkLinux, as in nearly all Mach-based systems, the OS personality is provided by a "single server". This is Mach terminology for a single process that handles all of a given operating system's personality.

The FSF's Hurd, also based on Mach, uses a "multiple server" design, with a small number of processes sharing the OS duties. (We have received some interest, by the way, in porting the Hurd onto OSF Mach 3 alongside MkLinux. Could be interesting...)

The MkLinux Server

The server that MkLinux uses looks quite a bit like a standard Linux kernel. In fact, it *is* a copy of the Linux kernel, modified to use Mach's low-level functionality. In the first two Developer Releases, the MkLinux server was based on Linux 1.2.13. Recent updates to DR2, however, as well as the new

DR2.1, are based on Linux 2.0 (specifically, 2.0.28). This kernel has many new features, along with large improvements in performance and stability.

Operating system developers will be pleased to know that 2.0-based MkLinux allows more than one (e.g., Linux or Hurd) server to run at the same time. This is extremely convenient to anyone who wishes to debug a new server.

With this capability, you can start up the debug version alongside of the production version. If (when :-) the debug version goes down in flames, the system just continues to work, saving you a great deal of time and trouble. Not only that, you can simply "fire up" gdb and debug the second server as you would any ordinary application.

Linux Goodies

Operating system elitists (read, some kernel hackers) may disagree, but the rest of us know that a kernel, however wonderful, isn't enough. We need more: shells, utilities, a window system, and all those other little toys we've grown to love. Don't worry; MkLinux has everything you've come to love in Linux.

Based largely on the RedHat Linux distribution, and making heavy use of the RedHat Package Manager (RPM), the default MkLinux installation includes a full set of user commands, as well as the complete X11R6 Window system. Many other commands are available in RPM archives, either on the Apple MkLinux CD-ROM or by FTP from `ftp.mklinux.apple.com`.

In fact, a complete MkLinux system is anything but small or spartan. Even the Developer Releases are quite substantial. (The Installation Guide recommends 16 MB of RAM and at least 500 MB of dedicated disk space.)

So, Why Linux?

Need you ask? Linux is the overwhelming favorite among users of free UNIX clones. Linux provides UNIX features such as true multitasking, virtual memory, shared libraries, demand loading, TCP/IP networking, and many other advanced features. Versions of Linux have been ported to a wide variety of platforms, including other PowerPC-based computers, making the Power Macintosh port that much easier.

The Linux community is large, growing, active, and involved. This community promotes development and exchange of software and ideas, making it an excellent environment for a new OS product. And, last but not least, Linux is covered by the GNU General Public License, ensuring that Apple's contributions will not be used in some other vendor's proprietary product.

GNU... And Apple?!?

We have to admit, Apple and the GNU Project have had their differences in the past. Nor can we suggest that Apple has given up on the idea of proprietary software. So, it comes as a surprise to many (and a shock to some!) that Apple is openly funding a project to develop MkLinux and port it to the entire family of Power Macintosh systems.

Not only that; except for the chance to sell more Power Macintosh systems (a strong inducement indeed :-), Apple is not making any profit from the MkLinux port. Distribution and sales of the Apple MkLinux disc, as well as this product, are being handled by Prime Time Freeware.

In full compliance with the best freeware etiquette, Apple is releasing the source code for all of their Linux and Mach changes under the appropriate (GPL, OSF, etc.) licenses. The entire distribution, in fact, is available via anonymous FTP. Third parties are encouraged to mirror the site, create their own CD-ROM distributions, or share the software with their friends. This is free software at its finest.

Why Power Macintosh?

You may be asking yourself: "Why would I want to run Linux on Power Macintosh?" After all, the Linux community is overwhelmingly oriented toward Intel hardware. Why change?

For one thing, it's good for Apple and Apple enthusiasts. As noted above, Linux opens the door to a new Macintosh market. Many researchers and scientists, who might well find the Macintosh a useful tool, cannot justify the purchase of a second computer system. If their shop runs UNIX, a Macintosh just didn't fit in – until now!

University laboratories and dorm rooms are another target. With the availability of MkLinux, users can benefit from the best of both worlds: using Linux for research and batch data processing and Mac OS for graphical applications, desktop publishing, and much more. So, Apple may sell the machine, but you get the fun. Think of all those cool Mac OS applications, just waiting to be explored, not to mention the joy of using the Power Mac's multimedia capabilities under (Mk)Linux!

In keeping with Apple's traditions, the highly integrated Power Macintosh hardware greatly eases Linux system administration. Power Macs are delivered as complete systems. Thus, a Power Macintosh normally can run MkLinux "straight out of the box", without the addition of cards, chips, and other components. Because Power Macs use intelligent busses such as NuBus and PCI, the OS can deal with hardware configuration concerns such as DMA addressing and interrupt vectors.

In fact, as we tell folks at trade shows: "Once you've installed it, MkLinux is really just Linux. You'll have to give up a few things, of course – DMA vectors, IRQ settings, jumpers, incompatible BIOS code – but basically, it's just Linux..."

What About Intel?

By porting MkLinux to the Power Macintosh, Apple opens the doors for a new market, but that's only half of the story. As a bow to the Linux community's Intel orientation, Apple has also made sure that an Intel port of Mk-Linux is available. In fact, the Mklinux/Intel port was developed first and was completely funded by Apple. The Intel port is tracking the Power Macintosh version; although you may not see it prominently displayed on the Apple Web pages, it's still quite alive.

By porting MkLinux to the Intel platform, Apple also opens the door for Intel and Power Macintosh users to try each other's systems, trade software and ideas, and generally enlarge the Linux world. For instance, we expect some valuable and interesting interchange in PCI driver software and multimedia applications.

Nitty Gritty Details

OK, you're almost convinced. You understand why Apple is funding a Linux project, and you've begun to believe in Linux on the Power Macintosh. But it's still called a Developer Release. How complete is MkLinux? Are all Power Macintoshes supported? What's there, and, perhaps more important, what's not there? The following summary describes the MkLinux DR2 release with all posted updates (through early February 1997) applied:

Supported Machines:

> Power Macintosh 61xx, 71xx, 81xx, Power Computing 100 & 120; Power Macintosh 72xx, 75xx, 76xx, 82xx, 85xx, 95xx, PCI clones

MACH Version:	3.0 (MK7.2)
Linux Version:	2.0.28
Disk Space:	minimum 400 MB; recommended minimum 500 MB
RAM:	minimum 8 MB; recommended minimum 16 MB
SCSI:	Disk & CD-ROM; Jaz drives and (possibly) other removables
Serial:	DMA & Modem Control supported
Floppy, Audio:	Not Yet. (Coming soon!)
Video:	Motherboard Video or Video Card, including A/V and HPV card; no multiple screen support, yet; up to millions of colors.
X11 support:	X11R6.3; 1, 8, and 24-bit pixel depth support; no support yet for 16 bit
Mouse support:	3-button mice conforming to Apple's multi-button mouse protocol; 1-button mice use keyboard keys (Option-2, -3) to emulate the 2nd and 3rd buttons.
Ethernet:	Yes
TCP/IP:	Ethernet and PPP only
Appletalk:	supported over Ethernet via netatalk
NFS, SLIP/PPP:	supported
HFS:	Native filesystem support is provided

The first two MkLinux Developer Releases were fairly complete, in terms of the base operating system and command set, but were still lacking in a few areas. As noted above, these versions were based on Linux 1.2.13, a somewhat dated version of the Linux server. Linux 2.0 support has recently been added, however (officially as of the December 1996 update). The MkLinux kernel changes have been offered to Linus Torvalds for inclusion in future revisions of Linux; we hope they will be incorporated soon.

From the beginning, MkLinux has had full SCSI support, including the ability to mount (and eventually boot from) removable disks such as Iomega's Jaz. It supports a wide range of monitors connected to the motherboard video or the HPV and A/V cards. It includes serial support for DMA and modem control, plus support for SLIP and PPP connections, as well as Ethernet. The X11R6 implementation supports a wide range of multiple-button pointing devices, as long as they conform to Apple's ADB protocol.

Several things are still missing, to be sure. Both Audio and Floppy disk support are still in development. Serial support does not yet extend to printers. At this writing, multiple monitors are not supported; in fact, no NuBus or PCI bus cards are supported yet. Shared libraries are almost ready; they should be available in Developer Release 3.

To the dismay of many early adopters, MkLinux initially lacked support for most current Power Macintosh models. DR1 and (as shipped) DR2 supported only the NuBus, PowerPC 601-based systems (Power Macintosh 6100, 7100, 8100 series, Power Computing 100 and 120 clones). The Apple products were discontinued shortly before MkLinux was announced, making it impossible for users to buy a new system "for MkLinux".

Following the release of DR1, however, the Apple MkLinux Team posted a survey, asking the MkLinux user (and prospective user) community to help choose the next set of machines to be ported. Not surprisingly, the overwhelmingly popular choice was the latest and fastest family of machines – the PCI-bus, PowerPC 604-based systems (Power Macintosh 7200, 7500, 7600, 8200, 8500, 9500, and clones).

Things always take longer than hoped; DR2 was released in September, still without PCI support. We promised support by Christmas, however, and managed to keep our promise. The DR2 update in mid-December contained (beta) support for the aforementioned PCI-based machines, rolled in the 2.0 Linux server, and was a major hit with our long-waiting and patient MkLinux fans.

With PCI support well underway, the team can concentrate on supporting the remaining systems (primarily Performas and Powerbooks) and begin to think about the upcoming CHRP (Common Hardware Reference Platform) systems. The only difficult decision will be which to work on first.

Unfortunately, although many machines seem similar on the surface (and Apple's System Software teams do an excellent job at making them look the same!), they're really all a little bit different inside. So, it may take a while... But rest assured; the team is committed to making MkLinux available on all of the Power Macintosh platforms in time.

The History And The Team

MkLinux was started as the dream of Brett Halle, then manager of Apple's kernel team within the Modern OS department. With the blessings of Apple vice president Ike Nassi, Brett began sponsoring a handful of OSF Research Institute employees to port the Mach 3.0 microkernel, and Linux, to the first Power Macintosh platform. Several months into the project, the first Apple engineer, Michael Burg, came on board to work part-time on the MkLinux effort.

Shortly before the DR1 release, Apple decided that the project was worth a little more backing, and spun the two Apple employees off into their own, dedicated team. Apple's Leveraged Technologies Group is now up to five (!) employees (with two additional engineers at the OSF Research Institute) and hopes for reasonable growth in the future.

Unfortunately for our anxious and growing body of MkLinux fans, this is still a very small team. While we concentrate on porting the next series of Power Macintoshes, keeping our Web pages and FTP site up to date, and managing the whole project, many interesting developments are "resource-limited".

Fortunately, this is Linux, where "everything is done by someone else". The MkLinux Developer's Corner is a small but intrepid band of MkLinux programmers who are willing to take on (and complete!) needed projects. Our Developers Corner has provided us with the X11R6 port, netatalk, GNU-step for MkLinux, HFS filesystem utilities, and a number of other interesting and desirable additions. We're happy to count these developers as members of the MkLinux team.

Last, but not least, our thanks go to all the MkLinux users who bravely download and install each new update as it is posted. In a small internal project such as MkLinux, we don't have access to Apple's dedicated software testing organizations. We've tried to test and debug our Developer Releases and updates before they are released, but we rely on our user community to stress test our releases in a wide range of network environments and hardware configurations. We've been most impressed by the helpful comments, willingness to get involved, cogent bug reports, and sensible Email we've received from all of these folks.

You Can Join Our Team!

The MkLinux team currently numbers over 15 registered developers, some 4000 registered users, and 5000 mailing list subscribers. (We admit that some of the mailing list subscribers are also registered users :-) If you haven't joined our team, we'd be happy to welcome you.

Visit our web site (`www.mklinux.apple.com`) and look around, then join some email lists. We strongly recommend that you join mklinux-announce and mklinux-answers; these are moderated lists (low in volume, high in relevant information) which will keep you abreast of important events in the MkLinux community. The remaining (topical) groups provide a means for you to interact with other MkLinux developers and users, sharing ideas, problems, and solutions. See you on the net!

Preface

The Macintosh has been tied, historically, to a single operating system, known variously as the Finder, Macintosh OS, and lately, Mac OS. After more than a decade of careful, innovative design, Mac OS is acknowledged as an industry leader in simplicity of use and administration. Its clean, safe, and consistent user interface encourages exploration, whether by novices or experienced users.

Because Mac OS is so well tuned to the interactive needs of individual users, it has gained a substantial and loyal following among "the rest of us", its chosen audience. In particular, Mac OS has become the dominant operating system in the fields of commercial art, graphic design, etc.

Over roughly the same period of time, UNIX has been ported to almost every modern computer system. It is available for many personal computers, most scientific and technical workstations, and a variety of mainframes, supercomputers, and large-scale multiprocessor systems.

In contrast to Mac OS, which was developed by a single company, UNIX was developed by companies, universities, and research laboratories around the world. In the process, it acquired a diverse set of data analysis and manipulation tools, along with subsystems for document preparation, software development, and more.

Not surprisingly, UNIX has developed a large and dedicated following in the scientific and technical communities. UNIX systems are commonly used for software development, batch and multi-user operation, network servers, and so forth.

Mac OS is a proprietary operating system; its source code is available only within Apple. UNIX source code is available for license, but the cost is not insignificant. Consequently, neither operating system is available for casual inspection and/or modification by most programmers.

For more than a decade, however, the GNU Project has been assembling the components of the GNU system, a freely redistributable clone of UNIX. In addition, a recent court decision has made the vast majority of the source code base for "Berkeley UNIX" (4.4BSD) available to any and all interested parties.

Parallel development of major components such as Mach (CMU, OSF) and the X Window System (MIT), along with the efforts of hundreds of public-spirited programmers, have added dramatically to this base. As a result, interested programmers are free to work with complete operating systems (e.g., Linux, FreeBSD, and NetBSD) and a large body of add-on programs (e.g., perl, gcc, httpd, tex).

MkLinux is a natural outgrowth of these developments. It is based on Linux, so it can take advantage of the immense amount of freely redistributable source code that is available for Linux (and other UNIX-related) systems. At the same time, because of its Mach roots, it is able to expand the already substantial capabilities and portability of Linux. Finally, because it runs on the powerful and highly integrated Power Macintosh, it can bring new ease of installation and use to the Linux community.

Linux And MkLinux

MkLinux runs on Power Macintosh hardware, using the Mach microkernel to handle low-level resource allocation tasks. The Linux kernel is rebuilt as a user-mode "single server". How similar can such a system be to traditional Intel-based Linux? What problems should the aspiring MkLinux administrator, programmer, or user expect to encounter?

Once MkLinux is running, it is essentially indistinguishable from Linux. It has all the same commands, library functions, and system calls. Source code that builds and runs correctly on Intel-based Linux systems generally has few problems building and running on MkLinux. The most common problems – byte ordering and signed-character dependencies – are typically trivial to resolve.

There are some differences, to be sure. For instance, MkLinux is remarkably free of BIOS incompatibilities, conflicting DMA vectors and IRQs, and the host of jumper settings that seems to be required for Intel-based machines to operate. But then, we think you'll get used to these differences in time (:-).

Mac OS And MkLinux

Although Mac OS and MkLinux both run on Power Macintosh hardware, they have very different historical backgrounds, goals, and (in general) user communities. In fact, they are an interesting study in contrasts:

- Access to source code

  Mac OS source code is highly proprietary and very carefully protected. Even Apple engineers do not have totally free access to system code.

  MkLinux source code is free software. The source code may be examined, modified, and even incorporated into other software, as long as certain minimal restrictions are met.

- Administration

  Mac OS typically requires little or no system administration, save for the occasional backup. Network servers require some administration.

  Small (e.g., single-user) MkLinux systems require little administration. Larger systems tend to require more administrative effort, depending on the number of users and services supported.

- Application software

  Mac OS does not include very many bundled applications. Macintosh Performa systems remedy this, including a large amount of software. Thousands of commercial applications are available for Mac OS.

  The Mac OS community has developed a large amount of shareware and freely redistributable applications. In general, this is distributed only in binary form.

  MkLinux includes hundreds of commands, ranging from data analysis and document preparation tools to a complete software development environment. No commercial applications are available at present, but some are reported to be on the way.

MkLinux is able to use a wealth of Linux (and more generally, UNIX) freeware, which is available as source code.

- Learning curve

  Mac OS has a very shallow learning curve. Mac OS users are famous for their habit of running applications long before they read the manual.

  MkLinux has a long and steep learning curve, supported by a vast body of online and printed documentation. Novice users who ask too many questions are typically advised to "Read The Fine Manual" (RTFM).

- Multiple users

  Mac OS is a single-user operating system; only one person may use the computer at a given time.

  MkLinux is capable of supporting dozens or even hundreds of users at the same time, limited only by the hardware's speed and memory capacity.

- Multitasking

  Mac OS does not currently support pre-emptive multitasking. Each application must tell Mac OS when it is willing to be interrupted.

  MkLinux supports fully pre-emptive multitasking. Programs may be interrupted by the system, re-scheduled, and even swapped out.

- Network support

  Mac OS systems can share resources (e.g., files and devices) with each other and with systems which emulate Apple's protocols. By means of third-party programs, Mac OS systems can support FTP, HTTP, PPP, Telnet, and other networking protocols.

  MkLinux can share files with other NFS-capable systems. MkLinux has built-in support for most common networking protocols.

- Networked applications

  Mac OS and its applications are not, in general, designed to be used over a network. X Window servers are available from third-party vendors.

Both the MkLinux command-line interface and the X Window System support interactive use of applications over the network.

- Origins

Mac OS was developed (and is still owned) by Apple Computer.

MkLinux is the result of more than a decade of collaboration, involving AT&T, commercial vendors, research laboratories, universities, and interested individuals. Although the MkLinux source code contains many copyright notices, the owners place few restrictions on its use.

- Portability

Mac OS was developed to run on the Motorola 68000 series of processors, using specific sets of support chips. It has since been ported to use other support chips and to run on the PowerPC processor (largely in emulated mode).

Macintosh Application Environment (MAE) is a software application that provides a virtual Macintosh environment in an X window to users of selected Hewlett-Packard and Sun workstations. Through 68LC040 emulation and native extensions, MAE lets users run off-the-shelf Mac OS-compatible, 680x0-based business productivity applications. MAE provides significant interoperability with other Mac OS-based systems in the enterprise, while giving users the ability to easily manipulate UNIX files and execute UNIX applications from within a Macintosh environment. Users can also copy and paste text and graphics between UNIX and Mac OS-compatible applications.

MkLinux currently runs on Intel and Power Macintosh hardware; other ports are quite feasible. The Linux kernel (upon which MkLinux is based) runs on a wide range of hardware. And, of course, there is some flavor of UNIX for almost any modern computer system.

- Real-Time support

Mac OS applications are free to retain control of the processor for as long as they need it. This lets them meet essentially any needed real-time requirements.

MkLinux does not currently have real-time support; future versions are expected to gain access to real-time features of the Mach kernel.

- Security

Mac OS has very little explicit support for security. Anyone who has physical access to a Mac OS system has complete authority to make any desired (or other :-) changes. Because Mac OS has no internal firewalls, it is quite susceptible to attacks by viruses, trojan horses, etc.

On the other hand, because Mac OS does not provide support for remote logins or many network services, Mac OS systems are relatively safe from attack over network links.

MkLinux has a comprehensive and reasonably robust security system, with internal firewalls, user accounts, file and directory permissions, network access controls, etc. For proper security, however, all of these features must be carefully administered.

- Structure

Mac OS is a rather monolithic system, with very little externally visible structure. Modifications to system behavior are made by installing Extensions (e.g, drivers) and by installing and/or interacting with Control Panels.

MkLinux consists of thousands of files, any of which can be examined, modified, or replaced as desired. Typically, modifications to system behavior are made by editing textual control files.

- User interface

Mac OS and its applications are strongly oriented toward graphical user interfaces, making heavy use of pull-down menus, dialog boxes, and mouse interaction.

Mac OS is highly optimized for interactive use, but has little support for "batch processing". Thus, users can perform simple tasks quickly, but may find themselves repeating actions for larger tasks. Most users tend to stay in single programs for extended periods of time.

Note: Mac OS programmers should be aware of Apple's **Open Scripting Architecture (OSA)**, a powerful cross-platform messaging and scripting system that can support multiple scripting languages. OSA has three basic components: the Apple events messaging system, the Apple events object model, and one or more scripting systems.

MkLinux has a command-line interface, supplemented by the X Window System, a mouse-driven windowing environment. Only a few MkLinux applications use the mouse.

MkLinux is highly optimized for batch use. MkLinux users frequently make use of "shell scripts" and "wild cards", greatly reducing the number of commands that have to be typed. Nonetheless, a typical MkLinux session may involve dozens or even hundreds of commands.

Audience

MkLinux isn't an attempt to dislodge Mac OS from its traditional audience; that would be silly. It can, however, open up the Power Macintosh to additional users and to additional forms of use. Many computer science students and programming professionals will be very happy that they can run Linux on their Power Macintosh systems.

By the same token, MkLinux is not for everyone. Casual computer users, users of commercial packages, and game enthusiasts will not find much in MkLinux to delight them. On the other hand, some (adventurous) users will find MkLinux very pleasant, indeed.

The target MkLinux user is interested in gaining access to the world of Linux software, while retaining the benefits of the well-designed, powerful, and highly-integrated Power Macintosh platform. This user probably owns at least one Power Macintosh, but may purchase one just for use with MkLinux.

We expect many students and computer professionals to use MkLinux as an economical way to experiment with Linux. The MkLinux distribution is very economical (even free, via FTP). The additional hardware (typically, 500 MB of disk storage) is very cheap, especially when compared to the cost of a dedicated system. This sort of user may alternate between Mac OS and MkLinux use, depending on the nature of the tasks to be performed.

Some network administrators may also choose MkLinux for LAN servers (compute, file, etc.), Internet servers (FTP, WWW, etc.), and other systems of that nature. MkLinux combines:

- the strengths of traditional UNIX (preemptive multitasking, multi-user support, security controls, etc.),

- the low cost and source availability of Linux,

- the portability, programming features, and robustness of Mach,

- and the known reliability of Power Macintosh hardware.

Why Mach, Linux, Power Macintosh?

MkLinux combines several disparate technologies. It is reasonable to ask why these particular technologies were chosen and why, in any case, they should be put together in this fashion.

The Mach microkernel is efficient, powerful, and mature. Originally developed by Carnegie Mellon University, it now forms the basis for several commercial and research operating systems. Mach provides (at least potentially) features such as:

- Portability to several platforms

- Real-Time capabilities

- Robustness

- Scalability (SMP, clusters, etc.)

- Security

- Unique OS debugging capabilities (e.g., multiple Linux servers)

- User-mode system extensions

Linux is a popular and rapidly developing "clone" of UNIX, based on the aforementioned GNU system. Linux source code, being protected by the GNU General Public License, cannot be "taken proprietary" by commercial enterprises. Many Linux programmers consider this to be an important part of their reason for contributing development work to the Linux community.

The Power Macintosh is a very widely deployed system. Several million systems are already in place and millions more are installed every year. The Power Mac is particularly popular in the research and higher education communities, where dozens of Power Mac systems can be found in virtually every building.

In addition, the Power Macintosh platform's integrated nature allows it to support true plug-and-play installation. Intel-based personal computers may have several busses, use any combination of controller cards, and in general offer a wealth of opportunities for confusion and error. The Power Mac, in contrast, is delivered as a reasonably complete system, with few additions that are likely to cause problems.

Finally, the Power Macintosh is based on the PowerPC CPU architecture. The price/performance ratio of the PowerPC is already far better than that of the Pentium; this disparity will only grow larger over time. Several key differences contribute to this disparity:

- Competition – The PowerPC, although standardized in architecture, is being designed and produced in a competitive manner. This encourages innovation, while keeping PowerPC prices far below those of Intel's proprietary offerings.

- Historical baggage – Unlike the Pentium, the PowerPC is not required to emulate a series of processors going nearly two decades into the past.

- RISC vs CISC – The RISC architecture of the PowerPC allows it to take advantage of hardware developments that the Pentium cannot.

- Simplicity – The PowerPC uses far fewer transistors than the Pentium does for its base logic. This translates to lower power consumption, smaller die sizes, more room for cache, and many other benefits.

In summary, MkLinux brings together good hardware, good software, and a pair of substantial and enthusiastic user communities.

Product Abstract

MkLinux: Microkernel Linux for the Power Macintosh is a combination of three items:

- The Apple MkLinux disc – a MkLinux snapshot, with source code

- The PTF Reference disc – a collection of Linux, Mach, NeXT, and Power Macintosh documentation, with other "added value" from PTF

- The book – this introductory and reference handbook

By keeping the snapshot and documentation on separate discs, we are able to update them separately. This should prove very useful over the next year or so, as new kernels and documentation become available. By keeping in touch with the MkLinux mailing lists and Web site, you will be able to decide which of these updates you wish to obtain.

In any event, the combined product is Apple's Reference Release of MkLinux for the Power Macintosh. As such, it must serve as a resource for MkLinux users and programmers and act as a common point of contact for the MkLinux community. Although it may be used as an operating system release, it is not intended to be a "commercial OS", with the polish and support that would imply. Instead, it is a well-annotated snapshot of a "Work In Progress", with more snapshots to come.

Like many products, this one is a compromise. It cannot be, for instance, a complete guide to any of the technologies found in MkLinux, let alone all of them at once. So, it attempts to:

- get new MkLinux users started, with a minimum of pain

- provide potentially useful reference information

- provide an organized set of pointers to other resources

Space on paper is much more expensive than CD-ROM bandwidth. Instead of trying to print up hundreds of pages of Apple, Linux, Mach, and NeXT documentation, we are providing most of this material in online form. This should let our users read, search, and if desired, print any of material that is relevant to their needs (while saving a few trees for our children!).

Updates, Patches, Etc.

Because of the evolving nature of MkLinux (and Linux, in general), this cannot be a "Final Release". So, it provides a snapshot of the current release, while providing opportunities for users to acquire patches and updates (via FTP), ancillary information (via WWW), and complete new snapshots (via CD-only distributions and/or FTP).

By planning for this sort of extension, we hope to make this book last longer than it otherwise might (despite the moving target MkLinux is certain to present). So, for instance, we have included information on hardware configurations that current MkLinux versions do not support. Apple has promised that future versions will support these configurations, so the information should eventually be quite useful.

To keep up with current bug fixes, updates, and other developments, visit the MkLinux Web site (`www.mklinux.apple.com`) on a regular basis. While you're there, join the mailing lists that seem most relevant. Be sure, in any case, to join the **announce** and **answers** groups, as they carry critical information from Apple's MkLinux team.

You should also visit PTF's MkLinux Pages (`www.ptf.com/mklinux`). We use these pages to give useful pointers and other information, reprint articles, report on MkLinux news, and (of course :-) announce products.

Plans And Prospects

The current version (DR3) supports most Power Macintosh systems, including most Power Macintosh systems, many PowerPC-based Performas, and some PowerBooks. Apple continues to port the MkLinux to new systems as they emerge, as well as filling in some of the empty spots in the line-up.

Apple's MkLinux team has taken on the responsibility for this effort. With members of The Open Group Research Institute, they are porting the Mach kernel to a wide range of Power Macintosh systems, adding support for common devices, and generally solving a large number of low-level technical problems.

The MkLinux Team is also looking at areas, such as ease of use and hardware support, where MkLinux can take advantage of traditional Apple and Macintosh strengths. The team's access to internal Apple information is of course very valuable to these sorts of efforts.

With the advent of MacOS X, the Mach microkernel has become of greatly heightened interest to Apple. MkLinux has served Apple well as an experimental Mach-based platform. As Mac OS X develops, we may see it returning the favor, in terms of device drivers, microkernel enhancements, etc.

Finally, the team performs a variety of support functions: answering email from users, maintaining a bug database and several email lists, and running a very substantial Web site. Consequently, the team members are far too busy to port large numbers of application programs to MkLinux, let alone track all of the new releases and updates that come along.

Fortunately, this is Linux, where "everything is done by someone else". The needed application ports are being handled by a combination of commercial vendors and interested individuals. (See the web site for information on how to volunteer!)

Prime Time Freeware plans to track these ports, putting them into future snapshots, as appropriate. PTF has some ideas of its own about adding value to MkLinux, stay tuned (`info@ptf.com`) to find out what they are...

Apple has made no formal statements about Mac OS interaction. Linux is already capable of handling Mac OS file systems (HFS) and supporting AppleTalk, so MkLinux gets these capabilities for free. Launching Mac OS applications and emulating the Finder, however, are a lot trickier. It will be interesting to see what develops...

Who "We" Are

This book is largely written in the first-person plural, using the editorial "we". In practice, most of the material in the book was:

- provided by Apple and/or OSF staff, with attribution,

- abstracted from published Apple documentation,

- or written by the Editor, Rich Morin.

Nonetheless, final editorial responsibility rests with the Editor. Any mistakes are his responsibility; any opinions expressed in the unattributed portions of this work are likely to be his, and should not be attributed to Apple, The Open Group, or other parties. Please address any corrections, suggestions, or other comments to Rich Morin (rdm@ptf.com).

- *MkLinux*
- *Mach*
- *Linux*
- *Documentation*

Acknowledgements

This product, more than most, is the result of a collaborative effort. It is, in fact, the result of many layers of collaboration. Although it is impossible to detail all of the contributors specifically, a few notes may give the reader an idea of the nature and scope of this far-reaching cooperation.

MkLinux

The most recent collaboration resulted in MkLinux itself. Apple Computer, largely in the persons of Brett Halle and Ike Nassi, came up with the idea of sponsoring The Open Group Research Institute (RI) to port Linux to Mach and Mach to the Power Macintosh. Nick Stephen and François Barbou des Places were the primary RI staff involved in this effort, but contributions have also been made by Franklin Reynolds and Gary Thomas. Apple also looked the other way while Brett Halle and Michael Burg spent many hours writing drivers, porting applications, and fixing bugs.

After a while, Apple asked PTF if we wanted to get involved. For a firm of PTF's size, getting into a contractual arrangement with Apple is a bit like dancing with an elephant. Apple's Larry Lowe helped us draft a mutually agreeable contract, calmed our fears, and generally made the experience very tolerable. Jeff Roberts also worked with us, telling us what Apple could (and could not) do to publicize MkLinux. The efforts of these two gentlemen were critical to our getting involved in the project and have been extremely useful to the present day.

Vicki Brown came on board about then. Vicki maintains PTF's MkLinux Pages (www.ptf.com/mklinux). In addition, Vicki wrote the Foreword and major sections of several chapters of this book. As the editor's spouse and a former member of Apple's MkLinux team, Vicki has gotten a double dose of MkLinux, so her efforts (and tolerance) are doubly laudable.

The Apple MkLinux Team, although miniscule, gets occasional unofficial help. Gilbert Coville was the buildmeister for DR3, but Michael Burg,

Mark Hatle, Brad Midgley, Gary Thomas, and Eryk Vershen helped to fill in some major gaps; their efforts are greatly appreciated by all of us.

Finally, MkLinux would not have anything like its current level of polish without the amazingly gracious assistance of the stalwart hackers who have been trying out a seemingly endless series of Developer Releases and updates. These folks continue to send in bug reports, questions, and useful suggestions, accompanied by a very minimal level of flames. Their help was absolutely critical to MkLinux in its early days. It will become even more important as the task list shifts from kernel hacking to driver writing, application porting, and overall system maintenance.

Mach

The possibility of porting *anything* to Mach depended, of course, on the existence of Mach itself. David Golub, Randall Dean, Alessandro Forin, and Richard Rashid of Carnegie Mellon University wrote *Unix as an Application Program*, the paper that announced the Mach effort, but the RI and many others can claim substantial credit, as well. For more information on Mach (and Mach contributors), see the Software Bibliography chapter.

Linux

Linux is named for Linus Torvalds, the principal author of the kernel. As he would be quick to point out, however, the kernel is the joint creation of dozens of volunteer programmers, in more or less formal capacities. If you care to look at the Linux source code, you will see some of these names.

More generally, Linux consists of far more than the kernel itself. It contains many thousands of files, including commands, control files, libraries, and more. Some of this material was developed by the Linux community, per se, but the vast majority was not.

Most of the commands and libraries found in MkLinux are the result of work by the Free Software Foundation's GNU Project. This project, which has been under way for more than a decade, has produced an immense body of software and documentation. Much of this software emulates traditional UNIX functionality (frequently with improved features and performance). The remainder adds facilities never found in traditional UNIX systems.

Linux also borrows heavily from the efforts of the BSD (Berkeley UNIX) and X Window System communities, as well as the many other freeware authors who have written so much code for the UNIX community. The particular version of Linux found in MkLinux is largely based on materials provided by Red Hat Software.

Finally, the entire UNIX community owes an immense debt to AT&T and its inspired band of early developers. The insights these folks brought to the UNIX environment continue to inspire the best efforts in C and UNIX today.

Documentation

We are particularly grateful to the technical writers who have helped to make all this code accessible and understandable. MkLinux users are very well served by the books, magazines, and volunteer documentation efforts of the Apple, GNU, Linux, Mach, UNIX, and X communities.

In addition, our own attempts to produce clean, correct, and understandable documentation have been greatly assisted by the efforts of the Apple Computer and Open Group Research Institute staff members mentioned above, as well as volunteers such as Rick Auricchio, Gene Dronek, Phil Glenn, Doug McNutt, Ann Reynolds, Adam Richter, and Isaac Wingfield. As always, however, the editor bears full responsibility for any errors or omissions.

Chapter 1:

- *Product Overview*
- *Some History*
- *The UNIX Dialectic*
- *Richard M. Stallman*
- *Linux And The GNU Project*
- *Legal Battles, Etc.*
- *Convergence?*

Introduction

Most users will want to install MkLinux immediately, then return later to whichever documentation is of most interest. If you are new to Linux, however, we suggest that you spend a few minutes looking over the introductory material in this book. A little light reading now could save you a great deal of trouble down the road.

Product Overview

This product is made up of several interrelated components, stored on a book and two CD-ROMs. The book contains, primarily:

- Help for installation and initial use

- Hints on system administration

- Selected information on advanced topics

- Pointers to additional resources

Note: In the initial version, both CD-ROMs are snapshots of Mac OS hard disks. This may change in future releases; see the online notes for details.

The "Apple MkLinux disc" is an installable snapshot of a distribution:

- Several useful Apple utilities, including a hard disk formatter

- The MkLinux installation program

- A complete, installable MkLinux system, including source code

- Archives of optional software packages, in executable form

The "PTF Reference disc" is largely occupied by online reference material:

- Adobe Acrobat Reader, Apple's SimpleText, etc.

- Apple reference documents, primarily in Acrobat's Portable Document Format (PDF) or HyperText Markup Language (HTML) format

- Linux, Mach, and NeXT documentation, in assorted formats

- Other additions (documentation, etc.) from Prime Time Freeware

Some History

The following quote, from Dennis Ritchie and Ken Thompson's landmark paper, *The UNIX Time-Sharing System*, rather understates the current situation. On the other hand, knowing that it was written in 1978, we can appreciate both its prescience and its charming modesty:

> UNIX is a general-purpose, multi-user, interactive operating system ... It offers a number of features seldom found even in larger computer systems, including:
>
> (i)　　A hierarchical file system incorporating demountable volumes,
>
> (ii)　　Compatible file, device, and inter-process I/O,
>
> (iii)　The ability to initiate asynchronous processes,
>
> (iv)　System command language selectable on a per-user basis,
>
> (v)　　Over 100 subsystems including a dozen languages,
>
> (vi)　High degree of portability.

Bell Laboratories' withdrawal from the Multics project left Ken Thompson and Dennis Ritchie, among others, without access to a time-sharing system. Fortunately for all of us, Ken and Dennis had the energy, initiative, and creativity to do something about it.

Equally fortunately, their managers and colleagues assisted and supported their efforts. This early crew of UNIX users established a tone and a way of doing things that continues in the better parts of UNIX (and Linux) to this day. Much of the power of MkLinux is a direct result of decisions made by the early UNIX programmers.

It may be a bit daunting, but try to imagine the environment these folks had to work with. Instead of a bit-mapped screen, picture a ten character per second teletype machine with a handy (!) paper-tape reader/punch.

No soft-touch keyboard on this baby; these keys go Ker-CHUNK! (It has been suggested that the awkward nature of these early keyboards was largely responsible for the fabled brevity of UNIX command names.)

For your multi-megabyte memory system, substitute about that many kilobytes of core memory. Perform equally drastic surgery on the disk space.

Now think about writing an operating system for this turkey. Lessee now, the first things we'll need are what, a cross-assembler and a program loader? Yeah, we can assemble the code down the hall and carry over the paper tapes. Once we get that working, we can start on a file system...

Then, step by step, claw your way up to the sort of system described in the quote above, moving to better hardware when it is made available. This sort of thing is said to build character, but we applaud the character of these early pioneers, however they came by it!

After a fairly brief incubation period, UNIX emerged from the Labs. It was not a commercial, supported operating system; far from it! Instead, it was a source code tape, a license agreement, and the Lab's best wishes. (Not too different from the present-day situation with MkLinux, for that matter. :-)

Possibly in response to this rather complete lack of formal support, UNIX hackers in laboratories and universities around the world got used to fixing their own bugs, writing their own tools, and helping each other out. This tradition, which is largely missing from today's binary-only commercial UNIX systems, endures today in the freeware (e.g., Linux) community.

The UNIX Dialectic

With so many people doing UNIX development, it is not surprising that multiple solutions were developed to many of the same problems. Human nature being what it is, it was all too frequently "impossible" for these differences to be reconciled.

Complicating the issue somewhat, AT&T changed the licensing terms on UNIX, making it much more expensive for license-holders to upgrade than to stick with the version(s) they already had. This hardened divisions that already existed, forming the basis for the current BSD/SYSV schism.

Although the differences in UNIX versions have bedeviled programmers and users alike for nearly two decades, they also have a positive side. With two major (and many minor) versions of UNIX around, there has been plenty of room for experimentation and intellectual interchange.

Developer conferences put on by vendors of proprietary operating systems tend to rather one-way in nature. Vendors announce and demonstrate their wonderful new technology. Audience members may complain, but do not have any sort of veto capability. More to the point, they don't have copies of the source code!

UNIX conferences, in contrast, are chock full of hackers telling each other about the wonderful new ways they have found to "improve" the kernel or some other part of UNIX. Heated arguments can develop over these ideas, though a tradition of academic respect tends to prevent outright violence.

This ferment has led to the creation of thousands of pages of papers and untold numbers of lines of source code. More to the point, it has polished and honed UNIX into the sturdy, powerful system it is today. Consequently, although we support standardization most heartily, we are equally fervent in our desire to see this intellectual anarchy continue!

Richard M. Stallman

The existence of free UNIX-like systems today is largely due to the idealism of Richard M. Stallman (**rms**), who in the 1980s worked persistently towards this goal, even though most of us thought it was an impossible dream. By doing a large part of the job himself, he showed us it wasn't too far to aim for, and then we could do the rest.

The free software community owes a tremendous debt to this pioneering work. rms has made fundamental contributions to the technical, organizational, and legal aspects of free software. It is unlikely that the free software community would have developed in anything like its current form, to say nothing of its current size and robust state of health, without him.

rms has written (and overseen the development of) immense amounts of free software, including substantial and innovative software systems. GNU Emacs and the GNU C Compiler (GCC) are just two examples of his work. The utility and overall quality of this software is so high that it is often used by commercial developers in preference to proprietary software.

rms founded the Free Software Foundation and the GNU Project, creating an organizational framework for collecting, developing, and distributing free software. The mission of the project was the creation of the GNU system: a freely redistributable, UNIX-like operating system. To this end, the project created many dozens of commands, ranging from trivial to very complex, and is now working on an advanced Mach-based kernel, known as the Hurd.

By instigating and promoting the use of the GNU **General Public License** (**GPL**), rms has changed the legal foundations of free software. The GPL allows individuals and organizations to examine, use, and modify the free software it covers. It even allows companies such as PTF to sell collections of free software.

The GPL does not, however, allow anyone (save, in general, the original author) to distribute binaries without source code, modify the licensing terms, or in any other way convert free software into proprietary products.

It is important to realize that the Linux operating system, more commonly known as Linux, is really a Linux-flavored version of the GNU system, with historical roots going back more than a decade. GNU utilities form a large fraction of the code of every Linux system; without these, it is very unlikely that Linux would exist.

It is also important to understand *why* rms and his compatriots did all the hard work of writing compilers, assemblers, and libraries. After all, much of this work is not glamorous computer science!

Although each of the GNU developers has his or her own motivation, rms is motivated by the belief that proprietary software is inimical to good will in society; that the presence of software on his system which he is forbidden to share with his neighbors prevents him from living ethically.

By writing software, founding organizations, and establishing a legal basis for protecting free software, rms has changed the landscape of the computer community. We all owe rms (and all the other GNU contributors) a debt of gratitude.

How can we pay this debt? rms says, "The best way to thank us for writing GNU is to write more of it. Write a new free application that does a substantial job which no free software exists for – and then we can thank you too."

Linux And The GNU Project

The remainder of this section is reprinted, with permission, from a short article of the same name. It summarizes the GNU (and to a large degree, our) perspective on Linux. We think it is well worth reading...

Linux And The GNU Project

Richard M. Stallman
The GNU Project

Many computer users run a GNU system every day, without realizing it. Through a peculiar turn of events, the version of GNU which is widely used today is more often known as "Linux", and many users are not aware of the extent of its connection with the GNU project.

There really is a Linux; it is a kernel, and these people are using it. But you can't use a kernel by itself; a kernel is useful only as part of a whole system. The system in which Linux is typically used is a modified variant of the GNU system – a Linux-based GNU system.

Many users are not fully aware of the distinction between the kernel, which is Linux, and the whole system, which they also call "Linux". The ambiguous use of the name doesn't contribute to understanding.

Programmers generally know that Linux is a kernel. But since they have generally heard the whole system called "Linux" as well, they often assume that there must be a good reason for this. For example, some believe that once Linus Torvalds finished writing the kernel, his friends looked around for other available free software, and just happened to find everything necessary to make a UNIX-like system.

What they found was no accident – it was the GNU system. The available free software added up to a complete system because the GNU project had been working since 1984 to make one. The GNU Manifesto set forth the goal of developing a free UNIX-like system, and after more than a decade of work, we have one.

Most free software projects have the goal of developing a particular program for a particular job. For example, Linus Torvalds set out to write a UNIX-like kernel (Linux); Donald Knuth set out to write a text formatter (TEX); Rob Scheiffler set out to develop a window system (X). It's natural to measure the contribution of this kind of project by specific programs that came from the project.

If the GNU project were a project of this kind, and its contribution were measured in this way, what conclusions would follow? One CD-ROM vendor counted how much of their "Linux distribution" was GNU software. They found that GNU software was the largest single contingent, around 28% of the total source code, and this included some of the essential major components without which there could be no system. Linux itself was about 3%.

So if you wanted to pick a name for the system based on credit for the programs in the system, that name would be "GNU".

But choosing the name in this way would overlook a fundamental distinction. The GNU project was not a project to develop specific software. It was not a project to develop a C compiler, although we developed one. It was not a project to develop a text editor, although we did so. The GNU project's aim was to develop *a complete free UNIX-like system*. And that is what we have done, more or less – with many people's help.

Many people have made major contributions to the free software in the system, and they all deserve credit. But the reason it is *a system* – and not just a collection of useful programs – is because the GNU project set out to make it one. We chose what programs to write based on what was needed to get a *complete* free system. We wrote essential but unexciting major components, such as the assembler and the C library, because you can't have a complete free system without them.

By the early 90's, when Linux was ready, we had put together the whole system, aside from the kernel (and we were working on a kernel, the GNU Hurd, which runs on Mach). So it was possible to put Linux, a free kernel, together with the GNU system which had everything but the kernel, to make a complete free system.

Putting them together sounds simple, but it was not a trivial job. The GNU C library had to be changed substantially. And integrating a complete system as a distribution that would work "out of the box" was a big job, too. It required addressing the issue of how to install and boot the system – a problem we had not tackled, because we hadn't yet reached that point. The peo-ple who developed the various system distributions made a substantial contribution. Seen in perspective, their contribution was to combine Linux and the GNU system to produce a Linux-based modified GNU system.

Aside from GNU, one other project has independently produced a free UNIX-like operating system. This system is known as BSD, and it was developed at UC Berkeley. The BSD developers were inspired by the example of the GNU Project, and occasionally encouraged by GNU activists, but their actual work had little overlap with GNU. BSD systems today use some GNU software, just as GNU systems use some BSD software; but taken as wholes, they are two different systems which evolved separately. A free operating system that exists today is most likely either a GNU system or a BSD system.

We use Linux-based GNU systems in the GNU project today, and we encourage you to use them too. But please don't confuse people by using the name "Linux" ambiguously. Linux is the kernel, one of the essential major components of a system. The system is GNU.

Legal Battles, Etc.

Although UNIX System V adopted many of the advances made by the BSD community, the reverse was not the case. Indeed, the vast majority of the BSD releases was written by universities and research laboratories and was not, in fact, descended from the original UNIX source code base.

At some point, it became apparent that a relatively small amount of AT&T licensed source code was preventing free distribution of the entire 4.xBSD system. The folks at UC Berkeley's Computer Science Research Group (UCB CSRG) reacted to this situation in a characteristically upfront manner.

They performed triage on the code base, dividing it (roughly) into clean, doubtful, and dirty. The clean code was released (in BSD NET1). The doubtful code was re-examined, cleaned up, and released (in NET2). The dirty code was recapitulated or, in some cases, ignored.

AT&T brought suit, alleging that CSRG was giving away material covered by trade secret, unpublished copyrights, etc. To make a long (and rather interesting) story short, they lost. CSRG then published 4.4BSD-Lite, an almost complete (and freely redistributable!) subset of 4.4BSD.

Meanwhile, Linus Torvalds was off writing his own kernel, Linux. Many OS hackers, tired of waiting for the AT&T/UCB legal battle to sort itself out, decided to get involved with Linux, instead. Thus, by the time 4.4BSD-Lite emerged, a healthy and popular competitor was already in place.

NET1, NET2, and 4.4BSD-Lite are the basis for the current raft of BSDish UNIX clones: 386BSD, FreeBSD, NetBSD, OpenBSD, etc. They also supply a large part of the application code found in today's Linux systems. Finally, Apple's Mac OS X is largely based on 4.4BSD-Lite technology. Look at any current UNIX (or clone) system, in fact, and you will find a great deal of BSD-derived technology.

Convergence?

The UNIX community has had a long history of incompatible programming interfaces, proprietary user interfaces, and other compatibility problems. It is unclear whether the current organizational arrangement will resolve any more of the problems than previous ones have.

The Open Group, formed out of X/Open and the Open Software Foundation, is the current owner of the name "UNIX" and the POSIX standards which attempt to define it. Most commercial operating system vendors are looking for ways in which they can adapt and then certify their systems for POSIX compliance.

The free software community has been very supportive of standardization in general and POSIX in particular. Until recently, however, few freeware releases could be certified, due to the high cost of the POSIX certification test suite.

Fortunately, this situation has changed. The U.S. Government's National Institute of Standards and Technology (NIST) has released a free version of their Federal Information Processing Standard (FIPS) 151-2 compliance test software, which tests for compliance with a superset of POSIX. Over time, this should result in POSIX certification of most freeware UNIX releases.

Chapter 2:

Preparation

Unlike Intel-based Linux systems, MkLinux has few requirements that aren't met by standard system hardware. Basically, if MkLinux has been ported to your system, you won't need to add much in the way of new hardware. Nor, in general, will you need to spend much time preparing your system. A bit of disk formatting is all you need to do.

System Requirements

MkLinux requires a Power Macintosh (or equivalent) system with at least eight megabytes of RAM (found on all Power Macintosh systems) and 100 MB of free disk space. For best results, you should have at least 16 MB of RAM and 500 MB or more of free disk space, preferably on a separate drive.

DR3 supports most Power Macintosh (including Performa and PowerBook) systems; many clones also work, but add-in boards are unlikely to function. Support for IDE drives is spotty; USB is not supported at all. For current information, see the MkLinux web site (`www.mklinux.apple.com`).

File System Basics

By default, each Mac OS disk drive contains a single **file system**. MkLinux disk drives, in contrast, frequently have multiple file systems, each located on its own physical disk **partition**. In particular, the main system drive will have at least two partitions and may well have three or more. The added partitions allow the administrator to:

- back up selected subsets of the system data.

- increase the efficiency of file allocation on very large disk drives (by reducing the minimum block size).

- prevent problem areas (e.g., spool directories) from causing the rest of the system to run out of space.

A skeletal MkLinux system can be made to work in 100 MB of disk space; however, this will be almost unusable for most purposes.We recommend a minimum of 500 MB (and preferably, more) if you intend to load a full system, install additional software, add user accounts, re-build kernels, etc.

You may use **Apple HD SC Setup** or any disk partitioner that can create A/UX type partitions. Your target drive may have any legal SCSI ID (0-6). The MkLinux distribution also contains a copy of **Apple Drive Setup**; this can be used to initialize and partition IDE drives.

Note: Although MkLinux uses the Linux EXT2 file system format, the partition map is not compatible with Intel-based Linux systems. Upcoming versions of MkLinux may address this issue, however.

Existing Macintosh drives usually come pre-configured such that the entire drive is taken up with one or more Mac OS (HFS format) file systems. This does not work for MkLinux, which uses a number of file systems, typically in its own formats (e.g., EXT2 or swap). Consequently, your disk must be partitioned properly in order for you to install and use MkLinux.

Note: Partitioning is a tricky business. Be sure to save any important files that are on the drive (programs, data files, etc.) *before* you try to repartition the disk!

Unfortunately, at this writing, partitioning is a manual process that must be performed before you begin the actual installation. The process you will use to create the disk partitions will vary, depending on the utility you are using. MkLinux currently uses the same basic partitioning structure that was used for Apple's **A/UX** product, so most utilities should support setting up the partitions.

The two most important partitions are **Swap** and **Root** – you cannot run MkLinux without these. The Swap partition is used as backing store for the MkLinux virtual memory system. The Root partition holds the core elements of the MkLinux system: utilities, drivers, etc.

It is common to create a **Usr** partition for the more dynamic portions of the operating system, leaving relatively static items on the root partition. Local applications should go into the **/usr/local** directory. This allows them to be backed up for safety, updates, etc.

The swap partition must be at least 8 MB and will usually be at least 32 MB. It can be no larger than 128 MB, but additional swap partitions can be used. The Root partition normally should be at least 100 MB; Usr should be at least 350 MB. If you combine these into a single Root&Usr partition, set the size to at least 400 MB.

Other partitions can/may exist but we're not going to cover those in any detail here (in any case, note that MkLinux currently supports fifteen partitions per physical disk. These additional partitions may be used for personal (user) files, source code building, or other desired uses.

If you have trouble setting up your partitions, review the documentation for your partitioning utility. If you are still having trouble, look for help on our web site. Finally, the various MkLinux mailing lists (e.g., **mklinux-setup** :-) stand ready to help you get things running.

Creating the partitions in preparation for installing MkLinux will require your becoming intimately familiar with a disk drive setup utility. You may want to use HD SC Setup, which came with your Macintosh (and which we've included on the Apple CD-ROM) or **Drive Setup** (which ships with later Power Macintosh systems and Mac OS System Software releases).

No matter which utility you use, you will need to go into the partition setup portion of the utility. You will also, in all probability, need to use the more advanced (e.g., custom) modes of partitioning. The Apple MkLinux Team hopes to simplify this process in a future release of MkLinux.

The first step in repartitioning is making sure there is sufficient free space available on the drive. This does not mean free space as listed in the Finder window. Instead, it refers to space that is not assigned for use by any filesystem such as HFS. You may have to shrink or delete existing Mac OS filesystems before you proceed. Remember that you should have at least 500 MB of otherwise unassigned drive space.

Note: If you are upgrading an existing MkLinux system and do not wish to change your partitioning, you do not need to repartition your drive. Skip to the next chapter.

Preparing The Hard Disk

Before you can prepare your hard disk for use with MkLinux, you will need to answer several questions.

- What is the total capacity of the disk drive?

  The larger the available disk space, the more flexibility you have in designing your system. Remember that you should have a minimum of 500 MB available. (Although MkLinux can run in less space, you will find that it will get crowded quickly!)

- How much disk space do you require for user accounts, source code examination, and utility building?

  This will help you decide how much additional disk space you need.

- How much space do you require for large programs you might add?

When calculating the required size for any partition, increase your figure by at least 15 percent to allow space for file system maintenance.

Initializing And Partitioning

The disk preparation procedure consists of two distinct parts: **initializing** and **partitioning**. Initializing (sometimes called **formatting**) prepares a hard disk to receive information (e.g., by organizing its surface into tracks and sectors, looking for bad sectors, and allocating spare sectors). Partitioning divides the disk into separate areas for different parts of MkLinux and/ or Mac OS.

Note: We recommend that you use separate disk drives for Mac OS and MkLinux. This provides increased convenience, flexibility, and safety, all of which are useful in an experimental environment such as MkLinux.

Most third-party disks are delivered in initialized, but not partitioned, form. If a disk is partitioned, it typically will be set up as a single Mac OS volume. Your decision to initialize and partition your hard disk depends on the current status of your hard disk:

- If you have a hard disk with a partitioning scheme that can accommodate all of MkLinux, there is no need for you to prepare the hard disk. This is the most likely case if you have already installed and been running a previous release of MkLinux. If so, you may proceed to the next chapter, which covers MkLinux installation.

- If you have a new hard disk that has not been initialized, you will need to initialize the disk and create disk partitions. This is the most likely case if you purchased a new hard disk from a vendor who does not specialize in Macintosh products.

- If you have a new hard disk that is already initialized, you will need to create disk partitions. This is the most likely case if you purchased a new hard disk from a vendor who specializes in Macintosh drives.

- If you have a hard disk that has been previously used with an operating system other than MkLinux or Mac OS, or you've been trying to use the disk with MkLinux or Mac OS but it has been giving you trouble, go through the initialization procedure to ensure that the hard disk is initialized with the current software, and then create partitions.

- If you have a Mac OS hard disk with enough extra space to support a set of MkLinux partitions, you will need to (a) back up any information you wish to retain, (b) partition the drive as needed, and (c) reload any partitions that have been damaged.

    Even if you do not intend to move or resize an existing partition, be sure to back it up! (A backup is cheap insurance against a disaster.)

Disk Preparation Software

You can reinitialize and/or partition your hard disk using Apple HD SC Setup (included on the Apple MkLinux disc) or with another Macintosh third-party partitioner of your choice. Macintosh hard disks are usually sold with disk preparation software; such software is also available commercially as a separate product.

If you are using an Apple drive, we recommend that you use Apple HD SC Setup. It is easy to use and is known to do everything needed by MkLinux. In addition, we have documented its use, later in this chapter.

Note: pdisk, which runs under both Mac OS and MkLinux, is a useful tool for partitioning secondary MkLinux disks. It creates "A/UX" partitions on Apple or third-party disks, reporting partition numbers that match MkLinux usage. It cannot, however, install a Mac OS driver or build an HFS filesystem. See the last section in this chapter for detailed information.

If you have a third-party disk drive, however, you probably will not be able to prepare it using the standard version of Apple HD SC Setup. Specifically, Apple HD SC Setup may not recognize your hard disk. In this event, you have two choices:

- Obtain a third-party hard disk utility (e.g., Silverlining) which will recognize and prepare your hard disk. (Some drives are shipped with this sort of utility.) This is a safe, well-supported, and conservative solution. For sales information on Silverlining, contact:

  La Cie Limited   www.lacie.com
  8700 SW Creekside Place   sales@lacie.com
  Beaverton, OR   +1 800 999-1179
  97008 USA   +1 503 520-9000, 9100 (fax)

The instructions in this chapter assume that you are using Apple HD SC Setup. If you are using another disk preparation utility, follow the initialization and partitioning instructions for that software.

Note: Be sure to use a hard disk utility which can create "A/UX" partitions. The MkLinux Installer program depends on the disk preparation software to create partitions of this type.

- Modify Apple HD SC Setup to recognize your hard disk. This is a bit more radical; we don't really recommend it unless you feel comfortable using ResEdit or a similar Macintosh resource editor. If you wish to use a modifed version of Apple HD SC Setup (totally at your own risk!), follow the steps below:

  - Copy Apple HD SC Setup 7.3.5 (included on the Apple MkLinux disc) to a writable Mac OS disk drive.

- Using ResEdit or a similar utility, change the one byte in the "wfwr" ID 67 resource from "00" to "FF".

- Prepare your disk, using the modified copy of ResEdit.

This solution was originally posted on

```
www.euronet.nl/users/ernstoud/patch.html
```

More information and a copy of ResEdit are available there.

Initializing The Hard Disk

Note: Initializing the hard disk destroys everything previously contained on the disk. If you have existing files on the hard disk, be sure to back them up before initializing the hard disk.

Follow these steps to initialize a hard disk:

- Launch Apple HD SC Setup.

A copy of Apple HD SC Setup 7.3.5 is included on the Apple MkLinux disc in the Apple Utilities folder. The dialog box appears as follows:

Next to the words "SCSI Device", you should see a number whose value ranges from 0 to 6, representing the SCSI ID value for the selected hard disk. (SCSI ID 7 is reserved for the Power Macintosh CPU.)

Make sure that the selected disk is the one you want to use for MkLinux. If the wrong disk is listed, click the Drive button until the correct disk is indicated. (If you are uncertain of your hard disk's SCSI ID number, look in the small window on the hard disk's back panel or see the documentation that came with the disk.)

Updating the Hard Disk Driver.

If you have a hard disk that is already initialized, you may want to update the hard disk driver, which controls the communication between the hard disk and your computer. To update the driver, click the Update button in the Apple HD SC Setup dialog box. This copies the most recent hard disk driver to your hard disk.

Click the Initialize button.

A dialog box will appear, reminding you that initializing erases all the information from the hard disk:

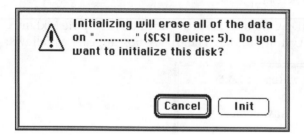

Click the Init button.

If you want to cancel the procedure, click the Cancel button.

Messages explaining the course of the initialization will appear in the Apple HD SC Setup dialog box. Initialization will take at least several minutes; on very large drives, it could take an hour or more.

If you see a message stating that the hard disk failed to initialize properly, check all your SCSI cables and terminators. Make sure that all the connections are tight; then try again. If you are still unable to initialize the disk, contact your Apple dealer.

At the end of the initialization process, the main setup dialog box will appear, letting you know that the initialization was successful. If this is a new disk drive, the program will ask you to name the disk.

* Name the Macintosh volume (disk).

  A dialog should now appear, asking you to name the disk. If the name prompt does not appear, it means the disk already has a name. Type the name (e.g., "Mac Partition"), then press RETURN; you can edit the disk name later in the Finder, if desired.

  If you are planning to use the entire disk for MkLinux, you will soon remove this partition, so it doesn't matter what you name it. If you are planning to install a Mac OS volume on this disk, choose a name that seems appropriate for the volume's intended use.

Space Considerations

In selecting predefined partitions or creating custom partitions, remember to include enough space for the basic MkLinux installation. If your root and usr filesystems are combined, we recommend 400 MB for the Root&Usr filesystem. If they are not combined, we recommend at least 100 MB for the Root filesystem and 350 MB for Usr.

In determining the size of your partitions, note that filesystems require a certain amount of overhead or **user free space.** If you are creating any "Free UNIX" partitions, to be used for user data, be sure to include this overhead in your calculations.

The user free space is used by the operating system to ensure efficient access to the files in the file system. The recommended free space is five to ten percent. Our recommendation for the minimum sizes of the Root and Usr filesystems includes this overhead.

Be sure to create a Swap partition. MkLinux uses space on a hard disk to increase the computer's effective memory (RAM) capacity. This space is used to exchange, or swap, data in the computer's memory with copies being kept temporarily on the hard disk.

The swap space must be at least 16 MB; 32 MB is about right for a 16 MB system. To take advantage of the MkLinux virtual memory system, you should allocate 1-3 MB of swap space for each megabyte of RAM. Thus, a system with 16 MB of RAM should have 32-64 MB of swap space. MkLinux allows the swap space to be as large as 128 MB.

Predefined Partitioning Schemes

The Apple HD SC Setup program offers several predefined partitioning schemes; one of these may meet your needs. If you want to create your own partitioning scheme, go on to "Custom Partitioning Schemes".

Note: Most of the predefined partitioning schemes in versions of Apple HD SC Setup at or before version 7.3.5 are not applicable to MkLinux. Be sure to check for adequate partition sizes, etc.

Follow these steps to use a predefined partitioning scheme:

- Click the Partition button.

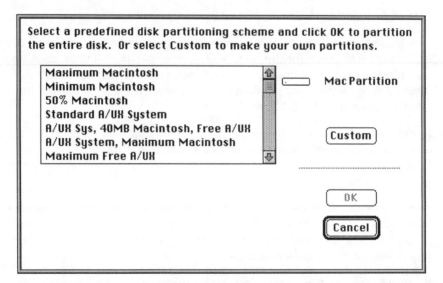

The Partition dialog box will appear. Make sure that the hard disk icon on the right represents the disk you just initialized and named.

The predefined partitioning options are listed in the scrolling panel on the left side of the dialog box. (You may need to use the scroll arrows to view the complete list of schemes.)

Select a predefined disk partitioning scheme. An information box will appear in the lower-left corner of the Partition dialog box. The box provides a brief description of the partitioning scheme you've selected.

Alternatively, click the Custom button to specify your own partitioning scheme. If one of the predefined schemes is close to what you want as your final partitioning scheme, you may want to start with that, then edit the resulting partitions.

- Click the OK button to partition the entire disk.

In most cases, a dialog box will now appear, reminding you that partitioning erases the information on your hard disk.

> **Warning: Removing a partition will destroy any data in that partition.**

- Click the OK or Cancel button.

If you have any data on the hard disk that you do not want to lose, click the Cancel button. Quit the Apple HD SC Setup program and back up any data you want to save before partitioning the hard disk. If you know the hard disk is empty, or if it contains data that you have already saved, click the OK button.

Partitioning usually takes a minute or two. When partitioning is complete, a message should appear, saying that partitioning was successfully completed.

- If a message asks you to name the Macintosh volume (disk), type an appropriate name and click the OK button.

If the disk has not been partitioned with a Macintosh partition before, and you have chosen an option which includes a Macintosh partition, you will be asked to name the volume. Type the desired name (e.g., "Mac Partition"), then press RETURN.

Note: A hard disk partition may be used for arbitrary purposes, including Mac OS (HFS) volumes, MkLinux partitions, swap space, or raw data storage.The name you supply here will appear in the Finder to identify the Macintosh file system (volume) that has been written into the partition.

- Click the Drive or Done button.

    If you have more than one hard disk to prepare, click the Drive button to select the next hard disk; then repeat the steps in this section to partition the disk. (If you need to initialize the hard disk first, return to the section on "Initializing the Hard Disk".)

    If you wish to edit the partitioning scheme you have just created, see the next section, "Custom Partitioning Schemes".

If you are finished preparing the hard disk, click Done to exit Apple HD SC Setup. Skip now to the Installation chapter to begin the MkLinux installation.

Custom Partitioning

As an alternative to selecting one of the predefined disk partitioning options, Apple HD SC Setup lets you define your own custom disk partitioning scheme. In the following steps, the figures illustrate a particular partitioning scheme, but you can easily modify these steps to adjust the sizes for other partition types as well.

- Click the Partition button.

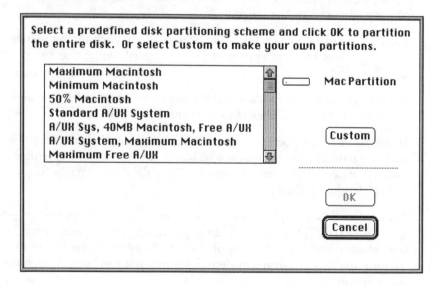

The Partition dialog box will appear. Make sure that the hard disk icon on the right represents the disk you just initialized and named.

The predefined partitioning options are listed in the scrolling panel on the left side of the dialog box. (You may need to use the scroll arrows to view the complete list of schemes.) If one of the predefined schemes is similar to your desired partitioning scheme, you may want to start with that, then edit any differing partition definitions.

Select a predefined disk partitioning scheme. An information box will appear in the lower-left corner of the Partition dialog box. The box provides a brief description of the partitioning scheme you've selected. Alternatively, click the Custom button to specify your own partitioning scheme.

- Click the Custom button.

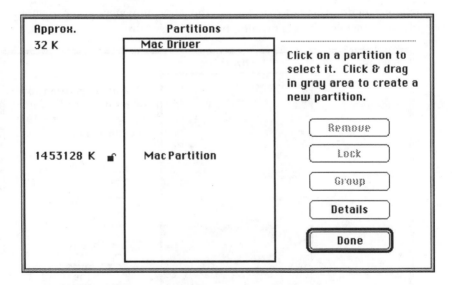

The Custom Partition dialog box will now appear. What you see in the dialog box will depend on how your hard disk is currently partitioned. If you have recently initialized the disk, you will probably see one large Macintosh Volume and one or more additional (much smaller) partitions.

Each partition is represented by a rectangle. Its size, in kilobytes (K), is shown on the left. Sections of free space – any portions of the disk not contained in a defined partition – appear in gray.

• Remove all partitions except the Mac Driver partition.

Click on the partition you want to eliminate, then click the Remove button. A message will warn you that removing the partition causes a loss of all data on that partition. Click the OK button to proceed.

Repeat this process until only the Mac Driver partition remains. The Mac Driver partition is necessary on any disk containing a Macintosh file system.

• Press and drag downwards from the top of the gray area, releasing the mouse button when the partition is approximately the size you want.

Note: You don't have to be exact in this allocation step; you can enter the exact size in the next dialog box.

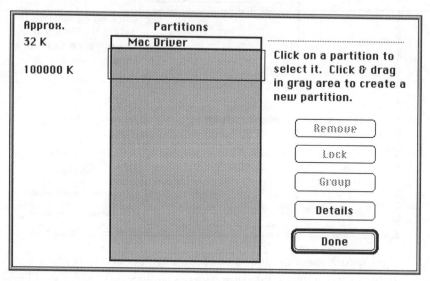

Note: Don't click the Mac Driver partition or you will move this partition instead of selecting the free space.

When you finish dragging, you should see a list of individual partition types on the screen. The size of the partition you are creating, in kilo-bytes, will appear selected in its own box on the right.

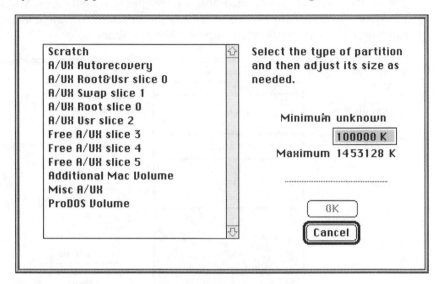

- Select the type of partition you want to create.

  Select a partition type from the list on the left side of the dialog box by clicking on the name of the partition type.

- If you wish, type a number to specify an exact size for the partition.

  Dragging provides only an approximate size for the partition. You can specify the exact size of the partition by typing in the amount.

- Click the OK or Cancel button.

  Click the OK button to proceed; click the Cancel button to cancel the action. In a moment, you will return to the Custom Partition dialog box, where you will see a representation of the partition you just created.

- Repeat the preceeding four steps for each partition you want to create.

  Repeat these steps as many times as needed to create your partitioning scheme. Each time, you will return to the Custom Partition dialog box, which will show a representation, or map, of the current scheme. Remove and readjust partitions until you are satisfied with the results.

The figure below shows an incomplete partitioning scheme for a MkLinux disk. The gray (unpartitioned) area could be used to create user partitions for personal work or perhaps a Mac OS volume:

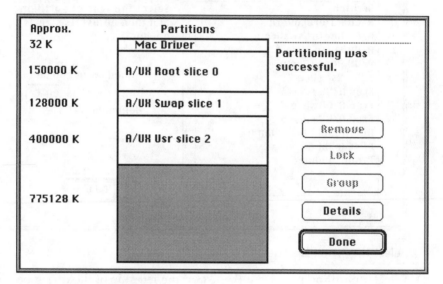

- Click the Done button.

  When you have finished creating all the partitions you need, click the Done button. A message will tell you that custom partitioning is done.

- Click the Done button to exit Apple HD SC Setup.

The pdisk Utility

The MkLinux **pdisk** utility provides a useful supplement to the partitioning tools described above. As of DR3, pdisk cannot install a driver nor build an HFS file system. On the other hand, you are free to supplement pdisk with other tools, using each for its strengths.

Now for some of pdisk's highlights. pdisk is a menu-driven, interactive program that runs under Mac OS and MkLinux. It is available as freely redistributable source code, allowing you to examine, modify, and/or port it to another system. pdisk generates "A/UX-style" partitions by default, reporting partition numbers in MkLinux-compatible form.

If you are partitioning a secondary drive, intended solely for use under Mk-Linux, pdisk can do the entire job by itself. If, however, you wish to use the drive under Mac OS, you will need to create Mac OS (HFS) file systems and possibly install a Mac OS "driver". These can be accomplished in one of two ways, depending on your needs and preferences:

- Partition the drive with a Mac OS-specific tool, creating any desired HFS file systems and (if desired) installing a Mac OS driver. Then, use pdisk to add A/UX-style partitions.

- Use pdisk to partition the drive and create the desired partitions. Then, use **Disk First Aid** to create any desired HFS file systems.

The pdisk manual page is the official word on detailed usage instructions and late-breaking changes to the program's capabilities. Here, however, is a gentle introduction to pdisk's user interface, when used under MkLinux.

Like many MkLinux tools, pdisk is happy to tell any user its version number and commonly used options:

```
[linus@penguin linus]$ /usr/sbin/pdisk --version
version 0.4a2 (15 January 1997)
[linus@penguin linus]$ /usr/sbin/pdisk --help
    pdisk [-h|--help]
    pdisk [-v|--version]
    pdisk [-l|--list [name ...]]
    pdisk [-r|--readonly] name ...
    pdisk name ...
```

Note: Because /usr/sbin is not on most user's search paths, we have specified the full path to the command. The directory is on root's search path, however, so the commands below do not require this.

Before you can get pdisk to examine, let alone modify a disk drive, you will need to become root. For a safe walkthrough, try using pdisk in "readonly" mode:

```
[root@penguin /root]# pdisk -r /dev/sda
/dev/sda
Command (? for help): ?
```

```
Notes:
  Base and length fields are blocks, which are 512
  bytes long. ...

Commands are:
  h    help
  p    print the partition table
  P    (print ordered by base address)
  ...
Command (? for help): P
/dev/sda
  #:            type name     length  base       (size)
  1      ..._SVR2 Usr...      200000 @ 1         (97.7M)
  2      ..._SVR2 Usr...      200000 @ 200001 (97.7M)
  ...
Command (? for help): q
[root@penguin /root]#
```

Once you feel comfortable with the program, you can try partitioning a drive for real. Just be careful; `pdisk` will do exactly what you tell it to do; which may or may not be what you actually *wanted*.

Drive Setup

Drive Setup is the standard partitioning utility that is shipped with Mac OS. It can create multiple Mac OS partitions on your drive, leave free partition space (e.g., for use by pdisk), deposit the latest Apple disk drivers onto the disk, and create actual Mac OS standard and extended volumes in created partititions. It can partition (Apple-branded) SCSI and IDE drives.

Drive Setup cannot create the A/UX-style partitions used by MkLinux. One common method is to use Drive Setup to create free partition space on your drive, then use pdisk to create MkLinux partitions in the free space. Alternatively, you can have Drive Setup create extra Mac OS partitions, then use pdisk to change them to MkLinux partitions before use.

Chapter 3:

- *MkLinux Installation*

Installation

The current (DR3) MkLinux system installation procedure, although very flexible, is quite a bit more complex than the previous (DR2.1) one. On the other hand, it is still far simpler than installation would be on an IBM PC.

This chapter, in any case, describes the procedures for installing MkLinux DR3. It is *not* guaranteed to be accurate for any succeeding release. Be sure to read the README files and any other initial documentation on the Apple MkLinux disc before starting your installation!

There are five files in the **Mac Files** folder on the CD-ROM:

- The **MkLinux Booter** starts up the MkLinux system. The **Mach Kernel** takes over from the booting process and performs the interprocess communication, low-level I/O, scheduling, and virtual memory functions of MkLinux. Copy these files to the **Extensions** folder.

- The **MkLinux** Control Panel controls your system's booting behavior (via **MkLinux.prefs**). Copy the **MkLinux** file to the **Control Panels** folder.

- **lilo.conf** is a text file which is read by the Mach Kernel. It contains settings which control the default behavior of MkLinux (e.g., the boot device). Copy this file to the **Preferences** folder.

- **MkLinux.prefs** is a text file which is read by the MkLinux Booter. It controls the default operating system and timeout behavior of the MkLinux splash screen. Copy this file to the **Preferences** folder.

The initial boot of MkLinux runs the installer. In DR3, it is set up to install from a SCSI CD-ROM drive. If your system has a SCSI CD-ROM drive, you will not need to change anything; skip ahead to "MkLinux Installation". (If you aren't sure which kind of CD-ROM drive you have, read on...)

ATAPI CD-ROM Drives

Several of Apple's more recent machines have ATAPI CD-ROM drives. For example, if you have one of the following machines, you probably have an ATAPI CD-ROM drive:

- PowerBook 3400 or G3

- Power Macintosh 4400 or G3

- "Tanzania"-based clone

To determine whether your machine has an ATAPI CD-ROM drive, insert a disc into your drive, click once on the disc's desktop icon, and run "Get Info" (from the File menu). If the "Where:" line ends in "(ATAPI ...)", you have an ATAPI drive and you will need to change a setting.

To change MkLinux so that it will retrieve the installer from an ATAPI CD-ROM, launch the **MkLinux** Control Panel and select "Custom...". SimpleText will be launched to edit your **lilo.conf** file. Change your root device (rootdev) according to the instructions in the lilo.conf file.

MkLinux Installation

Before you begin the installation, make sure that your primary monitor is set to "256 colors". Use the "Monitors and Sound" Control Panel to choose a 256-color scheme.The first page of the installer should then display a blue background and a white text window with black characters.

Restart your Macintosh. Upon reboot, you should see the MkLinux "splash screen". By default, it is set to boot into Mac OS. Click on the "MkLinux" button; the MkLinux installer should run from your CD-ROM drive.

The DR3 installer is adapted from the well-known "Red Hat Linux" installer, originally written by Red Hat Software. The installer was ported to MkLinux with the intent of making as few changes as possible.

Consequently, there are still many references to "Red Hat Linux", as well as options that are inappropriate for MkLinux. Don't worry; with some basic instruction, you will be able to get your system installed with the desired complement of packages.

The following keys will help you navigate while using the installer:

Tab	Move to the next field
Return	Select the current highlighted choice
Up/Down Arrow	Move up/down in a list of items
Space	Check /uncheck the selected list item

Installation Screens

The installer will present you with a series of screens, generally requiring some sort of decision. The entries below are a step-by-step description of the installation screens you should encounter. Review them carefully before attempting your MkLinux installation.

"Welcome to MkLinux" Screen

Simply press Return to continue to the next screen.

"Keyboard Type" Screen

Select a keyboard type. This controls the keyboard mapping. Not all of the listed keyboard mappings work properly. If you find that this is the case for your selection, start over and select "us" as your keyboard type. You should then be able to continue through the installation.

"Installation Method" Screen

Since the packages to be installed reside on the CD-ROM, choose "Local CD-ROM".

"Installation Path" Screen

Choose "Install". The other option, "Upgrade", adds packages to an already installed Red Hat system, and is not supported under DR3.

"Partition Disks" Screen

The installer will show you a list of disks on your system that MkLinux has recognized. If you select one and choose "Edit", you will be able to view and optionally change that disk's partition map, using the MkLinux version of pdisk. When you have finished viewing/editing the partition maps on various disks, choose "Done".

Note: Don't confuse this screen with the "Partition Disk" screen, below.

"Select Root Partition" Screen

The installer will list every partition that is appropriate for an MkLinux filesystem. Pick one to use for your "root" partition.

"Partition Disk" Screen

This page will list the other partitions that are available to be mounted. Use the arrow keys to highlight a particular partition, then press Return. A follow-on dialog will tell the installer where you would like to have the filesystem in that partition mounted. You may also use this page to mount Mac OS Standard (HFS) volumes. Please note, however, that the HFS volumes will be mounted read-only.

Note: Don't confuse this screen with the "Partition Disks" screen, above.

"Active Swap Space" Screen

The installer will give you a list of every partition that is suitable to be a MkLinux swap partition. Remember, use the Space bar to set/unset which partitions you want to use for swap.

"Find installation files" Screen

This isn't a real screen (that is, you aren't being asked to decide anything). However, you may notice a significant pause here. Be patient.

"Format Partitions" Screen

The installer will give you a list of partitions. You will need to use the arrow keys and space bar to select which partitions to format. If you have never used MkLinux in these partitions, you must reformat all of them. If you have used MkLinux DR2.1 (or an earlier version), we suggest that you reformat *all* your MkLinux partitions. If you have used MkLinux "pre-DR3", we suggest that you format at least the operating system partitions, such as / (the root partition), /usr, or /var.

"Components to Install" Screen

At this point, the installer will present you with a list of selected collections of packages. Use the Space bar to select the collections that seem appropriate for your installation.

At the very end of the list, there is an item labelled "Everything". Selecting this item will install every package (all 420 of them!) in the main package set, even those not represented in the other groups.

There is also a box that is labelled "Select individual packages". If this box is checked when you leave this screen, you will go to a set of screens where you can select the packages individually.

Note: Be sure to scroll down and view all of the selections!

"Install log" Screen

This is just an informative message explaining that an installation log will be saved and will be viewable after the installation in the file "/tmp/install.log".

"Install System" Screens

At this point, the installer will proceed to create the filesystems in your MkLinux partitions, then install the packages that you selected. A progress bar will be displayed, along with estimates of how much time it will take to complete installing the packages.

Note: A few packages write to the installer screen, making the display somewhat messy. You may safely ignore these messages.

"Configure Mouse" Screen

Choose ADB Mouse.

Note: The "emulate three buttons" option is not applicable under DR3.

"Network Configuration" Screen

If your MkLinux system is connected to a TCP/IP-based Local Area Network, and you want to configure your system to operate on this network at this time, choose "Yes".

The installer will bring up two screens: "Configure TCP/IP" and "Configure Network". You will need to know an IP address for your system, the Net Mask, a Default Gateway address, and a DNS nameserver address. If you don't know these values, you should ask your Network Administrator.

Checking "Configure device with bootp" (with the Space bar) indicates that you want to query the network for a set of values appropriate for your machine.

The "Configure Network" screen allows you to enter your domain name and host name. Hostnames normally consist of 1-8 lower-case alphabetic characters [a-z] and/or digits [0-9] (e.g., penguin). Avoid 8-bit characters (e.g., alphabetic characters with accents, etc.). If you have any alternate nameservers, you should enter them on this screen.

"Configure Timezones" Screen

This is the place to set your local timezone. Use the up and down arrow keys to select the correct timezone from the list.

You should always check the "Hardware clock set to GMT" box. Don't worry; this will not affect your Mac OS clock in any way.

"Services" Screen

The installer will present a list of the services that can be started automatically when your MkLinux system boots. If you do not know which services you want (and which ones you *don't* want), it is safe to simply leave the checkboxes unchanged.

"Configure Printer" Screen

If you choose "Yes" on this screen, the installer will present you with a few more screens asking fairly straightforward questions about your printer. Please note that, as of DR3, you cannot set up an AppleTalk printer using this mechanism.

"Root Password" Screen

You must pick a password for the "root" account. Remember this password, because the "root" account will be the first thing you need once the MkLinux installation is complete. Note that when you type the password, the letters do not appear.

"Info" Screen

Be sure to remember or write down the "rootdev" value that the installer tells you on this screen. You will need it in a few steps.

"Done" Screen

When you press ok, the system will reboot. You will need to go into Mac OS at least one more time to change the rootdev setting (mentioned in the previous screen).

When the system reboots, the MkLinux "Splash Screen" will appear again. Select "Mac OS". Once Mac OS has booted, invoke the MkLinux Control Panel. Press the "Custom..." button in the control panel. The SimpleText editor will be launched, editing the "lilo.conf" file. Make sure that the line containing "`rootdev=/dev/XXXX`" uses the value that the installer gave you. Save the file and quit.

This is a good time to choose your "Startup Selection". Click the button next to either Mac OS or MkLinux. (This sets the default choice at the MkLinux Splash Screen. At the splash screen, you can always override the default choice.)

Close the MkLinux Control Panel and restart your Macintosh. Choose MkLinux. (If MkLinux is the default OS, you may simply choose to wait 10 seconds.) MkLinux should now boot, placing you at the "login prompt".

Chapter 4:

Getting Started

If you are an old hand at Linux, feel free to skim this chapter; it is a very brief introduction to MkLinux in particular and Linux in general, aimed largely at Mac OS users.

If you are new to Linux, you should read this introduction fairly carefully, then follow up your reading with a few exploratory sessions. We suggest *The UNIX Programming Environment* as a clear and concise introductory text on UNIX command syntax, tools, and philosophy.

More generally, you should look over the extensive lists of reading matter and other resources included in the Hardware and Software Bibliography chapters at the end of this book. MkLinux is a very large system, but it is well served by books, magazines, mailing lists, web sites, and other sources of information. You are not alone...

Logging In

Unlike Mac OS, MkLinux will not interact with a user until the user has **logged in**. Further, it allows different users to log in, maintaining unique sets of information for each **login session**. Finally, when a user is finished with a session, s/he is responsible for **logging out**, as discussed below.

A brand-new MkLinux system has only one user account, named **root**. Start your session by logging in as root:

```
penguin login: root
...
[root@penguin /root]#
```

Once you are logged in, the system prints a **prompt**, giving certain useful information. The prompt shown above indicates that your **username** is root and that you are logged into a machine named penguin.

The prompt also indicates that your **current directory** is **/root**. This is the root account's **home directory**, used for private administrative files. (We will discuss home directories at some length a bit later in the chapter.)

Note: The prompt is entirely customizable, as are many of the user interface features of MkLinux. For now, however, we will assume that you are getting the default MkLinux prompt, as shown above.

Logging Out, Rebooting, And Shutting Down

Having just logged in, you probably aren't ready to log back out or shut down the machine. On the other hand, we always find it annoying to have to hunt around for these kinds of instructions, so here they are!

The following notes assume that you are sitting at the main system console display, logged in as an ordinary user (named Linus :-), and that you are not running X11 or any other window system:

- Here is how to log out, leaving MkLinux to its own devices. This is not the same as shutting down!

  ```
  [linus@penguin linus]$ exit
  ```

- You can now log back in as root and reboot the system:

  ```
  penguin login: root
  Password: [...silent...]
  [root@penguin /root]# shutdown -r now
  ```

This will kill off any running programs, shut down MkLinux, and reboot the system. At the MkLinux startup dialog, you will have a chance to specify whether you wish to restart under Mac OS or MkLinux.

- Alternatively, you can log in as root and shut down (halt) the system:

```
penguin login: root
Password: [...silent...]
[root@penguin /root]# shutdown -h now
```

This will kill off any running programs, shut down MkLinux, and power down the computer (assuming that your computer system supports software power down).

Setting The root Password

Even if your computer isn't on a network, it is still vulnerable to straying fingers. If it's on a network, the fingers could stray onto your system from anywhere in the world. For safety, therefore, set the root **password**:

```
[root@penguin /root]# passwd
Changing password for root
...
New password (? for help): [...silent...]
New password (again): [...silent...]
Password changed for root
[root@penguin /root]#
```

The password you enter is not echoed to the screen. In fact, unlike Mac OS practice, MkLinux doesn't even print bullets to show you how many characters you have typed. This may seem a bit awkward, but it is a valuable precaution. Someone might be looking over your shoulder at the screen or even coming by when you're not around! Why give them any clues (including the number of characters) about your password?

When picking a password, use a (six or more) character string that you can remember. Avoid passwords that can be guessed easily (e.g., names, birthdays, etc.) or found in a dictionary. Some reasonable strategies are:

- including a mixture of UPPER and lower-case alphabetic characters

- including numbers and special characters

- combining words

Thus, you might create a password such as *none2good*, *Im_D_Bo$$*, or *Its4sure*. Of course, be sure not to use one of these examples (:-).

Although we don't recommend writing passwords on whiteboards or miscellaneous pieces of paper, you *should* prepare some method for obtaining the `root` password in case of emergencies. Here is one effective strategy:

- Write the `root` password on a piece of paper, fold the paper (to make it opaque), then put it in an envelope.

- Give the envelope to some person who is trustworthy, well-organized, and typically available during normal working hours. Alternatively, put it in a place with guaranteed limited access.

- Allow any of a small set of authorized persons the privilege of "signing out" the envelope and retrieving the password. Require them to report why they needed the password and (specifically!) how they used it.

- Set a new `root` password and repeat the setup procedure. Analyze the report to see if your administration procedures need improvement.

Note: MkLinux will not save your password, *per se*. Instead, it will encrypt it and save the encrypted form. Then, the next time you log in, it can encrypt your entered password and see if the result matches what it has saved. This distinction is very important: a MkLinux administrator *cannot* find out a user's password, even by looking in the **password file (/etc/passwd)**. S/he can only install a new password and then ask the user to change it promptly. Consequently, losing the `root` password is a *real* problem!

Setting The Time Zone

By default, MkLinux is set to use the Pacific Time Zone. To change the time zone to the appropriate configuration for your location, create a symbolic link from `/etc/localtime` to the correct **timezone file** for your location.

For example, to set the correct time zone for Apple Computer in Cupertino, California, USA, type:

```
# cd /etc
# ln -fs /usr/lib/zoneinfo/US/Pacific localtime
```

To set the correct time zone for The Open Group Research Institute in Grenoble, France, type:

```
# cd /etc
# ln -fs /usr/lib/zoneinfo/Europe/Paris localtime
```

Additional time zone files can be found in `/usr/lib/zoneinfo`.

Note: When you are back in Mac OS, use the Date & Time Control Panel to verify that the Date, Time, Time Zone, and Daylight Savings option are set correctly for your location.

Adding User Accounts

Initially, MkLinux has only one login account, `root`. The `root` account is very powerful; it can read (and write!) any file at all.

So, unless you never make misteaks (:-), you probably should not stay logged in as `root` all the time. Pick a personal **username** for your regular system use. In theory, your username can contain:

- lower-case letters (a-z)

- digits (0-9)

- periods (.) and underscores (_)

In practice, it's best to use only letters, avoiding ones that aren't found in English (i.e., 8-bit characters). You will be giving your username to folks around the world; pick something they can use and remember!

If at all possible, let users pick their own usernames. First names (brett) and nicknames (lion) work very well on smaller systems. They tend to be short, memorable, and emotionally satisfying.

If you are administering a system on a network or there are lots of users on your system, consider using initials (vlb) or combinations of first initials and surnames (gcoville). Avoid using artificial usernames (q123456); they are hard to remember and tend to depersonalize your users.

Note: Teach your users how to change their passwords. Instruct them to set a new password *whenever* the current one may have become compromised!

To add a user account (create a home directory, etc.), use the **adduser** command, then use `passwd` to set an (initial, if for someone else) password:

```
[root@penguin /root]# adduser linus
...
[root@penguin /root]# passwd linus
```

```
Changing password for linus
...
New password (? for help): [...silent...]
New password (again): [...silent...]
Password changed for linus
[root@penguin /root]#
```

Logging In As Yourself

Now that you have your own account, you can try it out:

```
[root@penguin /root]# exit

penguin login: linus
Password: [...silent...]
...
[linus@penguin linus]$
```

Note that the prompt has changed in a few ways. The username is different, as is the home directory. Finally, the last character of the prompt is now a dollar sign (**$**), rather than a sharp sign (**#**). These are cues that you are no longer logged in as root.

Your options in this account are more limited, but they are powerful enough for most purposes. And, if you need more privileges, you can always log back in as root. Alternatively, you can **set user** to root, as:

```
[linus@penguin linus]$ su -
Password: [...silent...]
[root@penguin /root]#
...
[root@penguin /root]# exit
exit
[linus@penguin linus]$ su
Password: [...silent...]
[root@penguin linus]#
...
[root@penguin linus]# exit
exit
[linus@penguin linus]$ su
```

Note: The "-" option tells su to give you root's typical login environment. If you wish to retain your normal PATH and such, omit this flag.

Commands And Shells

As you have no doubt noticed, MkLinux requires users to enter **commands** (e.g., adduser, exit, passwd, su) in order to request desired actions. We think of these commands as verbs, asking the system to perform one or more desired actions. **Command lines** frequently include **arguments** (nouns) and/or **flags** (adverbs), which specify and/or modify the requested behavior.

MkLinux commands may be built into the **shell** (command line interpreter). Alternatively, they may be pre-defined macro strings (also known as **aliases** or **shell functions**) or names of application programs.

Note: Mac OS and MkLinux both have aliases, but they are quite different in nature. Specifically, a Mac OS alias is approximately what MkLinux would call a **symbolic link**. More generally, be careful not to confuse Mac OS and MkLinux jargon!

Viewed from a distance, all shells are pretty much equivalent. They all support a common set of **built-in commands** and they are all able to invoke application programs. The differences between shells lie in their interactive and programming features.

Note: If you are familiar with other shells (e.g., **csh** or **ksh**), you may find **bash** (the default MkLinux shell) a little peculiar. Give bash a chance; it combines the programming power of ksh with the interactive features of **tcsh**.

Trying Out Some Commands

```
[linus@penguin linus]$ pwd
/home/linus
```

The **pwd** command tells MkLinux to Print (to the screen) the Working (current) Directory. Although the prompt lists linus as your current directory, pwd reveals the **full path** to be /home/linus. This is the complete name of your home directory, loosely equivalent to a Mac OS name like *:penguin: home:linus*.

```
[linus@penguin linus]$ cd /
[linus@penguin /]$ ls
bin    home        mach_servers    root    usr
dev    lib         mnt             sbin    var
```

```
etc   lost+found   proc        tmp
```

The **cd** command lets us Change to a specified Directory. The **ls** command gives a minimal listing of the contents of the current directory, showing both files and directories. To get a more complete listing, we can add a flag to the command line (e.g., "**ls -l**").

Note: Both MkLinux and Mac OS allow the use of mixed case in file names. Under MkLinux, however, case is significant. That is, MkLinux treats "foo", "Foo", and "FOO" as three different entities, whereas Mac OS does not. In addition, although MkLinux *allows* the use of special characters in file names, you should be conservative in using them, as the shell may see them as wild cards, token separators, etc.

Each command has its own unique set of flags, which can be used to modify aspects of the command's operation. There are no universal rules regarding flag formation or meaning, but there are a couple of common conventions.

Traditional UNIX flags consist of single letters, each prefaced with a dash (-). You generally can combine these flags for brevity (e.g., writing "**-a -l**" as "**-al**").

If more than one of the flags takes an **argument**, however, be careful to keep the arguments in the same order as the flags. Thus, a set of flags and arguments such as:

```
-a foo -b -c bar
```

may be combinable as:

```
-abc foo bar
```

In general, however, it is best to keep your flag use simple, at least until you are quite comfortable with the syntax and range of possible parameters for the command in question.

Note: You will see quite a bit of **foo** and **bar** in this book and elsewhere in the UNIX community. Derived from fubar (Fouled Up Beyond All Recognition), these are used as "placeholder" names, when no specific file is intended. For accurate, enlightening, and frequently amusing definitions of assorted UNIX jargon, see *The New Hacker's Dictionary*.

Many MkLinux commands also have GNU-style flags, as well. These flags are entire words, prefaced by a pair of dashes (--). Because GNU-style flags require more typing (and cannot be combined for brevity) you may not wish to use them on the command line. Their meanings tend to be obvious on inspection, however, making them very helpful in shell scripts.

The **-l** flag causes ls to give a very complete listing. The listing is similar to the Mac OS View by Name, but it also shows MkLinux characteristics such as **file type**, **modes** (also known as **permissions**), **links**, **owner name**, and **group name**.

```
[linus@penguin /]$ ls -l
total 29
drwxr-xr-x  2 root    root  1024 Aug 21 10:12 bin
drwxr-xr-x  2 root    root  5120 Aug 25 21:23 dev
. . .
```

Note: Using other commands (e.g., **chmod**), you can adjust some of these characteristics (e.g., modes), allowing files to be read and/or written as you determine. Group access, for instance, can be used to let a selected set of users access a given file or directory. Managing file modes is an important part of MkLinux system administration.

```
[linus@penguin /]$ cd /root
bash: /root: Permission denied
```

The command above asks MkLinux to Change our Directory to **/root**. This is an instance of the use of a command-line **argument** (sometimes called a **parameter**). The argument tells the command what entity (file, directory, etc.) to act upon.

As mentioned above, **/root** is the home directory of the root account. It is used for private administrative information and should not be accessible to ordinary users. Consequently, MkLinux denies us permission to enter /root.

Note: The word **root** has two separate meanings in MkLinux. All files and directories in the entire file system are connected to the **root directory** (**/**, pronounced **slash**). The **root account**, in contrast, is the all-powerful administrative login account.

```
[linus@penguin /]$ cd /tmp
[linus@penguin /tmp]$ touch foo
```

```
[linus@penguin /tmp]$ ls -l foo
-rw-rw-r-- 1 linus  root  0 Aug 25 21:56 foo
[linus@penguin /tmp]$ touch /foo
touch: /foo: Permission denied
```

The system lets us go to **/tmp**, and even **touch** (create and/or update the time and date stamp on) a file there, because /tmp is a shared community work space. On the other hand, although the root directory is readable by ordinary users, it is not writable by them. So, we can't create **/foo**.

```
[linus@penguin /tmp]$ rm foo
[linus@penguin /tmp]$ ls -l foo
ls: foo: No such file or directory
```

Note: MkLinux systems, unlike Mac OS, believe that users know what they are doing. If we tell MkLinux to remove (**rm**) a file, it will do so at once (assuming, of course that we have the necessary permissions). It won't ask if we're sure, put the file into a temporary holding area (e.g., Trash), trying to protect us from the consequences of our actions. MkLinux commands are like sharp knives, invaluable in a kitchen, but not to be handled carelessly.

The Home Directory

When used with no arguments, cd returns us to our **home directory**. This can be very useful if we have wandered off to some far corner of the file system.

```
[linus@penguin /tmp]$ cd
[linus@penguin linus]$
```

The home directory is the user's primary storage area for private files. Although the root account is perfectly free to examine (and indeed, modify) any file in the system, the files in users' home directories are generally considered to be private. In short, your home directory is the proper place to put your working files and directories.

Note: If you are working on multi-person project, you may wish to create a shared area for project files. You can use group access permissions to protect the files from unauthorized intrusion. Just warn the project members to be careful, lest two of them modify the same file at the same time!

Let's take a look at the contents of our home directory:

```
[linus@penguin linus]$ ls
```

Hmmm. Nothing there yet, or is there? Let's try again:

```
[linus@penguin linus]$ ls -alG
total 17
drwxrwxr-x  2 linus   1024 Sep 21 15:15 .
drwxr-xr-x  4 root    1024 Sep 21 15:15 ..
-rwxr-xr-x  1 linus    186 Sep 16 13:11 .Xclients
-rw-r--r--  1 linus   1126 Sep 16 13:11 .Xdefaults
-rw-r--r--  1 linus    674 Sep 16 13:11 .aliases
-rw-r--r--  1 linus     24 Sep 16 13:11 .bash_logout
-rw-r--r--  1 linus    226 Sep 16 13:11 .bash_profile
-rw-r--r--  1 linus    618 Sep 16 13:11 .bashrc
. . .
```

Aha! By using the **a** flag , we can get MkLinux to list *all* the files and directories in the directory. By default, items whose names begin with periods (usually pronounced as "dot", as in "dot-aliases") are not listed. The **G** flag, by the way, suppresses printing of group information.

The first two items we see are the **.** and **..** directories. We can tell that they are directories by the leading **d** in the first (permissions) field. The first of these directories (**.**) is an alternative name for the **current directory** (wherever we might be).

The second directory (**..**) is an alternative name for our **parent directory**. So, if you know that a file **bar** is located in a sibling directory named **foo**, you can access it as **../foo/bar**.

Although everything else in the listing is owned by linus, the parent directory is owned by root. Most of the directories and files in MkLinux are owned by administrative accounts like root and bin, with read-only permissions for the rest of the world. This allows ordinary users to examine the files, but not to modify them, lest critical files be damaged or lost.

The rest of the listing is taken up by user configuration files of one sort or another. The **.bashrc** file, for instance, is read by bash whenever it starts up a new instance of the shell.

As a new user, you will want to try creating files, removing them, and generally fooling around. Let's create a playground directory, to keep all these files together:

```
[linus@mkloner linus]$ mkdir play
[linus@mkloner linus]$ cd play
[linus@mkloner play]$ touch foo
[linus@mkloner play]$ ls -al
total 2
drwxrwxr-x  2 linus  linus  1024 Sep 21 16:02 .
drwxrwxr-x  3 linus  linus  1024 Sep 21 16:02 ..
-rw-rw-r--  1 linus  linus     0 Sep 21 16:13 foo
```

Note: By creating hierarchies of directories, you will be able to keep large numbers of files under control. MkLinux commands work most conveniently when all of the files in a given directory are related to a single topic.

Manual Pages

MkLinux comes with an extensive set of online **manual pages**. Each manual page nominally describes a command, file, library function, or other feature of the operating system. (In practice, a manual page may cover numerous related features and may be dozens of printed pages in length.) Let's look at a few manual pages.

```
[linus@penguin linus]$ man foo
No manual entry for foo
```

No luck here! If MkLinux doesn't have a requested manual page, it says so!

```
[linus@penguin linus]$ man ls
Formatting page, please wait...
```

Note: MkLinux stores its manual pages in unformatted (and possibly compressed) form. The first time a manual page is requested, MkLinux prepares it for display. After that, the page will be ready for use when requested.

The text on the screen should now be replaced by the first part of the manual page:

```
LS(1L)                                                    LS(1L)

NAME
    ls, dir, vdir - list contents of directories
```

SYNOPSIS
  ls [-abcdfgiklmnpqrstuxABCFGLNQRSUX1] [-w cols]
  [-T cols] [-I pattern] [--all] [--escape]
  [--directory] [--inode]
    . . .

DESCRIPTION
  This manual page documents the GNU version of **ls**.
  dir and **vdir** are versions of **ls** with different
  default output formats. These programs list each
  given file or directory name. Directory contents
  are sorted alphabetically. . . .

OPTIONS
  -a, --all

:

The manual pages are displayed by the **less** command, which allows the
user to scan forward and backward, search for desired character strings, etc.
less is based on the UNIX command **more** (more or less :-).

The colon (:) at the bottom of the screen is the prompt from less, asking
you if you wish to move forward, backward, quit, etc. Spend some time
playing with less; it is a handy tool for examining MkLinux text files.

You will also need to spend some time looking at manual pages before you
will know where to find information, what the different sections mean, etc.
Don't be overwhelmed; manual pages pack a lot of information into a very
small area. Indeed, they often appear to contain only reminders, rather
than explanations. In time, however, you will find them indispensible.

To go down one line in a manual page, hit the **return** key. To go down an
entire screenfull of text, hit the **space bar**. To leave a manual page, type **q**.

Trying Out X11

The discussion thus far has assumed that we are sitting at the system console, which is operating in "glass teletype" mode. MkLinux supports other
forms of interaction, however, through the **X Window System** (also known
as **X11**). This system allows the user to use multiple windows in both textual and graphical modes.

Note: X11 may *look* a bit like the Mac OS Finder, but it does not *act* at all like it. X11 uses more buttons on the mouse (emulating them via keyboard combinations, if need be), has totally different scrolling, cut-and-paste, and other semantics, and is able to operate over a network to applications running on other computers.

So, let's try out the X Window System. Start up the X11 server for `penguin`:

```
[linus@penguin linus]$ startx
```

By default, MkLinux sets users up with **KDE** (K Desktop Environment), a (mostly) free collection of window management software, productivity tools, etc. See one of the references on X for information on customizing KDE and other X commands. In the meanwhile, here are some useful pointers on our default X setup:

- To bring up a terminal window, first click the "K" icon at the left-hand end of the toolbar. Then, select "Terminal" from the "Utilities" menu. Browse around in the K menu to see what other facilities are available.

- KDE's windows, like those of Mac OS, are "click to type". If the cursor is over a window, that window "hears" the keyboard. (Different window managers have different ways of changing this; see the appropriate documentation.)

- X expects the mouse to have three buttons. If you are using a one-button mouse, use Option-2 and Option-3 to emulate the "middle" and "right" buttons, respectively.

  Note: MkLinux supports mice (and other pick devices) that conform to the ADB **multi-button mouse protocol**. Before you buy a multi-button pick device, be sure to find out whether it complies with this standard.

- To exit X, use the "Logout" item at the bottom of the K menu.

You can set your system up to default to KDE, causing the system to use X-based interaction throughout. In `/etc/inittab`, change the runlevel of `initdefault` from 3 to 5. A system reboot will allow this to take effect; alternatively, you can use the `telinit` command (as root), as follows:

```
# telinit 5
```

Chapter 5:

Essential System Administration

Mac OS systems don't require very much administration. This is fortunate: most Mac OS systems never receive *any* regular system administration. If this sounds like your common mode of operation, *please* read this chapter.

Unlike Mac OS, MkLinux requires a certain amount of administration. Not all that much: an hour a month is more than enough for most small systems. If your system does not receive this attention, however, **bad things** can start to happen. File systems can fill up, files can get lost or corrupted, and users can find that key system facilities are starting to break down.

We don't want this, you certainly don't want it, and it isn't all that hard to avoid. So, do your homework and keep your system running cleanly!

Some Philosophy

We have been using and administering computer systems for nearly three decades. This doesn't make us wizards, but it *has* given us a few opinions on the subject. Please bear with us while we pontificate a bit...

System administration mythology. We occasionally encounter some rather peculiar mythology concerning system administration. We know that *you* don't believe these myths, but you may be able to use some ammunition when discussing these issues with your peers (and/or management):

- **System administration is optional.**

  Unlike Mac OS, MkLinux loves to create files: log files, temporary files, spool files, and more. And, unfortunately, it doesn't always clean up after itself.

  With all this activity, it is quite possible for things to break. If they don't get fixed, they can break worse. File system damage, in particular, tends to propagate over time.

- **System administration is just "housekeeping".**

  No more than ordinary "housekeeping" is. A properly administered system runs efficiently and cleanly, presenting an image of order. A poorly administered system causes inefficiency and frustration for all of its users.

- **Anyone can do it.**

  No. A system manager must be a competent MkLinux user and must have a reasonable set of attitudes (more on this later) about the task. There is also some basic knowledge that is needed, but much of this can be picked up along the way.

- **Only gurus can do it.**

  No. Some parts of system administration are very tricky, to be sure, but most system administrators are not gurus. It *is* helpful to have a guru on call, however. If you haven't joined some MkLinux **email lists** yet, get over to the MkLinux web site (`www.mklinux.apple.com`) and do it!

- **Somebody else will do it.**

  Not if you're the only user or the owner of the system. This makes *you* the system administrator! Aside from occasional "help" from passing system crackers, you're on your own. Nor can you count on the vendor to automate everything or even to set things up right in the first place.

- **Security isn't important *here*.**

  OK, you run a nice, loose shop, and everyone is completely honest. Or perhaps this is your own private system, sitting in your den. Well, there are nasty people out there with modems and Internet connections, for starters. Failing that, some of your employees and/or friends may not be as honest as you'd like.

The best reason for security, however, has to do with human error and damage control. A secure system will keep your users from shooting off each others' feet *when* they make mistakes.

Attitude is an important component of effective system administration, particularly if the system is going to have more than one user. It can be very tempting, on receiving the `root` password, to decide that you are now the local deity. Avoid the temptation; this isn't MS-DOS, let alone Mac OS...

Moving from the general to the specific, here are some useful cautions:

- **Omniscience.** Read the manual; don't just assume you know everything. Besides, vendors occasionally change things around. It is also useful to ask your users about their needs and preferences. They have a totally different perspective from your own, so you may be surprised (and enlightened) by what you hear.

- **Infallibility.** Don't stay logged in as `root` all the time, and be very careful when you take on `root` authority. Fingers have been known to slip and MkLinux assumes that anyone who is logged in as `root` knows what s/he is doing.

- **Omnipotence.** As the system administrator, you are pretty much in charge of things. You can take the system down whenever you like, throw away anybody's files, and generally do whatever you like. In a word, don't. Users have a right to expect courteous behavior on your part; it is only proper to provide it.

  Scheduled down time, for instance, should be announced well in advance. It should also take place during times (e.g., weekends) when the system would normally have few users online and when you will have time to fix anything you break.

- **Immortality.** You won't be around forever, so leave some notes around for your successor(s). Be sure to write the *really* critical information into a notebook: when the system is down, so is your online documentation!

So much for political indoctrination. Now let's look at some specific reasons for performing system administration.

- **To protect the integrity of programs and data.**

  You don't want things to get lost, stolen, or sabotaged. Neither do your users. As the system administrator, your task is to make sure that bad things either don't happen, or can be resolved with minimal losses.

- **To help the system run smoothly.**

  MkLinux isn't MS-DOS or Mac OS. It is a big, hairy, complex operating system, requiring proper setup and continuing support to work properly.

- **To integrate new devices and users into the system.**

  As new devices and users are added to the system, the system administrator must modify and/or create assorted files to reflect this. If this is done in a sloppy manner, the result will be security holes, inefficiency, and possible loss of data.

- **To add desired features to the system.**

  The MkLinux distribution can't possibly include every package you might want. There are many freely redistributable utilities you may want to add and you may wish to install occasional proprietary tools.

Levels of system administration. There are several levels of system administration:

- **Elementary.** These tasks constitute most of an administrator's duties. They involve adding and removing users, backing up files, moving files around, and so forth.

- **Intermediate.** Now we get into trickier stuff: restoring files, installing new devices and/or versions of MkLinux, adding applications, setting up **ppp** links or other network connections, etc.

- **Advanced.** These activities should really be done by gurus, but ordinary system administrators sometimes get pulled into them. They include hacking **sendmail**, modifying device drivers, and repairing clobbered file systems.

- **Specialized.** Each site has certain subsystems it cherishes, each one requiring a certain amount of administration. The necessary skills may range from elementary to advanced; the system manager simply gets to cope as best s/he can.

This chapter introduces most of the elementary tasks, touches on a couple of intermediate tasks, and leaves the rest alone. If you are running a small standalone system, making few changes to the configuration, this chapter may meet most of your needs. If not, we suggest that you peruse some of the administration texts listed in the Software Bibliography chapter.

Bringing It Up, Shutting It Down

System startup. MkLinux usually can handle startup by itself, unless something has gotten severely damaged. Let the normal startup procedure take care of things, noting any peculiarities. If it has real trouble, it will let you know about it.

Normal shutdown. The system will need to be shut down occasionally for preventative maintenance, adding devices, etc. Use the `shutdown` command, as `root`, giving an explanation and a reasonable amount of warning:

```
# shutdown -h 5 "Need to add a disk drive."
```

When the machine has successfully shut itself down, you may power it off. (If your Power Mac can turn off its own power, this command will cause it to do so.) Attitude hint: On multi-user systems, don't schedule shutdowns during normal working hours without a very good reason.

Rapid shutdown. Occasionally, something will make it is necessary to shut the system down at once. If possible, follow the instructions above, using a suitably short amount of time. Otherwise, use the following command:

```
# shutdown -h now "Disk drive is screeching."
```

Panic shutdown. Smoke has just started to pour out of a critical piece of system hardware. Pull the plug! (You can clean up the mess later.) You may lose some files, but you *should* have backups for most of them. In any case, the hardware is a bit more critical at this point.

Accidental shutdown. A large truck has just eaten your utility pole. The power will be off until the utility company gets things put back together. Unplug the system and leave it that way until the power seems to have stabilized. Power companies have a tendency to switch things on and off a bit when they are getting the power back in service. Your computer system is very vulnerable when it is just starting up; being interrupted could well cause it to lose or damage files...

Where Things Live

Unlike Mac OS, MkLinux views all of its file systems as parts of a unified "tree". The `root` file system forms the base of the tree, but other file systems can be added as desired. Once a file system has been mounted, its directories act just like directories on the root file system. In fact, very few MkLinux commands can determine whether a file is on a mounted file system or not.

By unifying the file systems, MkLinux can keep its file names very consistent. Here are some sample **full path names**:

```
/
/bin
/bin/cp
/usr
/usr/bin
/usr/bin/vi
```

Although `/usr` is frequently stored on a separate file system, nothing in these names indicates the fact. This allows users and programs to ignore the exact hardware configuration, preventing problems when and if it changes.

MkLinux file trees are generally drawn with the root directory at the top. This may seem peculiar, at first glance, but it turns out to be very convenient. Here, in any event, is a simplified summary of the distributed MkLinux file tree:

/	the root directory
bin	critical commands
dev	devices and other special files
etc	system administration data and commands
home	user home directories, etc.
lib	libraries, programs, etc.
lost+found	`fsck` drop-off point for / filesystem
mach_servers	Server processes (`vmlinux`, etc.)
mnt	convenient (temporary) mount point

proc	address spaces of processes, other system info
root	root's home directory
sbin	system administration commands
tmp	symbolic link to /var/tmp
usr	everything else (permanent)
var	everything else (transient)

The **/usr** sub-tree is a good candidate for removal to a separate file system. It tends to contain read-only files that are used by the system, but not critically needed for its operation.

/usr	everything else (permanent)
bin	less critical commands
doc	assorted documentation files
games	game commands, etc.
include	text for inclusion by compilers, etc.
info	texinfo-format documentation files
lib	(more) libraries, programs, etc.
libexec	subprograms for commands
local	good spot for local additions
lost+found	fsck drop-off point for /usr filesystem
man	on-line manuals (unformatted)
sbin	(more) system administration commands
share	common reference files (source code, etc.)
spool	symbolic link to /var/spool
src	source code
tmp	temporary storage

The **/var** sub-tree is a good candidate for removal to a separate file system. It tends to contain files that are maintained by the system, including lock files, log files, and directories used by spooling subsystems.

/var	everything else (transient)
adm	system administration data files
catman	on-line manuals (formatted)
lib	(more) libraries, programs, etc.
lock	lock (synchronization) files
log	system log files
preserve	system crash drop-off point for editors
run	miscellanous system status and log files

`spool`	storage for spooling subsystems
`at`	`at` control files
`cron`	`cron` control files
`lpd`	line printer data and lock files
`mail`	mail files for users
`mqueue`	mail queueing files
`rwho`	rwho
`uucp`	uucp data and lock files
`tmp`	temporary storage

Security Basics

Security issues have to do with protection of resources from loss or harm. Computer equipment is expensive and should be protected. Data can be far more valuable (often irreplaceable!) and deserves even more protection. We don't want to breed paranoia, but we do suggest that you treat security issues with respect: a modicum of caution now could prevent a great deal of anguish down the road.

Before we get into a discussion of software-related security issues, give some thought to the physical security of your installation. What would prevent someone from simply walking off with components or even entire systems? Is there anything to prevent a cracker from sniffing packets from your LAN?

Do you have a regular system in place for performing system back-ups? Are your back-ups cataloged and well protected? Do you cycle through your media, retiring it at some point? Do you keep some of your back-ups off-site, in case of disaster?

Mac OS was never intended to be a multi-user operating system. Designed to support personal machines, it has essentially no mechanisms for controlling user access. The standard Mac OS distribution, for instance, assumes that physical access to the system implies complete authority to perform any desired actions. Joe User is perfectly free to drag any file or folder to the trash can. Once the trash has been emptied, the data is gone, gone, gone!

On the other hand, most Mac OS systems *are* personal machines. Even in a household, only a few people will be using the machine. If everyone is trustworthy and reasonably cautious, little damage is likely to take place. And, because Mac OS systems don't support remote logins, they are safe from most modem- or Internet-based attacks. Finally, some system files are always "in use", and cannot be thrown away.

MkLinux systems, in contrast, assume that there could be a multitude of users, both local and networked. The system accepts the responsibility, by and large, for keeping these users out of each others' way. It does have an administrative account (`root`) with complete authority, but access to the `root` account is (or at least should be) guarded with extreme care.

MkLinux security is implemented via **access permissions** (**file modes**) for all **processes**, directories, and **files** on the system. The access permissions tell MkLinux which users have what kinds of access (e.g., read or write); the MkLinux file system code then enforces these restrictions.

As shipped, MkLinux has reasonably secure permissions. (Let us know if you find a problem!) As the local system administrator, you are responsible for maintaining this security. If you open up the permissions on a directory or a file, make sure you haven't allowed any undesirable access to take place.

User and Group id's. MkLinux tracks a **user id** (**uid**) and a **group id** (**gid**) for each file and process. The user id identifies the **owner** of the item in question. In most cases, the owner is the only user who will have anything to do with the item.

In cases where more than one user (but not everyone on the system) needs to have access to an item, the group id comes into play. The group id identifies a specific group of users (listed in the `/etc/group` file) as having a special (usually increased) amount of access to the item. For instance, a file might be totally accessible by its owner, readable by members of its group, and not accessible at all by anyone else.

Here is a brief summary of key points about user and group id's:

- Files get their user id's from their creator.

- By default, files get their group id's from the enclosing directory. It is possible, however, to have them take on the group id of their creator.

- Users get their (shell's) uid and gid from `/etc/passwd` at login time. They are:

  - Passed to all sub-processes

- Overridden by **setuid** and **setgid** routines

- Checked against every file at "open" time

- User and group **names** are translated to/from id's via **/etc/passwd** and **/etc/group**.

Permissions. Access to files and directories is controlled by their permissions and by those on the directories above. (To access a file, a user must satisfy the restrictions on the file and on each directory on its path.)

MkLinux supports three sets of permissions: **user**, **group**, and **other**.These are checked, in order, with the first matching test controlling access. That is, if you are the file's owner, *only* the first set of bits will be checked for you.

Each set contains three **mode bits**: **read (r)**, **write (w)**, and **execute (x)**. The interpretation of these bits varies somewhat, depending on the nature of the item. For files, the bits are interpreted as follows:

- Read permission allows data to be read from a file.

- Write permission allows data to be written into an existing file.

- Execute permission allows a file to be run as a command. In the case of shell scripts, read permission is also needed.

For directories, the interpretations are analogous, but a bit more subtle:

- Read permission allows a directory to be read, as by **ls** or shell **wild-carding** (use of pattern-matching meta-characters).

- Write permission allows a directory to be written, as in creating or removing files.

- Execute permission allows a directory to be used in a pathname (passed through on the way to a file).

Note: It is a relatively common practice to remove read permission from a directory, while retaining execute permission. This keeps stray users from snooping around, but allows the owner to say "Pick up ~linus/A123fW" to a friend without much fear of any unauthorized party gaining access.

Inspecting Files. Unlike Mac OS, MkLinux allows many sorts of things to reside in the file system. The file **/dev/cua1**, for instance, is actually a connection to driver for the modem serial port. The file **/dev/modem**, in contrast, is a **symbolic link** (alias, in Mac OS terms) to **/dev/cua1**.

This provides great convenience and flexibility for both programmers and users. On occasion, however, it's nice to know exactly what a given item is. We can inspect any item in the file system by means of the **ls** command:

```
% ls -al ~linus/foo
-rwxr-x--- ... linus staff ... /u/linus/foo
```

The first character in the output line is the **file type** flag, which indicates what kind of "file" this is. Here are some common file type flags:

- **-**   ordinary file

- **b**   block special file

- **c**   character special file

- **d**   directory

- **l**   symbolic link

- **p**   named pipe special file

In this case, the "file" is really a file. Further, it is owned by a user named linus, has group staff, and has permissions -rwxr-x---. (For more information on the flags and output of the ls command, try **man ls**.)

We discussed file mode bits above. Now we get to look at some. In this case, the first set of file mode flags (rwx) allows the file's owner (linus) to read, write, and execute the file. The second set (r-x) allows any member of the staff group to read and execute the file. Finally, the third set (---) prevents anyone else from accessing the file in any way.

The actual situation is a bit more complicated, of course. To gain access to the file, a user must also satisfy the permissions on directories **/**, **/u**, and **/u/linus**. And, of course, root can almost entirely ignore permissions.

Initial Permissions. The permissions acquired by a newly created file are determined by the creator's current **umask** (usage mask), as set by the **umask** command:

```
% umask 077  # create files as "rwx------"
% umask 027  # create files as "rwxr-x---"
% umask 002  # create files as "rwxrwxr-x"
```

The argument to umask is interpreted as an octal value. Each bit in the value masks (by means of an **exclusive or**) the default permission (777), yielding the permission bits for the resulting file. Thus, a mask value of 27 results in permissions of rwxr-x---, as:

Octal	Binary			Permissions			Notes
777	111	111	111	rwx	rwx	rwx	default (all on)
027	000	010	111	---	-w-	rwx	mask value
===	===	===	===	===	===	===	
750	111	101	000	rwx	r-x	---	resulting value

Changing Permissions. The owner of a file (or root) may change the permissions on a file, using the **chmod** command. Permissions may be specified either symbolically or numerically:

```
% chmod  go+x  foo
% chmod  750  foo
```

See the chmod manual page for more detailed coverage of its usage.

A file's group may also be changed by means of the **chgrp** command:

```
% chgrp  staff  foo
```

The file's owner can change a file's group to any group of which the owner is a member. (Group membership is controlled by the /etc/passwd and /etc/group files.)

Predictably, root may change a file's group to any group at all, even if it isn't listed in /etc/group:

```
# chgrp  fubar  foo
# chgrp  12345  bar
```

Alternatively, `root` may change both the ownership and the group, using the **chown** command:

> \# **chown root.fubar foo**

Finally, `root` may change just the ownership:

> \# **chown root foo**

Editing /etc/group. Each user has a default group, as specified in his or her `/etc/passwd` entry. Although it is not necessary to enter default groups into the `/etc/group` file, your `ls` output will be prettier if you do. It is also a good idea to list the membership of default groups in `/etc/group`, as a bit of useful documentation.

There are several ways of handling default group id's. On a small system, each account can have its own group, with all joint groups being explicitly defined. A dedicated group (and possibly a dedicated directory) is then created whenever users need to share a set of files. A "staff" group, for example, can let certain users do mundane system management functions without becoming `root`.

On larger systems, it is often useful to use default groups for project teams or user classes. Note, however, that the `umask` should be set appropriately to avoid accidental security holes.

Each line in `/etc/group` has four colon-separated fields:

1	group name	alphanumeric
2	group password	encrypted, but see below
3	group id	numeric
4	members	comma-separated login names

Note: Group passwords are poorly supported, and in any event are a **BAD IDEA**. Users don't tend to care for their own passwords very well; they take no care whatever of group passwords. Fill in this field with an asterisk!

Backing Up And Restoring Files

There are several reasons for doing backups, but the essential reason is risk avoidance. If you have adequate backups, few problems can do serious harm to your data. If you do not, almost anything can cause you serious grief.

Here is a sampling of the risks your data faces:

- Human error – MkLinux is quite willing to let users damage or delete their own files. More files are damaged by slipping fingers than by any other cause. And, of course, the `root` account can remove anything on the system.

- Software problems – If a data structure gets damaged, MkLinux may get confused and lose one or more files. Alternatively, a program could crash, damaging its working files.

- Hardware problems – Hard drives sometimes start getting read errors; less frequently, they simply jam and start smoking.

- Environmental problems – Mother nature can cause real problems for your data. How well are you prepared for an earthquake, fire, flood, wind storm, or other natural disaster?

- Intentional damage – Arson is always a possibility, as are theft and malicious tampering. Physical security reduces these threats, but cannot entirely eliminate them.

It is quite possible to do complete system backups on a daily basis. It is a lot of work, however, and is probably inappropriate for most MkLinux systems. We recommend a mixed backup strategy, which should meet your needs at a lower cost (and far less effort!) than a brute-force approach:

- Full backups – Every so often, you should make a full backup of your system. This ensures that you don't overlook something that may later turn out to have been critically important.

- Partial backups – By selecting important parts of your system for backup, you can reduce the amount of work involved. How many copies of the `/usr` partition do you really need?

- Delta backups – Some backup programs allow you to save only files that have been modified since the last full backup. If your data is relatively stable, this can greatly reduce the backup effort.

- "disk-to-disk" backups – Many risks (human error, hardware and software problems, etc.) can be reduced by automated disk-to-disk backups. Have **cron** run your favorite backup program during the middle of the night, compress the output, and save it on a different disk drive. (To save space, you can do mostly delta backups...)

Media considerations. Your backups are important; handle them with care:

- media security – Treat your backup media with care. You don't want it to be stolen, damaged, examined, or modified by malicious persons.

- multiple media – Your system could crash during the backup process. Alternatively, your backup tape (disk, etc.) could develop an error and become unreadable. If you only have one backup, you could be in big trouble. Use sets of at least three tapes, cycling through them as you perform your backups.

- off-site storage – If your building burns down, will you still have copies of your data? It is very easy to save copies of your backups in another location; the hard part is remembering to do it.

- retiring tapes – Even with occasional use, your tapes will wear out over time. Sheer age will also cause your tapes to degrade. Keep track of the age and usage of your tapes; after a few dozen uses or a couple of years of use, take them out of service.

  Note: Many sites are starting to use write-once media (recordable CD-ROMs) for archival purposes. These devices are physically robust, have long shelf lives, and are quite resistant to tampering.

- data retention – If you are taking frequent backups and saving them forever, you could easily run out of room to store them! On the other hand, how important is data from several months or years ago? In most cases, we recommend that you save some snapshots forever, but refrain from trying to save *everything*.

Backup frequency, etc. How often, when, and how should backups be done? These aren't easy questions; several interrelated factors are involved:

- How much data can you afford to lose? Your data is changing constantly; anything short of instantaneous backup (e.g., mirrored disk drives or
  a RAID system) may lose some amount of data.

- How often can you take your system down? Backups are best done while
  the system is quiescent, but kicking off your users too often has a cost, as
  well. You may want to take your chances on a few files being in transition during the occasional backup.

- How much resources do you want to allocate to doing backups? Your time
  has a value, even if you aren't getting paid for it. If you pay operators
  to load, fill, and inventory backup tapes, there is a real cost involved.

Like any other form of insurance, backups must be evaluated on a cost-bene-
fit basis. Decide how much risk you are willing to sustain and how much
effort you are willing to spend in risk reduction. Just don't let the decision
get made by default; you may not like the results!

Backup methods. MkLinux has several programs that can be used for
backups, including:

- `cpio` – The `cpio` utility will archive a specified list of files. It combines well with the **find** command, which can create file lists according to assorted criteria. The pass-through mode is particularly useful
  for making identical copies of directory trees.

- `dd` – The `dd` utility is able to copy a bit-for-bit image of a disk partition (or even an entire disk drive).

  Note: This is seldom a useful tool for general-purpose backups, but it can
  be quite useful for, say, copying one hard disk (partition) to another.

- `tar` – The `tar` utility is very facile at archiving specified directory
  trees, omitting specified sub-trees, etc.

How MkLinux Starts Up

The first parts of MkLinux start-up are rather unusual, by conventional
Linux standards. After that, however, things are totally standard:

- Boot Mac OS

  - Run MkLinux Booter (Mac OS INIT)

- Load Mach Kernel (Mac OS INIT)

- Run Mach kernel

  - Run bootstrap code

    - Start up `/mach_servers/default_pager`

    - Start up `/mach_servers/vmlinux`

      - Initialize internal data structures

      - Mount `root` file system

      - Start up `/mach_servers/mach_init`

        - Exec `/sbin/init` as process 1

          - Run commands from `/etc/inittab`

          - Run commands in `/etc/rc.d/rc`, ...

          - Fork and exec `/sbin/getty`, according to getty entries in `/etc/inittab`

            - Read login name from the `tty`

            - Exec `/bin/login`

              - Log in the user

              - Exec the requested shell

              - Fork and exec user commands

          - On SIGHUP, re-read `/etc/inittab` and start/terminate tasks accordingly

          - On TERM, go to single user mode

How Sessions Start Up

Each user session startup follows a predictable path, depending on the shell involved and the complement of start-up files. Here is a summary; for definitive explanations and variations, see the online manual pages:

If the login shell is bash, it starts up as:

- Source /etc/profile

- Source $HOME/.bash_profile, $HOME/.bash_login, or $HOME/
  .profile, in that order

  - Source $HOME/.bashrc

    - Source /etc/bashrc

- Run user commands

- Source $HOME/.bash_logout

If a new interactive instance of bash is spawned:

- Source $HOME/.bashrc

  - Source /etc/.bashrc

If the login shell is (t)csh, the startup goes like:

- Source /etc/csh.cshrc

- Source /etc/csh.login

- Source $HOME/.cshrc

  - Source $HOME/.aliases

- Source $HOME/.login

- Run user commands

- Source $HOME/.logout

If a new interactive instance of (t)csh is spawned:

- Source /etc/csh.cshrc

- Source $HOME/.cshrc

- Run user commands

Setting Up Disks

MkLinux allows disks to be added, but a number of things have to be done correctly, and in the right order, as:

Wiring it up. A MkLinux system will have one or more **SCSI** busses, each of which can support several devices. Each device is addressed by means of its **SCSI ID**. Devices on the bus are "daisy-chained", usually by means of external cables. **Termination** must be provided at each end of the bus.

Each device on a given SCSI bus must have its own unique ID, ranging from 0 to 6 (the CPU uses ID 7). Most external devices have switches to set the ID. Internal devices typically use removable jumpers for this purpose.

SCSI devices are commonly "daisy-chained", with several units being linked in series. Each end of the bus must be terminated by a set of resistors or an active (solid-state) terminator. The inboard (CPU) end of the SCSI bus is normally terminated by the vendor; terminating the outboard end is the responsibility of the user.

Some SCSI devices are shipped with removable packs of resistors or other "internal" termination. We suggest that any such termination be removed or disabled, as it is a frequent source of confusion. Use an external terminator (preferably an active one), attached to the last device in the chain.

Formatting, labelling, etc. A newly acquired disk is a bit of an unknown. It may have bad tracks, inappropriate sectoring, or any number of other problems. Fortunately, Apple and other vendors provide tools for dealing with these issues. If your disk was manufactured by Apple, you will be able to use **Apple HD SC Setup**, **Drive Setup**, or **pdisk**, shipped with MkLinux, for this purpose. If not, you may need to acquire a third-party product. (See the Preparation chapter for detailed information on these topics.)

Disk formatting sets up the disk correctly for the system, scans for bad spots, and generally readies the disk for use. On Mac OS and MkLinux systems, disk labelling is then performed. The label allows the system to know what kind of disk is being used, how it is laid out (partitioned), etc.

Making a node for the device. MkLinux wants to find all of its devices in /dev, even the disks themselves. In general, however, any needed entries will be present in the standard MkLinux system.

If you need a device entry that is not present, try to use the **MAKEDEV** script, located in /dev. If this does not meet your needs, you can use the mknod command to make a file system node for a device and the chmod command to set appropriate permissions. (If you are getting this far into things, you should either be a UNIX guru or have one available!)

Making a file system. If a disk partition is to be used for storing MkLinux files, it first must be partitioned into MkLinux file systems. The **mkfs** and **mke2fs** commands do this, setting up the assorted control blocks and directories that MkLinux needs. (You normally should use mke2fs.)

Creating a free directory. When a file system is "mounted" on a directory, the original contents of the directory disappear. The contents reappear when the disk is dismounted, but you might want to look at them before then. So, it is generally appropriate to create an empty directory to be used as the **mount point** for the new file system. (MkLinux provides **/mnt** as a mount point for temporary purposes.)

The mount point directory can have any desired name, but short names are preferable. Some administrators prefer to name mount points for the SCSI device ID and partition involved (e.g., /1a); others like to name them topically (e.g., /wombats). Be sure to set the mode of the directory to 777; other modes can cause the mounted file system to behave weirdly:

```
# mkdir   /1a
# chmod  777  /1a
```

Mounting the file system on a directory. Use the **mount** command to mount file systems, and the **umount** command to unmount them. If the umount command fails, check for a shell session (or a subsidiary process) whose current directory lies within the mounted file system. (MkLinux will not unmount a file system that is currently in use.) If you *cannot* find the guilty process, you can always do a reboot, but don't do this rashly...

If a file system is going to be mounted frequently, you should add a line for it in **/etc/fstab**. Use the **noauto** flag if the file system should *not* be mounted automatically at system boot.

Chapter 6:

- *Snapshots*
- *Updates*
- *RPM Binary Archives*
- *Installing RPM Binary Archives*
- *RPM Source Archives*
- *Building RPM Source Archives*
- *Other Freeware Archives*
- *Building Other Freeware Packages*

Upgrades And Enhancements

Unlike many commercial operating system products (but in common with most other Linux distributions!), no MkLinux release can really be considered a "final" product. MkLinux is constantly changing: bug fixes and enhancements are made frequently, **updates** are posted regularly, new applications are ported and added to the application base. For this reason, we refer to the published MkLinux releases as **snapshots**. Like their photographic counterparts, MkLinux snapshots represent static images, taken of the ongoing, ever-changing, "moving target" of MkLinux development.

Unlike physical photographs, however, MkLinux snapshots are frequently updated and enhanced. As mentioned above, updates are posted frequently by the MkLinux development team. These may include bug fixes or enhancements (new features) not present in the latest snapshot. So, be sure to stay current with the latest MkLinux updates; this will help ensure that your MkLinux system is operating at optimum reliability and performance.

A MkLinux snapshot distribution consists of the operating system (including the Mach kernel and Linux Server) and a basic set of tools and application programs. Each snapshot also includes installable, optional "Extras" – programs the Apple MkLinux team thought were interesting but not appropriate for inclusion in the basic installation set. These programs are shipped as **RPM archives**, in source and (often) binary form.

RPM stands for the **RedHat Package Manager**, a tool that creates, uses, and manages a convenient form of archives for application packages. **Binary RPM archives** contain only executable applications. **Source RPM archives** contain source code, which you can examine, use, and/or modify as you desire (subject, of course, to any redistribution or other legal restrictions).

If all this isn't enough, MkLinux is almost infinitely customizable, assuming that you possess some programming capability and wish to go exploring. A wealth of **freeware packages** is available on the Internet. Some **FTP** sites contain broad-spectrum collections, including many kinds of freely redistributable software. Other, more esoteric sites, may host only one or two specialized packages.

The bad news is that it may require considerable programming skill to port some of these packages to MkLinux. The good news is that, once you have ported them, you can post your results so that others may benefit from your explorations (and laud your achievements)! Again, be sure to pay attention to any restrictions before you post a package.

Snapshots

As described above, a **snapshot** is a single, documented point in the MkLinux development process. All updates, bug fixes, and enhancements to date are sifted, collected into a coherent whole, packaged with an installer and various documentation files, tested, and distributed.

Snapshots involve quite a bit of work for everyone involved: the MkLinux Team must create them and the MkLinux user community must install them, often removing the existing MkLinux system in the process. Consequently, snapshots occur fairly infrequently: historically, they have been at least three months apart.

Once a snapshot is ready for distribution, it is made available in two forms:

- **FTP** – snapshots are made available for anonymous FTP downloading on `ftp.mklinux.apple.com/pub/` (the official MkLinux FTP site) and various mirror sites, in the `Full_Release` subdirectory.

  Dartmouth's Fetch utility, included on the PTF Reference disc, allows FTP under Mac OS; under MkLinux, use the **ftp** command.

- **CD-ROM** – Prime Time Freeware publishes MkLinux snapshots as part of its CD-ROM "MkLinux Snapshot" distributions.

As each snapshot is released, it becomes the new **baseline** upon which all future updates and enhancements will be made. Support, in the form of bug fixes and enhancements, typically is greatly reduced (or nonexistent) for previous snapshots. **Bug reports** may still be accepted for recent snapshots, but reports receive far more attention if the problem has been reproduced under the current version of MkLinux.

Each snapshot has a **release designation**, such as DR1, DR2, or 1.0. This gives the MkLinux community a point of reference to use in discussing issues, porting applications, filing bug reports, or sharing ideas on the various mailing lists and similar forums.

Updates

Because MkLinux is constantly evolving, a given snapshot isn't completely current for very long. Bug fixes, enhancements, and updates are posted frequently (typically, every few weeks), replacing or augmenting portions of the current snapshot.

To keep your MkLinux system up to date, try to download and apply these updates on a regular basis. More critically, be sure you're updating the latest snapshot! Each set of updates is expected to be applied to the most recent snapshot, sometimes in a particular order.

Because updates happen so frequently, PTF does not include them on our CD-ROMs. Even if we tried to do so, it is likely a new update would be posted before the discs were ready for shipping! In particular, the snapshot CD-ROM associated with this Reference Release contains only the most current snapshot at the time of this writing.

RPM Binary Archives

The MkLinux Installer loads your MkLinux system disk drive, by default, with the MkLinux operating system (including the Mach kernel and Linux Server) and a basic set of tools and applications. However, the distribution also contains additional packages which you may (or may not!) find useful and interesting.

These packages, known as **RPM binary archives**, contain pre-built application programs which are believed to run on MkLinux. Many of these are included on the CD-ROM, ready to be installed at your convenience. RPM binary archive files typically have names like:

```
apache-1.1.1.3a.ppc.rpm
```

The name includes the package name (apache), version (1.1.1), release number (3a), machine architecture (ppc), and archive type (rpm).

Additional package archives may be made available on the MkLinux FTP site, in the contrib directory; these packages have been ported by MkLinux users like yourself and made available to the rest of the MkLinux community. If you port a package to MkLinux, consider making it available. See the MkLinux web site (www.mklinux.apple.com) for information on uploading procedures. Be sure to include all appropriate attributions, including your own contact information, with any uploaded archive.

Still more RPM packages may be found on other FTP sites. However, you should understand the RPM packaging mechanism is used for many kinds of Linux systems. Most frequently, RPM binary packages are intended for use on Intel-based Linux systems. Because of architectural issues, a binary archive intended for use on an Intel machine will *not* work under MkLinux.

If you find an RPM binary archive on a non-MkLinux FTP site, check carefully to see if the binary application is known to work on MkLinux (or at least PowerPC Linux) *before* attempting to install and run it. Look for the ppc architecture specification in the name. While this is no guarantee that the package is supported, it's a good starting point.

Installing RPM Binary Archives

Before you can unpack and install the contents of any RPM binary archive, you will need to load it onto your MkLinux disk. If you find an RPM archive on an FTP site, download it (using binary mode!) onto your MkLinux disk. If you wish to unpack one of the archives included on the Apple MkLinux disc, first copy the desired archive to an appropriate MkLinux directory.

Note: At this writing, several commands (e.g., **hmount**) are supplied to allow access to HFS filesystems. We expect future releases of MkLinux to make accessing files in HFS filesystems easier yet. Check the Release Notes or the MkLinux Web site for details.

Once you have the archive loaded into an appropriate MkLinux directory, you can examine it. Query the package to determine its contents and other information, such as description, release size, build date, etc.:

```
$ rpm -qip apache-1.1.1-3a.ppc.rpm
Name   : apache          Distribution: (none)
Version  : 1.1.1          Vendor: (none)
Release  : 3a            Build Date: Tue Aug...
Install date: (none)       Build Host: power120
Group  : Networking/Daemons Source RPM: apache-...
Size   : 1178576
Summary  : HTTP server daemon to provide WWW services
Description :
The Apache web server is the best free web server
available in the UNIX world today. It uses HTTP
(HyperText Transfer Protocol) to allow web browsers to
view documents and submit data remotely. It has...
```

The -q option specifies a query. The additional options modify the query. The -p option specifies that you are querying a specific package file. The -i option displays the retrieved information. Many other useful options are available. See the rpm man page or try **rpm --help** for details.

When you've examined the package and determined that it is what you want, su to root and install it:

```
# rpm -iv apache-1.1.1-3a.ppc.rpm
Installing apache-1.1.1-3a.ppc.rpm
```

The -i option specifies an installation. The -v option specifies verbose output. You may want to try the -h option (e.g., rpm -ivh), which prints a sequence of hash marks (###) as the installation progresses.

The RPM archive contains all of the information necessary to install the package. Each file is unpacked and installed in the appropriate place on your MkLinux system.

Usually, installation is straightforward; however, you may get errors under some circumstances. Errors will occur if the package you are trying to install is already installed, contains files which conflict with previously installed files, or depends on a package that has not yet been installed. The rpm utility has special options which can be used to override these situations, if that is appropriate. See the rpm man page for details.

If you ever change your mind and wish to uninstall a previously installed packages, this is also simple:

```
# rpm -e apache
```

(Note: as the uninstall process will need to delete files from privileged areas of the filesystem, you must become root to perform this operation.)

The -e option specifies that you wish to uninstall the package. Note that, whereas an installation requires the name of the RPM archive file containing the package, uninstall requires that you specify the package name. That is, type "apache" rather than "apache-1.1.1-3a.ppc.rpm".

RPM Source Archives

RPM source archives contain the source code for application programs. Like RPM binary archives, these may be included on the CD-ROM, served on the MkLinux FTP site (ftp.mklinux.apple.com) in the contrib directory, or found on other FTP sites. RPM source archive files typically have names like apache-1.1.1-3a.src.rpm. The name includes the package name (apache), version (1.1.1), release number (3a), source code indication (src), and archive type (rpm).

For each of the RPM binary archives included on the MkLinux CD-ROM , there is an associated RPM source archive. In most cases, however, the binary has already been built to run on MkLinux, so you will not need to deal with the source code.

Some packages have not yet been ported, however; if you wish to use them, you will need to unpack the source code and attempt a build. Alternatively, you may wish to examine the source code, just to see "how something was done". Finally, you may wish to make a modification or fix (gasp!) a bug.

Note: If you fix a bug, please send any changes you make to the original package author, for inclusion in future releases of that package. Be sure to indicate which version of the package you started with, what problem you were trying to resolve, etc. Package authors are generally very happy to get this kind of careful, detailed input; please don't send them the other kind!

RPM source archives can also be found in many of the freeware collections available on the net. This source code may not yet have been ported to MkLinux and/or Power Macintosh. Frequently, the port is as simple as compiling and building (via make) a binary executable. On the other hand, additional work may be required.

The amount of work will vary considerably. If you do not consider yourself a programmer, you may want to start with something simple, or get some help from a programmer friend, if you decide to port a source package.

RPM source packages, in general, have been ported to run on some flavor of Linux, so the port to MkLinux should not be very difficult. In our experience, the only problems users encounter have to do with processor architecture incompatibilities (e.g. byte ordering, signed vs. unsigned characters).

If you port a source package to MkLinux, we suggest that you share your results with the rest of the MkLinux community. See the MkLinux web site (www.mklinux.apple.com) for information on uploading procedures. Be sure to include all appropriate attributions, including your own contact information, with any uploaded archive.

We recommend that you use the RPM binary and source archive format; we've found it to be a good convention to follow. For information on creating RPM archives, including the application of **patches** (**diffs**) to existing archives, see the rpm man pages or the complete documentation on the Red Hat web site (www.redhat.com).

Building RPM Source Archives

Before you can unpack and build the contents of any RPM source archive, you will need to load it onto your MkLinux disk. If you find an RPM archive on an FTP site, download (using binary mode!) onto your MkLinux disk. If you intend to unpack one of the archives included on an Apple MkLinux disc, copy the desired archive from the Macintosh HFS filesystem on that disc to an appropriate MkLinux directory.

Note: At this writing, several commands (e.g., hmount) are supplied to allow access to HFS filesystems. We expect future releases of MkLinux to make accessing files in HFS filesystems easier yet. Check the Release Notes or the MkLinux Web site for details.

Once you have the archive loaded into an appropriate MkLinux directory, you can examine it. Query the package to determine its contents and other information, such as description, release size, build date, etc:

```
$ rpm -qip apache-1.1.1-3a.src.rpm
Name   : apache             Distribution: (none)
Version : 1.1.1             Vendor: (none)
Release : 3a                Build Date: Sat Aug...
Install date: (none)        Build Host: Atlas
Group  : Networking/Daemons Source RPM: (none)
Size   : 307189
Summary : HTTP server daemon to provide WWW services
Description :
The Apache web server is the best free web server
available in the UNIX world today. It uses HTTP
(HyperText Transfer Protocol) to allow web browsers to
view documents and submit data remotely. It has...
```

The -q option to rpm specifies a query. The additional options modify the query. The -p option specifies that you are querying a specific package file. The -i option displays the verbose information. Additional options are available. See the rpm man page or try **rpm --help** for details.

When you've determined that the package is what you want, building it is straightforward. Become root, then unpack and install the sources:

```
# rpm  -iv  apache-1.1.1-3a.src.rpm
Installing apache-1.1.1-3a.src.rpm
```

The -i option specifies an install. The -v option specifies verbose output. A **spec** file is extracted and placed in /usr/src/redhat/SPECS. A tar archive and any patch files are unpacked into .../redhat/SOURCES.

Next, "prep" and compile the source:

```
# cd  /usr/src/redhat/SPECS
# rpm  -bi  apache-1.1.1.spec
```

The -b option specifies a build. The -i option specifies the "installation stage", which includes **prep** (unpack sources and apply patches), compile, and install. The rpm utility provides options for running these stages separately – prep alone, prep and compile, or prep, compile, and install in one step. See the manual page for rpm or run **rpm --help** for details on these and other options.

This step prepares the source distribution files for the target machine. The archive is unpacked and any patches specified by the **.spec** file are applied. The prepared source is then compiled and installed into the appropriate location(s) on your MkLinux system.

You will see progress information scrolling down your screen:

```
* Package: apache
+ umask 022
+ echo Executing: %prep
Executing: %prep
+ cd /usr/src/redhat/BUILD
+ cd /usr/src/redhat/BUILD
+ rm -rf apache_1.1.1
+ gzip -dc /usr/src/redhat/SOURCES/apache_1.1.1.tar.gz
+ tar -xvvf -
drwxrwxr-x 129/9 0 Jul 8 12:05 1996 apache_1.1.1/
drwxrwxr-x 129/9 0 Jul 8 12:04 1996 apache_1.1.1/cgi-...
...
+ echo Executing: %build
Executing: %build
+ cd /usr/src/redhat/BUILD
+ cd apache_1.1.1
+ cd src
+ ./Configure
Using 'Configuration' as config file
+ make RPM_OPT_FLAGS=-O2 -fsigned-char AUX_LIBS=
gcc -c -O2 -fsigned-char -DSTATUS -DLINUX alloc.c
...
+ echo Executing: %install
Executing: %install
+ cd /usr/src/redhat/BUILD
+ cd apache_1.1.1
+ mkdir -p /home/httpd/html
...
```

If all goes well, your new package will now be installed and ready to run. Be sure to read any accompanying documentation.

If all does not go well, you should examine the source, make any necessary modifications, then try to rebuild and install the package. The unpacked and prepared source usually ends up in a subdirectory of /usr/src/ redhat/BUILD. Go to the appropriate source code directory, look at the README files and other documentation, and continue to debug amd compile the sources by hand.

Other Freeware Archives

There is a wealth of freely redistributable software available on the Internet, but only a small portion of it has been ported to MkLinux. Freeware is available on hundreds of FTP sites, scattered across the Internet. Unfortunately, the source code may be in any of several possible conditions:

- known to build on Linux

- known to build on some variant(s) of UNIX

- known to build on some other operating system

- condition unknown

Like their RPM source archive counterparts, these applications may or may not be useful and interesting. And, unlike most RPM source archives, some will require considerable porting effort; others will port very easily.

Thus, you should always look first for a version which has been ported to MkLinux. Failing that, try for a Linux version, etc., moving down the list given above. Each step in the list represents a new measure of complexity and potential dificulty in porting. (Note that this is only potential difficulty; you may find a program designed for some other operating system that ports with ease.)

If you port a freeware program to , we suggest that you contribute it to the large body of MkLinux source and binary archives. See the MkLinux web site (www.mklinux.apple.com) for information on uploading procedures. Be careful, however, to read and comply with any restrictions placed on the software. Also, be sure to include all appropriate attributions, including your own contact information, with any archive.

We recommend that you use the RPM binary and source archive format; we've found it to be a good convention to follow. For information on creating RPM archives, see the `rpm` man pages, or the complete documentation on the Red Hat web site (`www.redhat.com`).

Building Other Freeware Packages

Before you can build the contents of any Freeware source archive, you will need to load it onto your MkLinux disk. We recommend that you create a Working directory where you will load, unpack, modify, and build source archives.

Freeware source archives are often distributed as `tar` archives, compressed with `compress` or (increasingly) `gzip`. The former will usually end in the suffix ".`tar.Z`". The latter will often end in the suffix ".`tgz`" or perhaps ".`tar.gz`". If you are unsure about which utility to use to unpack the file, look at the associated README files and other documentation.

To unpack a `tar` archive that has been compressed with `gzip`, go to the desired destination directory, then use the following command:

```
# tar -zxpf archivename.tgz
```

(To ensure that ownerships, permissions, etc. of the extracted files are not inadvertently changed, you may want to become `root` before you do this.)

Once you have unpacked the archive, you can examine the source, make any necessary modifications, then attempt to build and install the package. Be sure to examine any README files and other documentation, especially any Configure scripts, before you attempt to build the package.

Chapter 7:

- *Preparatory Steps*
- *Building The Microkernel*
- *Modifying The MkLinux Server*

Building The System

Although the name of this chapter follows conventional UNIX practice, it may be misleading to the unwary. A "system build" in UNIX parlance is not the creation of binaries for the entire operating system, let alone the placement of these and other files into their designated places in the file system.

Rather, it is the creation of the operating system kernel, a low-level program which is responsible for the management of all system resources and for making these resources available to processes, via system calls.

In MkLinux, even these two functions are separated. The Mach microkernel is responsible for managing low-level system resources such as memory use and processor time, as well as device and inter-process communication.

Higher-level functions (e.g., file systems, networking) are provided by **server** tasks, whose binary files generally reside in **/mach_servers**:

- **default_pager**   Swap manager for virtual memory

- **mach_init**   Used by vmlinux to launch first MkLinux process (**/etc/init**, PID 1)

- **mach_perf**   Performance test suite, used for testing Mach microkernel (independently of any other tasks)

- **vmlinux**   MkLinux "single server"

It is very unlikely that you will need to modify any of the first three programs. If you need to build one of these, see the last part of the section on Building the Microkernel.

For most kernel-related changes, you should only need to modify vmlinux, the MkLinux server. If you are writing or modifying a device driver, you probably will need to modify the Mach microkernel, as well.

Note: It is quite possible that build procedures will change over time. See the README files at the top level of the distribution, as well as any README files located with the kernel source files. Finally, inspect the Apple MkLinux Web Server (www.mklinux.apple.com) for up-to-date information before attempting any of the procedures below.

Preparatory Steps

Before you can build anything, there are a few preparatory steps you will need to perform. These only need to be done once, but it is critical that they are done correctly.

- **Become root.** The following steps require root privileges. Be careful, however; like most UNIX-derived systems, MkLinux offers few protections against mistakes made by the root account!

  ```
  $ su -
  Password: [...silent...]
  #
  ```

- **Retrieve the source code.** The notes below assume that you will be performing your builds under the **/usr/src** directory. If you need to do your builds somewhere else, it is up to you to make any needed changes (e.g., modifying directory names and search paths).

  Retrieve and unpack copies of the MkLinux server and Mach microkernel source archives, the Mach include files and libraries, and the Mach build tools

  ```
  # mount  /mnt/cdrom
  # cd /usr/src
  # S=/mnt/cdrom/mklinux_source
  # for i in $S/*.tgz; do
  >   tar xzf $i
  > done
  ```

- **Set up the ML link.** To avoid rewriting your setup scripts every time you grab new sources, and to reduce typing (and mistakes) all around, we suggest that you create a link to the source directory, substituting the appropriate version string for **VER**, etc:

```
# ln -s VER ML
```

If and when you load in new source trees, you will need to replace this link. For example:

```
# rm OLD
# ln -s NEW ML
```

- **Change the ownership of the source code directory.** Decide which account will be used for doing the builds, then set the ownership (and group) of everything in the tree to that account. Finally, `exit` (or whatever) to get back to the build account.

```
# chown -R linus:linus VER
# exit
logout
$
```

Note: If you will be doing all of your builds as `root`, you can skip this step. Just be careful not to make any (Oops! #@%$) misteaks...

- **Make sure that bash is your default shell.** The helper scripts below assume that you will be using the `bash` shell for your build activities. Check to see if `bash` is the default shell:

```
$ echo $SHELL
/bin/bash
```

If the answer is not `/bin/bash`, you need to change your shell to `bash` before starting any builds. You have two options:

- **Start a copy of bash for each build session.**

```
$ bash
$
```

- **Declare bash as your default shell.**

```
$ chsh
Changing shell for linus.
Password: [...silent...]
```

```
New shell [/bin/sh]: /bin/bash
Shell changed.
$
```

Building the Microkernel

As noted above, it is seldom necessary to rebuild the Mach microkernel. So, unless you have a strong reason (such as one listed below), you probably should ignore (or merely skim, for background) this section.

- adding a patch – MkLinux microkernel patches are normally accompanied by patched binary images, but some may not be.

- creating or modifying a device driver – MkLinux device drivers do most of their work in the microkernel, rather than in the Linux Server.

- doing operating system research – Mach in general, and MkLinux in particular, can be a useful medium for OS experimentation.

- using a new compiler to build the microkernel – If a compiler promises added features or increased performance, a rebuild might make sense.

Before you modify the Mach microkernel, you should do a complete build of the existing microkernel. This assures you that the base distribution is complete, correctly installed, etc. It also ensures that all of the needed object files are available, with clean date stamps, etc. Even if you only intend to modify the Linux server, you will need to do a partial build.

- **Make sure you have a way to copy files to your boot partition.** The commands shown below assume that your boot partition is formatted as an "HFS" (as opposed to "HFS+") volume. If this is not the case, you will need to come up with a way to transfer the new microkernel. This may include using an HFS volume or another machine (via FTP) for temporary storage, but you'll need to come up with a working strategy!

- **Add the Mach and ODE tools to your search PATH.** In order to build the microkernel, you'll need the ODE (**OSF Development Environment**) tools. They are located in:

  ML/ode-bin/ppc_linux/bin/

  We recommend that you use the **set_ode_path.sh** script, which will automatically set your PATH variable to the correct value, depending on whether you're in an ODE sandbox or not. Just add the following line to **~/.bashrc**:

```
. /usr/src/ML/set_ode_path.sh
```

Also note that the .bashrc file is *not* executed by default at login time. Consequently, you should either:

- Source set_ode_path.sh from ~/.profile.

- Source ~/.bashrc from ~/.profile.

Note: The PATH cannot always be set to the same value. In some situations (e.g., when building the microkernel), you will need to use the ODE make command. In others (e.g., building the MkLinux server), you will need to use the MkLinux make command.

If make complains about the syntax of a Makefile, you're probably using the wrong make command. You can use **make -v** to find out which version of make is being executed:

```
$ make -v
program : make
release : ODE 2.3.4
built   : Fri Apr 19 16:03:02 EDT 1996
```

Some Mach tools are also needed to build the MkLinux server. The set_ode_path.sh script takes care of that too. The tools are in

```
ML/osfmk/tools/ppc/ppc_linux/hostbin/
```

- **Edit and install ~/.sandboxrc**. If you've never used ODE, use the sandboxrc.template file. Install this file as **.sandboxrc** in your HOME directory.

```
$ cp  ML/sandboxrc.template  ~/.sandboxrc
```

Then, edit it to reflect the place where you've installed the OSF MK sources (the base line should point to the ML directory).

- **Make sure USER is set.** The /etc/profile script sets this; just make sure that you have not disabled the setting.

```
$ echo $USER
```

```
linus
```

You may set USER to any desired name, but normally you will want it to be the same as your login name:

```
$ export   USER=$LOGNAME
```

It's a good idea to add this to your ~/.profile file.

- **Enter the OSF microkernel sandbox.**

```
$ workon  -sb  osfmk
cd'ing to sandbox source directory: ...
starting new shell: /bin/bash.
$
```

This command should start a shell after setting up the environment for ODE. The current directory should now be /usr/src/ML/osfmk/src.

Note: Don't forget to exit the workon shell when you're done building pieces of Mach software!

- **Build the OSF MK header files.**

```
$ build   MAKEFILE_PASS=FIRST
```

Note: There is a handy shell script named build_world, located in /usr/src/ML/osfmk/build_world. It can be configured to perform any of these build steps, as desired.

- **Build the OSF MK libraries.**

```
$ MS=mach_services
$ build   -here   $MS/lib/libcthreads
$ build   -here   $MS/lib/libsa_mach
$ build   -here   $MS/lib/libmach
$ build   -here   $MS/lib/libmach_maxonstack
```

Note: It is quite possible (and sometimes very convenient) to set a temporary shell variable (e.g., **MS**) to a frequently-typed piece of text.

- **More to build.** Some other parts of the microkernel source tree can be built on a MkLinux system.

- The **file_systems** library (for the bootstrap task):

  ```
  $ build  -here  file_systems
  ```

- The **bootstrap** task:

  ```
  $ build  -here  bootstrap
  ```

- The **default pager**:

  ```
  $ build  -here  default_pager
  ```

- The **name_server** and its libraries:

  ```
  $ build  -here  $MS/lib/libservice
  $ build  -here  $MS/lib/libnetname
  $ build  -here  $MS/servers/netname
  ```

- The **mpts** (microkernel performance test suite):

  ```
  $ build  -here  $MS/cmds/mach_perf
  ```

  Note that mpts is not written as a MkLinux application, but should
  run directly on top of Mach. Place an entry similar to:

  ```
  -w mach_perf /dev/boot_device/mach_servers/mach_perf
  ```

  in the /mach_servers/bootstrap.conf file. If this entry is
  before that for the MkLinux server, then MkLinux should boot after
  quitting mpts.

- **Building the microkernel itself.**

  Before you can build the microkernel, you must decide which type to
  build:

DEBUG	debug
DEBUG+MP+KDB	debug, MP-capable
PRODUCTION	optimized
PRODUCTION+KGDB	optimized, with kgdb support
PRODUCTION+MP+KDB	optimized, MP-capable

Other configurations are possible; see

```
ML/osfmk/src/mach_kernel/conf/POWERMAC/
```

for more information. Now, unless you are building an MP-capable microkernel, issue the **build** command, as:

```
$ build -here mach_kernel \
MACH_KERNEL_CONFIG=DEBUG
```

Note: Kernels which include debugging support suppress usage of DMA on the serial ports. The modem and printer ports are used for remote debugging and console interaction, respectively. They should be hooked up to a terminal or to another machine (standard RS-232, 9600 baud).

- **Building an MP-capable microkernel.**

  If you have a multiprocessor computer, you may wish to build an MP-capable microkernel. This allows programs to be run on different CPUs, yielding improved performance (i.e., throughput and response time).

  DR3 supports two-way (2 CPUs) multiprocessing on the Power Macintosh 9500/180MP and 9600/200MP, as well as on certain third-party processor replacement cards that are based on the Daystar design.

  Note: As of DR3, the source code to operate Daystar-style cards is under non-disclosure agreement between Apple Computer and Daystar. Consequently, only the object file (MP_2p.o) is distributed with the release.

  The build process for MP-capable microkernels is substantially more complicated than the normal build. You must create a dummy source file (MP_2p.s), do a partial build, wait for the link stage to fail, then add in the object file (MP_2p.o) and restart the build. Here goes...

```
$ touch  mach_kernel/ppc/POWERMAC/mp/MP_2p.s
$ build -here mach_kernel \
MACH_KERNEL_CONFIG=DEBUG+MP+KDB
...
$ su
Password: [...silent...]
# mount  /mnt/cdrom
# cp  /mnt/cdrom/mklinux_source/MP_2p.o  \
../obj/powermac/mach_kernel/DEBUG+MP+KDB/
```

```
# exit
logout
$ build  -here  mach_kernel  \
MACH_KERNEL_CONFIG=DEBUG+MP+KDB
. . .
```

- **Installing a new Mach microkernel.** To install a new Mach microkernel, you will need to have built the microkernel and the bootstrap. You will also need to know the partition name, in terms MkLinux understands. If you do not know this name, follow the procedure below:

```
$ pdisk  -l  |  more
. . .
Partition map ... on '/dev/hda'
. . .
5:    Apple_HFS ...
. . .
```

Write down the names of any listed "Apple_HFS" partitions. In the example above, the partition name would be "/dev/hda5". If more than one partition qualifies, you may have to try mounting each one, looking for a volume name that matches your Mac OS boot volume.

Once you are ready, hmount the Mac OS boot partition and change the hfstools current working directory to Mac OS Extensions folder:

```
$ su
Password:  [...silent...]
# hmount  /dev/hda5
Volume name is ...
. . .
# hcd  ":System  Folder:Extensions:"
# makeboot
# exit
logout
$
```

Note: If makeboot cannot find an existing microkernel image in the Mac OS System Folder, it will not install the new image. It will, however, give some instructions on what to do next. Be *sure* to save a copy of the Mach microkernel before you start generating new microkernels!

Modifying the MkLinux Server

Before you modify any part of the MkLinux server, you should do a complete build of the existing server. This assures you that your base distribution is complete, correctly installed, etc. It also ensures that all of the needed object files are available, with appropriate date stamps, etc.

- **Add the Mach tools to your PATH.** Some Mach tools are needed to build the MkLinux server. They are in:

  ```
  ML/osfmk/tools/ppc/ppc_linux/hostbin
  ```

  You need to add this path to your PATH environment variable. A good way to do that is to execute the commands in the script **ML/set_ode_path.sh** script as part of **~/.bashrc**. Just add the following line to the file:

  ```
  .  /usr/src/ML/set_ode_path.sh
  ```

  Note: The PATH cannot always be set to the same value. In some situations (e.g., when building the microkernel), you will need to use the ODE make command. In others (e.g., building the MkLinux server), you will need to use the MkLinux make command. For more details, see the notes in the section above on "Building the Microkernel".

- **Building multiple configurations.** We usually build multiple configurations of the server. The development (**dev**) version has **CONFIG_OSFMACH3_DEBUG** turned on; the production (**prod**) version does not.

  The easiest way to do this is to leave the original MkLinux source tree untouched (never build in it), but create some shadow trees that are fully populated with symbolic links to the original source tree.

  Shadow trees can be built with a utility provided with X (**lndir**) or an ODE utility (**mklinks**). Run one of these for each desired tree:

  ```
  $ cd  /usr/src/ML
  $ mkdir  ml_dev  ml_prod
  $ cd  ml_dev
  $ lndir  ../mklinux
  $ cd  ../ml_prod
  $ lndir  ../mklinux
  ```

- **Build the desired MkLinux server architecture.**

  The method used is essentially the same as that used in building a standard Linux kernel, save that there's no **zImage** to build. First, build the microkernel header files and libraries:

  ```
  $ cd /usr/src/ML/ml_dev/src
  ```

  If necessary, edit the Makefile to select the architecture you want to build: change the **ARCH** variable definition to one of the following:

  osfmach3_ppc   MkLinux server for PowerPC (default)

  osfmach3_i386   MkLinux server for i*86

  i386   original Linux kernel for i*86

  Note that the Intel builds will not work on the Power Macintosh, as we have not supplied the necessary cross-compiling tools.

  ```
  $ make config
  ```

  This will ask a number of configuration questions. You generally should accept the default answer, at least initially.

  Note: We haven't tested all the possible configurations. Some configurations may not compile, boot, or run correctly. Please report this kind of problem to the appropriate MkLinux mailing list.

  ```
  $ make dep
  $ make clean
  $ make
  ```

  This should produce a file named **vmlinux**, the MkLinux server.

- **Install the MkLinux server.** (Save the existing server first!)

  ```
  $ su -
  Password: [...silent...]
  # (cd /mach_servers; mv vmlinux vm-)
  # cp vmlinux /mach_servers
  ```

Note: If you don't use the default name (vmlinux) for the MkLinux server, update **/mach_servers/bootstrap.conf**, indicating which "startup" binary you want to use .

- **Reboot!**

```
# shutdown -r now
...
```

Chapter 8:

- *Proprietary Materials*
- *Freeware*
- *Apple License*
- *BSD License*
- *GNU GPL*
- *Linux License*
- *Mach Licenses*
- *X11 License*
- *PTF Legalese*

Licenses

MkLinux is composed of software from many disparate sources, including corporations, individuals, universities, and research laboratories. The licenses found on materials in this distribution reflect this diversity. This chapter attempts to give an overview of these licenses and their effect on users, programmers, and redistributors.

As a programmer or user, you are reasonably safe in ignoring most of the licensing issues discussed below. Nobody is likely to object to anything you do with the software in this collection, as long as you restrict the effects of your activities to the confines of your own organization.

If, however, you decide to redistribute these materials (possibly as part of another program or collection), the situation could change dramatically. Many of the items in this collection have restrictions that affect the manner in which they can be redistributed.

Proprietary Materials

Some of the material in this collection is proprietary, belonging to Adobe Systems, Apple Computer, Prime Time Freeware, etc. This material tends to be ancillary in nature, including:

- Documentation (e.g., materials from *Inside Macintosh*)

- Mac OS utilities (e.g., Apple HD SC Setup)

- Printed materials, such as this volume

Be very careful about redistributing any of these items. They have been obtained under license, and you have the right to use them, but you have no right, in general, to redistribute any of them without explicit permission.

Freeware

The vast majority of the materials in this collection is freeware (freely redistributable software). This does *not* mean, however, that it is in the Public Domain. Rather, it means that you are free to examine, use, modify, and redistribute the materials *as long as* you obey the licenses for the items in question. To motivate the discussion, let's dream up a worst-case scenario:

> Fred Frobozz is an engineer at Microlithic Systems. His boss has just asked him to create a very flexible inventory-control system for use inside Microlithic. As it happens, Fred has been working on the `gawk` code in his spare time. He realizes that he can turn `gawk` into a special-purpose inventory-control language with no real effort. So, he grabs the source code, modifies it to taste, and hands a working system to his boss.

At this point, it is quite unlikely that any rules have been broken. In any case, it would be impossible for anyone outside of Microlithic to know about any transgressions that *had* taken place. So, no real problem.

> The inventory-control system works very well, but Microlithic's stock gets in trouble. They get bought out by Megamorphic Enterprises, which immediately starts looking around for ways to make some money on the deal. The inventory-control system comes to light and is recognized as a rather salable piece of work. Megamorphic polishes it up, puts it in a pretty shrink-wrapped box, and offers it for sale as IC_BUX.

> Some time later, an inquiring hacker runs the `strings` command on IC_BUX , revealing something like:

> Copyright (C) 1989, 1991-1995 Free Software Foundation.

Now the fun begins, starting with a letter from the Free Software Foundation. The fun could go on to include:

- purchasing a license for `gawk` from its author(s),

- recapitulating the suspect portions of the system, or

- removing IC_BUX from the market.

After this, of course, Megamorphic 's stock collapses, causing a run on the stock exchange, financial collapse of the western world, and the explosion of a minor star in the Alpha Quadrant...

All of this could have been avoided, of course, had a few small precautions been observed. Avoid Megamorphic 's fate by following these rules:

- Don't use freeware code in projects that could become products.

- Leave all copyright notices in place.

- Note the fact of any modifications.

- Search for copyright strings before commercializing software.

As noted above, the MkLinux distribution comes from a variety of sources and is covered by a corresponding variety of licenses. This chapter summarizes some of the more prevalent and/or interesting of these.

Apple License

The proprietary Apple materials on this distribution are covered by the following license:

APPLE COMPUTER, INC.

License for Macintosh system software

PLEASE READ THIS LICENSE CAREFULLY BEFORE DOWNLOAD-ING THE SOFTWARE. BY DOWNLOADING THE SOFTWARE, YOU ARE AGREEING TO BE BOUND BY THE TERMS OF THIS LICENSE. IF YOU DO NOT AGREE TO THE TERMS OF THIS LICENSE, YOU ARE NOT AUTHORIZED TO DOWNLOAD THIS SOFTWARE.

1. **License.** The application, demonstration, system and other software accompanying this License, whether on disk, in read only memory, or on any other media (the "Apple Software"), the related documentation and fonts are licensed to you by Apple Computer, Inc. or its local subsidiary, if any ("Apple"). You own the disk on which

the Apple Software and fonts are recorded but Apple and/or Apple's Licensor(s) retain title to the Apple Software, related documentation and fonts. This License allows you to use the Apple Software and fonts on a single Apple computer and make one copy of the Apple Software and fonts in machine-readable form for backup purposes only. You must reproduce on such copy the Apple copyright notice and any other proprietary legends that were on the original copy of the Apple Software and fonts. You may use the Apple Software in a networked environment so long as each computer in such environment is the subject of a license for the Apple Software; however, you may not electronically transmit the Apple Software from one computer to another over a network. You may also transfer all your license rights in the Apple Software and fonts, the backup copy of the Apple Software and fonts, the related documentation and a copy of this License to another party, provided the other party reads and agrees to accept the terms and conditions of this License.

2. **Restrictions.** The Apple Software contains copyrighted material, trade secrets and other proprietary material and in order to protect them, and except as permitted by applicable legislation, you may not decompile, reverse engineer, disassemble or otherwise reduce the Apple Software to a human-perceivable form. You may not modify, network, rent, lease, loan, distribute or create derivative works based upon the Apple Software in whole or in part, except for the limited networking described above in Section 1. This Apple Software may not be imported to, used in, or reexported from France or any of its colonies or territories.

3. **Termination.** This License is effective until terminated. You may terminate this License at any time by destroying the Apple Software, related documentation and fonts and all copies thereof. This License will terminate immediately without notice from Apple if you fail to comply with any provision of this License. Upon termination you must destroy the Apple Software, related documentation and fonts and all copies thereof.

4. **Export Law Assurances.** You may not use or otherwise export or reexport the Apple Software except as authorized by United States law and the laws of the jurisdiction in which the Apple Software was

obtained. In particular, but without limitation, none of the Apple Software may be used or otherwise exported or reexported (i) into (or to a national or resident of) a United States embargoed country or (ii) to anyone on the U.S. Treasury Department's list of Specially Designated Nationals or the U.S. Department of Commerce's Table of Denial Orders. By using the Apple Software, you represent and warrant that you are not located in, under control of, or a national or resident of any such country or on any such list.

5. **Government End Users.** If the Apple Software is supplied to the United States Government, the Apple Software is classified as "restricted computer software" as defined in clause 52.227-19 of the FAR. The United States Government's rights to the Apple Software are as provided in clause 52.227-19 of the FAR.

6. **Disclaimer of Warranty on Apple Software.** You expressly acknowledge and agree that use of the Apple Software and fonts is at your sole risk. The Apple Software, related documentation and fonts are provided "AS IS" and without warranty of any kind and Apple and Apple's Licensor(s) (for the purposes of provisions 6 and 7, Apple and Apple's Licensor(s) shall be collectively referred to as "Apple") EXPRESSLY DISCLAIM ALL WARRANTIES AND/OR CONDITIONS, EXPRESS OR IMPLIED, INCLUDING, BUT NOT LIMITED TO, THE IMPLIED WARRANTIES AND/OR CONDITIONS OF MERCHANTABILITY AND FITNESS FOR A PARTICULAR PURPOSE. APPLE DOES NOT WARRANT THAT THE FUNCTIONS CONTAINED IN THE APPLE SOFTWARE WILL MEET YOUR REQUIREMENTS, OR THAT THE OPERATION OF THE APPLE SOFTWARE WILL BE UNINTERRUPTED OR ERROR-FREE, OR THAT DEFECTS IN THE APPLE SOFTWARE AND THE FONTS WILL BE CORRECTED. FURTHERMORE, APPLE DOES NOT WARRANT OR MAKE ANY REPRESENTATIONS REGARDING THE USE OR THE RESULTS OF THE USE OF THE APPLE SOFTWARE AND FONTS OR RELATED DOCUMENTATION IN TERMS OF THEIR CORRECTNESS, ACCURACY, RELIABILITY, OR OTHERWISE. WITHOUT PREJUDICE TO THE GENERALITY OF THE FOREGOING, APPLE DOES NOT WARRANT OR MAKE ANY REPRESENTATION OR GUARANTEE REGARDING THE AUTHENTICITY OR SECURITY OF ANY

DIGITAL SIGNATURE GENERATED USING THE APPLE SOFT-
WARE, OR ANY WARRANTY OR REPRESENTATION THAT
THE PERSON OR ENTITY THAT IS USING SUCH A DIGITAL
SIGNATURE HAS THE AUTHORITY TO DO SO. NO ORAL OR
WRITTEN INFORMATION OR ADVICE GIVEN BY APPLE OR
AN APPLE AUTHORIZED REPRESENTATIVE SHALL CREATE A
WARRANTY OR IN ANY WAY INCREASE THE SCOPE OF THIS
WARRANTY. SHOULD THE APPLE SOFTWARE PROVE
DEFECTIVE, YOU (AND NOT APPLE OR AN APPLE AUTHOR-
IZED REPRESENTATIVE) ASSUME THE ENTIRE COST OF ALL
NECESSARY SERVICING, REPAIR OR CORRECTION. SOME
JURISDICTIONS DO NOT ALLOW THE EXCLUSION OF
IMPLIED WARRANTIES, SO THE ABOVE EXCLUSION MAY
NOT APPLY TO YOU. THE TERMS OF THIS DISCLAIMER DO
NOT AFFECT OR PREJUDICE THE STATUTORY RIGHTS OF A
CONSUMER ACQUIRING APPLE PRODUCTS OTHERWISE
THAN IN THE COURSE OF A BUSINESS, NEITHER DO THEY
LIMIT OR EXCLUDE ANY LIABILITY FOR DEATH OR PERSON-
AL INJURY CAUSED BY APPLE'S NEGLIGENCE.

7. **Limitation of Liability.** UNDER NO CIRCUMSTANCES INCLU-
DING NEGLIGENCE, SHALL APPLE BE LIABLE FOR ANY INCI-
DENTAL, SPECIAL OR CONSEQUENTIAL DAMAGES THAT
RESULT FROM THE USE, INCLUDING BUT NOT LIMITED TO
THE IMPROPER, WRONGFUL, OR FRAUDULENT USE OF THE
DIGITAL SIGNATURES GENERATED USING THE APPLE SOFT-
WARE, OR INABILITY TO USE THE APPLE SOFTWARE OR
RELATED DOCUMENTATION, EVEN IF APPLE OR AN APPLE
AUTHORIZED REPRESENTATIVE HAS BEEN ADVISED OF
THE POSSIBILITY OF SUCH DAMAGES. SOME JURISDICTIONS
DO NOT ALLOW THE LIMITATION OR EXCLUSION OF LIA-
BILITY FOR INCIDENTAL OR CONSEQUENTIAL DAMAGES SO
THE ABOVE LIMITATION OR EXCLUSION MAY NOT APPLY
TO YOU.

In no event shall Apple's total liability to you for all damages,
losses, and causes of action (whether in contract, tort (including
negligence) or otherwise) exceed the amount paid by you for the
Apple Software and fonts.

8. **Controlling Law and Severability.** If there is a local subsidiary of Apple in the country in which the Apple Software License was purchased, then the local law in which the subsidiary sits shall govern this License. Otherwise, this License shall be governed by and construed in accordance with the laws of the United States and the State of California, as applied to agreements entered into and to be performed entirely within California between California residents. If for any reason a court of competent jurisdiction finds any provision of this License, or portion thereof, to be unenforceable, that provision of the License shall be enforced to the maximum extent permissible so as to effect the intent of the parties, and the remainder of this License shall continue in full force and effect.

9. **Complete Agreement.** This License constitutes the entire agreement between the parties with respect to the use of the Apple Software, related documentation and fonts, and supersedes all prior or contemporaneous understandings or agreements, written or oral, regarding such subject matter. No amendment to or modification of this License will be binding unless in writing and signed by a duly authorized representative of Apple.

APPLE COMPUTER, INC.
INTERNATIONAL SALES SUBSIDIARY LIST

COUNTRY	SUBSIDIARY
Canada	Apple Canada Inc.
South Africa	Apple Computer (Proprietary) Limited
United Kingdom	Apple Computer (UK) Limited
Sweden, Norway, Denmark	Apple Computer AB
Switzerland	Apple Computer AG (SA) (Ltd.)
Taiwan	Apple Computer Asia, Inc.
Netherlands, Belgium	Apple Computer Benelux B.V.
Brazil	Apple Computer Brasil Ltda.
Spain	Apple Computer Espana, S.A.
France	Apple Computer France S.A.R.L.
Austria	Apple Computer Gesellschaft m.b.H.
Germany	Apple Computer GmbH
Hong Kong	Apple Computer International Ltd
Ireland	Apple Computer (UK) Limited

Mexico	Apple Computer Mexico, S.A. de C.V.
Italy	Apple Computer S.p.A.
Singapore	Apple Computer South Asia Pte Ltd
Japan	Apple Japan, Inc.

BSD License

MkLinux contains a large number of utilities from the 4.4BSD (and earlier) UC Berkeley distributions. These are covered by the following terms:

> All of the documentation and software included in the 4.4BSD and 4.4BSD-Lite Releases is copyrighted by The Regents of the University of California.

> Copyright 1979, 1980, 1983, 1986, 1988, 1989, 1991, 1992, 1993, 1994 The Regents of the University of California. All rights reserved.

> Redistribution and use in source and binary forms, with or without modification, are permitted provided that the following conditions are met:

1. Redistributions of source code must retain the above copyright notice, this list of conditions and the following disclaimer.

2. Redistributions in binary form must reproduce the above copyright notice, this list of conditions and the following disclaimer in the documentation and/or other materials provided with the distribution.

3. All advertising materials mentioning features or use of this software must display the following acknowledgement:

   This product includes software developed by the University of California, Berkeley and its contributors.

4. Neither the name of the University nor the names of its contributors may be used to endorse or promote products derived from this software without specific prior written permission.

   THIS SOFTWARE IS PROVIDED BY THE REGENTS AND CONTRIBUTORS "AS IS" AND ANY EXPRESS OR IMPLIED WARRANTIES, INCLUDING, BUT NOT LIMITED TO, THE IMPLIED

WARRANTIES OF MERCHANTABILITY AND FITNESS FOR A PARTICULAR PURPOSE ARE DISCLAIMED. IN NO EVENT SHALL THE REGENTS OR CONTRIBUTORS BE LIABLE FOR ANY DIRECT, INDIRECT, INCIDENTAL, SPECIAL, EXEMPLARY, OR CONSEQUENTIAL DAMAGES (INCLUDING, BUT NOT LIMITED TO, PROCUREMENT OF SUBSTITUTE GOODS OR SERVICES; LOSS OF USE, DATA, OR PROFITS; OR BUSINESS INTERRUPTION) HOWEVER CAUSED AND ON ANY THEORY OF LIABILITY, WHETHER IN CONTRACT, STRICT LIABILITY, OR TORT (INCLUDING NEGLIGENCE OR OTHERWISE) ARISING IN ANY WAY OUT OF THE USE OF THIS SOFTWARE, EVEN IF ADVISED OF THE POSSIBILITY OF SUCH DAMAGE.

The Institute of Electrical and Electronics Engineers and the American National Standards Committee X3, on Information Processing Systems have given us permission to reprint portions of their documentation.

In the following statement, the phrase "this text" refers to portions of the system documentation.

Portions of this text are reprinted and reproduced in electronic form in the second BSD Networking Software Release, from IEEE Std 1003.1-1988, IEEE Standard Portable Operating System Interface for Computer Environments (POSIX), copyright ©1988 by the Institute of Electrical and Electronics Engineers, Inc. In the event of any discrepancy between these versions and the original IEEE Standard, the original IEEE Standard is the referee document.

In the following statement, the phrase "This material" refers to portions of the system documentation.

This material is reproduced with permission from American National Standards Committee X3, on Information Processing Systems. Computer and Business Equipment Manufacturers Association (CBEMA), 311 First St., NW, Suite 500, Washington, DC 20001-2178. The developmental work of Programming Language C was completed by the X3J11 Technical Committee.

The views and conclusions contained in the software and documentation are those of the authors and should not be interpreted as representing official policies, either expressed or implied, of the Regents of the University of California.

GNU GPL

The GNU (Gnu's Not UNIX) GPL (General Public License) covers a large part of the MkLinux system. There are two versions of the GPL. The one reproduced below is intended for use with independent programs. The other ("library") GPL is intended for use with linkable libraries such as `libc`.

GNU GENERAL PUBLIC LICENSE Version 2, June 1991

Copyright © 1989, 1991 Free Software Foundation, Inc., 675 Mass Ave, Cambridge, MA 02139, USA. Everyone is permitted to copy and distribute verbatim copies of this license document, but changing it is not allowed.

Preamble

The licenses for most software are designed to take away your freedom to share and change it. By contrast, the GNU General Public License is intended to guarantee your freedom to share and change free software to make sure the software is free for all its users. This General Public License applies to most of the Free Software Foundation's software and to any other program whose authors commit to using it. (Some other Free Software Foundation software is covered by the GNU Library General Public License instead.) You can apply it to your programs, too.

When we speak of free software, we are referring to freedom, not price. Our General Public Licenses are designed to make sure that you have the freedom to distribute copies of free software (and charge for this service if you wish), that you receive source code or can get it if you want it, that you can change the software or use pieces of it in new free programs; and that you know you can do these things.

To protect your rights, we need to make restrictions that forbid anyone to deny you these rights or to ask you to surrender the rights. These restrictions translate to certain responsibilities for you if you distribute copies of the software, or if you modify it.

For example, if you distribute copies of such a program, whether gratis or for a fee, you must give the recipients all the rights that you have. You must make sure that they, too, receive or can get the source code. And you must show them these terms so they know their rights.

We protect your rights with two steps: (1) copyright the software, and (2) offer you this license which gives you legal permission to copy, distribute and/or modify the software.

Also, for each author's protection and ours, we want to make certain that everyone understands that there is no warranty for this free software. If the software is modified by someone else and passed on, we want its recipients to know that what they have is not the original, so that any problems introduced by others will not reflect on the original authors' reputations.

Finally, any free program is threatened constantly by software patents. We wish to avoid the danger that redistributors of a free program will individually obtain patent licenses, in effect making the program proprietary. To prevent this, we have made it clear that any patent must be licensed for everyone's free use or not licensed at all.

The precise terms and conditions for copying, distribution and modification follow.

GNU GENERAL PUBLIC LICENSE

TERMS AND CONDITIONS FOR COPYING, DISTRIBUTION AND MODIFICATION

0. This License applies to any program or other work which contains a notice placed by the copyright holder saying it may be distributed under the terms of this General Public License. The Program, below, refers to any such program or work, and a work based on the Program means either the Program or any derivative work under copyright law: that is to say, a work containing the Program or a portion of it, either verbatim or with modifications and/or translated into another language. (Hereinafter, translation is included without

limitation in the term modification.) Each licensee is addressed as you.

Activities other than copying, distribution and modification are not covered by this License; they are outside its scope. The act of running the Program is not restricted, and the output from the Program is covered only if its contents constitute a work based on the Program (independent of having been made by running the Program). Whether that is true depends on what the Program does.

1. You may copy and distribute verbatim copies of the Program's source code as you receive it, in any medium, provided that you conspicuously and appropriately publish on each copy an appropriate copyright notice and disclaimer of warranty; keep intact all the notices that refer to this License and to the absence of any warranty; and give any other recipients of the Program a copy of this License along with the Program.

You may charge a fee for the physical act of transferring a copy, and you may at your option offer warranty protection in exchange for a fee.

2. You may modify your copy or copies of the Program or any portion of it, thus forming a work based on the Program, and copy and distribute such modifications or work under the terms of Section 1 above, provided that you also meet all of these conditions:

    a) You must cause the modified files to carry prominent notices stating that you changed the files and the date of any change.

    b) You must cause any work that you distribute or publish, that in whole or in part contains or is derived from the Program or any part thereof, to be licensed as a whole at no charge to all third parties under the terms of this License.

    c) If the modified program normally reads commands interactively when run, you must cause it, when started running for such interactive use in the most ordinary way, to print or display an announcement including an appropriate copyright notice and a notice that there is no warranty (or else, saying that you provide a warranty) and that users may redistribute the program under these conditions, and telling the user how to view a copy of this License. (Exception: if the Program itself is interactive but does not normally print such an announcement, your work based on the Program is not required to print an announcement.)

These requirements apply to the modified work as a whole. If identifiable sections of that work are not derived from the Program, and can be reasonably considered independent and separate works in themselves, then this License, and its terms, do not apply to those sections when you distribute them as separate works. But when you distribute the same sections as part of a whole which is a work based on the Program, the distribution of the whole must be on the terms of this License, whose permissions for other licensees extend to the entire whole, and thus to each and every part regardless of who wrote it.

Thus, it is not the intent of this section to claim rights or contest your rights to work written entirely by you; rather, the intent is to exercise the right to control the distribution of derivative or collective works based on the Program.

In addition, mere aggregation of another work not based on the Program with the Program (or with a work based on the Program) on a volume of a storage or distribution medium does not bring the other work under the scope of this License.

3.   You may copy and distribute the Program (or a work based on it, under Section 2) in object code or executable form under the terms of Sections 1 and 2 above provided that you also do one of the following:

   a)   Accompany it with the complete corresponding machine-readable source code, which must be distributed under the terms of Sections 1 and 2 above on a medium customarily used for software interchange; or,

   b)   Accompany it with a written offer, valid for at least three years, to give any third party, for a charge no more than your cost of physically performing source distribution, a complete machine-readable copy of the corresponding source code, to be distributed under the terms of Sections 1 and 2 above on a medium customarily used for software interchange; or,

c) Accompany it with the information you received as to the offer to distribute corresponding source code. (This alternative is allowed only for noncommercial distribution and only if you received the program in object code or executable form with such an offer, in accord with Subsection b above.)

The source code for a work means the preferred form of the work for making modifications to it. For an executable work, complete source code means all the source code for all modules it contains, plus any associated interface definition files, plus the scripts used to control compilation and installation of the executable. However, as a special exception, the source code distributed need not include anything that is normally distributed (in either source or binary form) with the major components (compiler, kernel, and so on) of the operating system on which the executable runs, unless that component itself accompanies the executable.

If distribution of executable or object code is made by offering access to copy from a designated place, then offering equivalent access to copy the source code from the same place counts as distribution of the source code, even though third parties are not compelled to copy the source along with the object code.

4. You may not copy, modify, sublicense, or distribute the Program except as expressly provided under this License. Any attempt otherwise to copy, modify, sublicense or distribute the Program is void, and will automatically terminate your rights under this License. However, parties who have received copies, or rights, from you under this License will not have their licenses terminated so long as such parties remain in full compliance.

5. You are not required to accept this License, since you have not signed it. However, nothing else grants you permission to modify or distribute the Program or its derivative works. These actions are prohibited by law if you do not accept this License. Therefore, by modifying or distributing the Program (or any work based on the Program), you indicate your acceptance of this License to do so, and all its

terms and conditions for copying, distributing or modifying the Program or works based on it.

6.   Each time you redistribute the Program (or any work based on the Program), the recipient automatically receives a license from the original licensor to copy, distribute or modify the Program subject to these terms and conditions. You may not impose any further restrictions on the recipients' exercise of the rights granted herein. You are not responsible for enforcing compliance by third parties to this License.

7.   If, as a consequence of a court judgment or allegation of patent infringement or for any other reason (not limited to patent issues), conditions are imposed on you (whether by court order, agreement or otherwise) that contradict the conditions of this License, they do not excuse you from the conditions of this License. If you cannot distribute so as to satisfy simultaneously your obligations under this License and any other pertinent obligations, then as a consequence you may not distribute the Program at all. For example, if a patent license would not permit royalty-free redistribution of the Program by all those who receive copies directly or indirectly through you, then the only way you could satisfy both it and this License would be to refrain entirely from distribution of the Program.

If any portion of this section is held invalid or unenforceable under any particular circumstance, the balance of the section is intended to apply and the section as a whole is intended to apply in other circumstances.

It is not the purpose of this section to induce you to infringe any patents or other property right claims or to contest validity of any such claims; this section has the sole purpose of protecting the integrity of the free software distribution system, which is implemented by public license practices. Many people have made generous contributions to the wide range of software distributed through that system in reliance on consistent application of that system; it is up to the author/donor to decide if he or she is willing to distribute software through any other system and a licensee cannot impose that choice.

This section is intended to make thoroughly clear what is believed to be a consequence of the rest of this License.

8. If the distribution and/or use of the Program is restricted in certain countries either by patents or by copyrighted interfaces, the original copyright holder who places the Program under this License may add an explicit geographical distribution limitation excluding those countries, so that distribution is permitted only in or among countries not thus excluded. In such case, this License incorporates the limitation as if written in the body of this License.

9. The Free Software Foundation may publish revised and/or new versions of the General Public License from time to time. Such new versions will be similar in spirit to the present version, but may differ in detail to address new problems or concerns.

    Each version is given a distinguishing version number. If the Program specifies a version number of this License which applies to it and any later version, you have the option of following the terms and conditions either of that version or of any later version published by the Free Software Foundation. If the Program does not specify a version number of this License, you may choose any version ever published by the Free Software Foundation.

10. If you wish to incorporate parts of the Program into other free programs whose distribution conditions are different, write to the author to ask for permission. For software which is copyrighted by the Free Software Foundation, write to the Free Software Foundation; we sometimes make exceptions for this. Our decision will be guided by the two goals of preserving the free status of all derivatives of our free software and of promoting the sharing and reuse of software generally.

NO WARRANTY

11. BECAUSE THE PROGRAM IS LICENSED FREE OF CHARGE, THERE IS NO WARRANTY FOR THE PROGRAM, TO THE EXTENT PERMITTED BY APPLICABLE LAW. EXCEPT WHEN OTHERWISE STATED IN WRITING THE COPYRIGHT HOLDERS AND/OR OTHER PARTIES PROVIDE THE PROGRAM AS IS WITHOUT WARRANTY OF ANY KIND, EITHER EXPRESSED

OR IMPLIED, INCLUDING, BUT NOT LIMITED TO, THE IM-
PLIED WARRANTIES OF MERCHANTABILITY AND FITNESS
FOR A PARTICULAR PURPOSE. THE ENTIRE RISK AS TO THE
QUALITY AND PERFORMANCE OF THE PROGRAM IS WITH
YOU. SHOULD THE PROGRAM PROVE DEFECTIVE, YOU AS-
SUME THE COST OF ALL NECESSARY SERVICING, REPAIR OR
CORRECTION.

12. IN NO EVENT UNLESS REQUIRED BY APPLICABLE LAW OR
AGREED TO IN WRITING WILL ANY COPYRIGHT HOLDER,
OR ANY OTHER PARTY WHO MAY MODIFY AND/OR REDIS-
TRIBUTE THE PROGRAM AS PERMITTED ABOVE, BE LIABLE
TO YOU FOR DAMAGES, INCLUDING ANY GENERAL, SPE-
CIAL, INCIDENTAL OR CONSEQUENTIAL DAMAGES ARIS-
ING OUT OF THE USE OR INABILITY TO USE THE PROGRAM
(INCLUDING BUT NOT LIMITED TO LOSS OF DATA OR DATA
BEING RENDERED INACCURATE OR LOSSES SUSTAINED BY
YOU OR THIRD PARTIES OR A FAILURE OF THE PROGRAM TO
OPERATE WITH ANY OTHER PROGRAMS), EVEN IF SUCH
HOLDER OR OTHER PARTY HAS BEEN ADVISED OF THE
POSSIBILITY OF SUCH DAMAGES.

END OF TERMS AND CONDITIONS

Appendix: How to Apply These Terms to Your New Programs

If you develop a new program, and you want it to be of the greatest possible use to the public, the best way to achieve this is to make it free
software which everyone can redistribute and change under these
terms.

To do so, attach the following notices to the program. It is safest to
attach them to the start of each source file to most effectively convey
the exclusion of warranty; and each file should have at least the copyright line and a pointer to where the full notice is found.

Copyright (C) 19yy

This program is free software; you can redistribute it and/or modify it
under the terms of the GNU General Public License as published by the

Free Software Foundation; either version 2 of the License, or (at your option) any later version.

This program is distributed in the hope that it will be useful, but WITHOUT ANY WARRANTY; without even the implied warranty of MERCHANTABILITY or FITNESS FOR A PARTICULAR PURPOSE. See the GNU General Public License for more details.

You should have received a copy of the GNU General Public License along with this program; if not, write to the Free Software Foundation, Inc., 675 Mass Ave, Cambridge, MA 02139, USA.

Also add information on how to contact you by electronic and paper mail.

If the program is interactive, make it output a short notice like this when it starts in an interactive mode:

Gnomovision version 69, Copyright (C) 19yy name of author.

Gnomovision comes with ABSOLUTELY NO WARRANTY; for details type "show w". This is free software, and you are welcome to redistribute it under certain conditions; type "show c" for details.

The hypothetical commands show w and show c should show the appropriate parts of the General Public License. Of course, the commands you use may be called something other than show w and show c; they could even be mouse-clicks or menu items whatever suits your program.

You should also get your employer (if you work as a programmer) or your school, if any, to sign a copyright disclaimer for the program, if necessary. Here is a sample; alter the names:

Yoyodyne, Inc., hereby disclaims all copyright interest in the program "Gnomovision" (which makes passes at compilers) written by James Hacker.

<signature of Ty Coon>, 1 April 1989

Ty Coon, President of Vice

This General Public License does not permit incorporating your program into proprietary programs. If your program is a subroutine library, you may consider it more useful to permit linking proprietary applications with the library. If this is what you want to do, use the GNU Library General Public License instead of this License.

Linux License

The MkLinux kernel is an offshoot of the Linux kernel. As such, it is covered by the GNU General Public License. Specifically, it is covered by the terms in the COPYING file:

> NOTE! This copyright does *not* cover user programs that use kernel services by normal system calls – this is merely considered normal use of the kernel, and does *not* fall under the heading of "derived work". Also note that the GPL below is copyrighted by the Free Software Foundation, but the instance of code that it refers to (the linux kernel) is copyrighted by me and others who actually wrote it.
>
> Linus Torvalds
>
> --
>
> GNU GENERAL PUBLIC LICENSE
>
> Version 2, June 1991
>
> ...

The remainder of the MkLinux system (commands, manual pages, etc.) is covered by a variety of licenses, the most common of which are:

- GNU General Public License

- University-style (e.g., BSD, X11) licenses

- Unique licenses, written by package authors.

  Licenses written by package authors vary widely, in both intent and clarity. If you are unsure of the meaning of an author's license text, get in touch with the author for a clarification.

In general, as noted above, you are quite free to examine, use, modify, and redistribute the freeware materials on this collection, as long as you do not attempt to claim ownership of them, modify their licensing, or (in some cases) make money from their sale. It is **your** responsibility, however, to make sure that you are complying with the restrictions on these packages.

Mach Licenses

The base Mach distribution comes from Carnegie Mellon University and is covered by the following license:

Mach Operating System

Copyright (c) 1991 ... Carnegie Mellon University

All Rights Reserved.

Permission to use, copy, modify and distribute this software and its documentation is hereby granted, provided that both the copyright notice and this permission notice appear in all copies of the software, derivative works or modified versions, and any portions thereof, and that both notices appear in supporting documentation.

CARNEGIE MELLON ALLOWS FREE USE OF THIS SOFTWARE IN ITS CONDITION. CARNEGIE MELLON DISCLAIMS ANY LIABILITY OF ANY KIND FOR ANY DAMAGES WHATSOEVER RESULTING FROM THE USE OF THIS SOFTWARE.

Carnegie Mellon requests users of this software to return to

Software Distribution Coordinator or
Software.Distribution@CS.CMU.EDU

School of Computer Science
Carnegie Mellon University
Pittsburgh PA 15213-3890

any improvements or extensions that they make and grant Carnegie the rights to redistribute these changes.

Many parts of the Mach code have been modified by the Open Software Foundation (now part of The Open Group). These portions are also covered by licenses of the form:

Copyright 1996 ... by Open Software Foundation, Inc. 1996 ...

All Rights Reserved

Permission to use, copy, modify, and distribute this software and its documentation for any purpose and without fee is hereby granted, provided that the above copyright notice appears in all copies and that both the copyright notice and this permission notice appear in supporting documentation.

OSF DISCLAIMS ALL WARRANTIES WITH REGARD TO THIS SOFTWARE INCLUDING ALL IMPLIED WARRANTIES OF MERCHANTABILITY AND FITNESS FOR A PARTICULAR PURPOSE.

IN NO EVENT SHALL OSF BE LIABLE FOR ANY SPECIAL, INDIRECT, OR CONSEQUENTIAL DAMAGES OR ANY DAMAGES WHATSOEVER RESULTING FROM LOSS OF USE, DATA OR PROFITS, WHETHER IN ACTION OF CONTRACT, NEGLIGENCE, OR OTHER TORTIOUS ACTION, ARISING OUT OF OR IN CONNECTION WITH THE USE OR PERFORMANCE OF THIS SOFTWARE.

Some parts of the Linux server code have been modified by the Open Software Foundation. In order to limit its liability, OSF includes the file OSF_FREE_COPYRIGHT in the source tree for the MkLinux server:

Copyright 1996 by Open Software Foundation, Inc.

OSF DISCLAIMS ALL WARRANTIES WITH REGARD TO THIS SOFTWARE INCLUDING ALL IMPLIED WARRANTIES OF MERCHANTABILITY AND FITNESS FOR A PARTICULAR PURPOSE.

IN NO EVENT SHALL OSF BE LIABLE FOR ANY SPECIAL, INDIRECT, OR CONSEQUENTIAL DAMAGES OR ANY DAMAGES WHATSOEVER RESULTING FROM LOSS OF USE, DATA OR PROFITS, WHETHER IN ACTION OF CONTRACT, NEGLIGENCE, OR OTHER TORTIOUS ACTION, ARISING OUT OF OR IN CONNECTION WITH THE USE OR PERFORMANCE OF THIS SOFTWARE.

X11 License

MkLinux contains a large amount of code from the X11 distribution. This code is, in general, covered by the following license terms, or ones of approximately the same nature:

X Window System, Version 11, Release 6 Contrib Manifest
Copyright © 1994 X Consortium

Permission is hereby granted, free of charge, to any person obtaining a copy of this software and associated documentation files (the "Software"), to deal in the Software without restriction, including without limitation the rights to use, copy, modify, merge, publish, distribute, sublicense, and/or sell copies of the Software, and to permit persons to whom the Software is furnished to do so, subject to the following conditions:

> The above copyright notice and this permission notice shall be included in all copies or substantial portions of the Software.

> THE SOFTWARE IS PROVIDED "AS IS", WITHOUT WARRANTY OF ANY KIND, EXPRESS OR IMPLIED, INCLUDING BUT NO LIMITED TO THE WARRANTIES OF MERCHANTABILITY, FITNESS FOR A PARTICULAR PURPOSE AND NONINFRINGEMENT. IN NO EVENT SHALL THE X CONSORTIUM BE LIABLE FOR ANY CLAIM, DAMAGES OR OTHER LIABILITY, WHETHER IN AN ACTION OF CONTRACT, TORT OR OTHERWISE, ARISING FROM, OUT OF OR IN CONNECTION WITH THE SOFTWARE OR THE USE OR OTHER DEALINGS IN THE SOFTWARE.

> Except as contained in this notice, the name of the X Consortium shall not be used in advertising or otherwise to promote the sale, use or other dealings in this Software without prior written authorization from the X Consortium. X Window System is a trademark of X Consortium, Inc.

PTF Legalese

We've tried to do a good job of getting the latest versions of code, checking that we have the right to distribute them, copying them accurately, etc. But we're mortal; we have certainly made mistakes, and you may be the lucky soul that finds one. Please don't sue us; we can't afford a lawsuit, and we don't have anything to give you, anyway.

Just tell us about the problem. We'll fix it in the next release and tell folks about it to limit the damage. For your part, try to use these packages as their owners (if any) have specified. Don't make MIT or CMU mad; they probably have the bomb. Just play nice, so we can all enjoy these goodies.

Now comes the difficult part. The packages in this distribution are all freeware, of one sort or another. What about the distribution itself, the doc files, the book, etc? Can a freeware distribution have (gasp) proprietary components? Well, yes, it can, and does.

We claim ownership of everything in the distribution *except* the packages themselves, about which we make **no claims whatsoever**, either singly or collectively. (PTF does not claim any form of "compilation copyright" or any other copyright affecting the packages themselves.) Thus, the book, annotation files, indices, and other things we have added all belong to us.

On the other hand, we make only one real restriction on their use: don't use them to make a competitive product. Copy the distribution to tape; post it to the net; serve it on archives; share it with a friend. Do anything the authors allow with the packages themselves. Make as many copies of the book as you like.

Just don't steal our added value to make a competing product. We wouldn't like it, it wouldn't help your name in the community, and you'd end up playing catch-up with us after every new PTF release. Besides, at our prices, is there really much room (or reason) for this kind of competition? We think not. And now, to satisfy our non-existent lawyers:

Trademarks, etc.

Various trademarks belong to various organizations and individuals. If you look into the packages, you will find specific statements on the subject. You will also find copyright notices and other legalistic verbiage. We have attempted to comply with these; go thou and do likewise. Portions of this distribution are Copyright © 1992-1997, Prime Time Freeware, San Bruno, CA.

Terms and Conditions

We provide this material AS IS. We make no warranties of any kind, whether expressed or implied, for the material contained in this book and the accompanying discs. We are not responsible for any damage of any kind that may result from your use of this material.

Chapter 9:

- *Introduction*
- *Architectural Model*

Mach   Overview

The material below is adapted from the OSF publication of the same name, published in June 1993. For a complete, online copy of the document below, and many other Mach-related documents, see the PTF Reference disc.

OSF Mach Approved Kernel Principles

Keith Loepere
Open Software Foundation and Carnegie Mellon University

Introduction

This paper documents the user visible architecture of the Mach 3 kernel. It is assumed that the reader is familiar with the basic ideas of Mach as are found in:

> Mike Accetta, Robert Baron, William Bolosky, David Golub, Richard Rashid, Avadis Tevanian, Michael Young, "Mach: A New Kernel Foundation for UNIX Development", in *Proceedings of the Summer 1986 USENIX Conference*, Atlanta, GA.

The notion of operating system functionality provided via a Mach user space server can be found in:

> David Golub, Randall Dean, Alessandro Forin, Richard Rashid, "UNIX as an Application Program", in *Proceedings of the Summer 1990 USENIX Conference*, Anaheim, CA.

Mach was developed as a new foundation for operating systems. It provides extensible memory management, multiple points of control (threads) and an extensive process (task) to process communication facility (IPC). The goals of Mach include:

- Exploiting parallelism in both operating system and user applications.

- Supporting large, potentially sparse address spaces with flexible memory sharing.

- Allowing transparent network resource access.

- Compatibility with existing software environments (BSD).

- Portability.

In versions 2.5 and earlier, Mach was combined with Unix to deliver a complete operating environment. Version 3, however, provides Mach as a pure kernel with no other operating system functionality in kernel space. Particular operating environments are provided by means of user space servers. To date, servers have been prototyped for BSD, SVR4, Sprite, OSF/1, and DOS.

Mach as a foundation technology for diverse operating environments subscribes to the philosophy of:

- A simple, extensible communication kernel.

- An object basis with communication channels as object references.

- A client/server programming model, using synchronous and asynchronous inter-process communication.

- User mode tasks performing many traditional operating system functions (e.g. file system, network access).

The fundamental idea is that of a simple, extensible communication kernel. It is a goal of the Mach project to move more and more functionality out of the kernel, until everything is done by user mode tasks communicating via the kernel. Of course, even in the extreme, the kernel must provide other support besides task to task communication, in particular:

- Management of points of control (*threads*).

- Resource assignment (*tasks*).

- Support of address spaces for tasks.

- Management of physical resources (physical memory, processors, device channels, clocks).

Even here, though, the goal is to move functionality outside the kernel. User mode tasks implement the policies regarding resource usage; the kernel simply provides mechanisms to enforce those policies.

Kernel Abstractions

Although it is a goal of the Mach kernel to minimize abstractions provided by the kernel, it is not a goal to be minimal in the semantics associated with those abstractions. As such, each of the abstractions provided has a rich set of semantics associated with it, and a complex set of interactions with the other abstractions. Although this makes it difficult to identify key ideas, the main kernel abstractions are considered to be the following:

- Task – The unit of resource allocation: large address space, port rights.

- Thread – The unit of CPU utilization, lightweight (low overhead).

- Port – Communication channel, accessible only via send/receive capabilities (rights).

- Message – Collection of data objects.

- Memory object – Internal unit of memory management.

The kernel provides some memory management, of course. Memory is associated with tasks. Memory objects are the means by which tasks take control over memory management.

Tasks And Threads

The Mach kernel does not provide the traditional notion of the *process*. This is for two main reasons:

- Any given operating system environment has considerable semantics associated with a process (such as user ID, signal state, etc.). It is not the purpose of the Mach kernel to understand or provide these extended semantics.

- Many systems (BSD, for example) equate a process with an execution point of control. Some systems (POSIX 1003.4a, for example) do not. Mach wishes to support multiple points of control in a way separate from any given operating system environment's notion of process.

Instead, Mach provides two notions: the *task* and the *thread*. A thread is Mach's notion of the point of control. A task exists to provide resources for its containing threads. This split is made to provide for parallelism and resource sharing.

A thread:

• Is a point of control flow in a task.

• Has access to all of the elements of the containing task.

• Potentially executes in parallel with other threads, even threads within the same task.

• Has minimal state for low overhead.

A task:

• Is a collection of system resources. These resources, with the exception of the address space, are referenced by ports. These resources may be shared with other tasks if rights to the ports are so distributed.

• Provides a large, potentially sparse address space, referenced by machine address. Portions of this space may be shared through inheritance or external memory management.

• Contains some number of threads.

Note that a task has no life of its own; only threads execute instructions. When it is said "a task Y does X" what is really meant is that "a thread contained within task Y does X".

A task is a fairly expensive entity. It exists to be a collection of resources. All of the threads in a task share everything. Two tasks share nothing without explicit action (although the action is often simple) and some resources cannot be shared between two tasks at all (such as port receive rights).

A thread is a fairly lightweight entity. It is fairly cheap to create and has low overhead to operate. This is true because a thread has little state (mostly its register state); its owning task bears the burden of resource management. On a multiprocessor it is possible for multiple threads in a task to execute in parallel. Even when parallelism is not the goal, multiple threads have an advantage in that each thread can use a synchronous programming style, instead of attempting asynchronous programming with a single thread attempting to provide multiple services.

Memory Management

The Mach kernel provides the mechanisms to support large, potentially sparse virtual address spaces. Each task has an associated address map (maintained by the kernel) which controls the translation of virtual addresses in the task's address space into physical addresses. As is true in virtual memory systems, the contents of the entire address space of any given task is most likely not completely resident in physical memory at any given time, and mechanisms must exist to use physical memory as a cache for the virtual address spaces of tasks. Unlike traditional virtual memory designs, the Mach kernel does not implement all of the elements of this caching itself; it endeavors to allow user mode tasks the ability to participate in these mechanisms.

Unlike other resources in the Mach system, virtual memory is not referenced via ports. Memory can be referenced only by using virtual addresses as indices into a particular task's address space. The memory (and the associated address map) that defines a task's address space can be partially shared with other tasks.

A task can allocate new ranges of memory within its address space, deallocate them, and change protections on them. It can also specify *inheritance* properties for the ranges.

A new task is created by specifying an existing task as a base from which to construct the address space for the new task. The inheritance attribute of each range of the memory of the existing task determines whether the new task has that range defined and whether that range is virtually copied or shared with the existing task.

Within Mach, most virtual copy operations for memory are actually achieved through copy-on-write optimizations. A copy-on-write optimization is accomplished by not directly copying the range, but by protected sharing. The two tasks both share the memory to be copied, but with read-only access. When either task attempts to modify a portion of the range, that portion is copied at that time. This lazy evaluation of memory copies is an important performance optimization performed by the Mach kernel, and important to the communication/memory philosophy of Mach.

Any given region of memory is *backed* by a *memory object*. A *memory manager* task provides the policy governing the relationship between the image of a set of pages while cached in memory (the physical memory contents of a memory region) and the image of that set of pages when not so cached (the abstract *memory object*). The Mach kernel comes with a default memory manager that provides basic non-persistent memory objects that are zero filled initially and paged against system paging space.

Task To Task Communication

Communication between tasks is a very important element of the Mach philosophy. Mach believes in a client/server system structure in which tasks (clients) access services by making requests of other tasks (servers) via messages sent over a communication channel. Since the Mach kernel provides very few services of its own (in particular, it provides no file service), a Mach task will need to communicate with a potentially great many other tasks that do provide these services. These communication channels in Mach are called *ports*. A port is a unidirectional channel consisting of a (bounded length) queue that holds *messages*. A message is a collection of data, memory regions and port rights. A port *right* is a name by which a task that holds the right names the port. A task can manipulate a port only if it holds the appropriate port rights. Only one task can hold the *receive right* for a port. This one task is allowed to receive (read) messages from the port queue. Multiple tasks can hold *send rights* to the port that allow them to send (write) messages into the queue. A task communicates with another task by building a data structure that contains a set of data elements, and then performing a message-send operation on a port for which it holds send rights. At some later time, the task with receive rights to that port will perform a message-receive operation. Note that this message transfer is an asynchronous operation. The message is logically copied into the receiving task (possibly with copy-on-write optimizations). Multiple threads within the receiving task can be attempting to receive messages from a given port, but only one thread will receive any given message.

The Mach kernel does not understand distribution at all (unless configured with the experimental multicomputer support, which provides distributed shared memory and IPC within a collection of Mach nodes). However, the

Mach IPC facility is designed so that a server task (a Net Message server) can transparently forward messages over a network.

Architectural Model

This section provides a brief, non-formal model of the system architecture supported by the Mach kernel. It attempts to discuss each feature of the kernel in an isolated way, building to an understanding of the programming model supported, without suggesting any particular method of use.

Like all systems, the Mach system has, as its primary responsibility, the provision of points of control that execute instructions within some framework. In Mach, these points of control are called *threads*. Threads execute in a *virtual* environment. The virtual environment provided by the Mach kernel consists of a *virtual* processor that executes all of the user space accessible hardware instructions, augmented by emulated instructions (system traps) provided by the kernel; the virtual processor accesses a set of (virtualized) registers and some *virtual* memory that otherwise responds as does the machine's physical memory; all other hardware resources are accessible only via special combinations of memory accesses and emulated instructions. Note that all resources provided by the Mach kernel are virtualized.

Elements

The Mach kernel provides an environment consisting of the following elements:

- thread – An execution point of control. A thread is a light-weight entity; most of the state pertinent to a thread is associated with its containing task.

- task – A container to hold references to resources in the form of a port name space, a virtual address space and a set of threads.

- security – Not really a kernel object. The privileged security port is used when setting (changing) task identity.

- ledger – A resource accounting device that counts and limits the amount of a type of kernel resource that may be consumed.

- port – A unidirectional communication channel between tasks.

- port set – A set of ports which can be treated as a single unit when receiving a message.

- port right – A capability allowing particular rights to access a port.

- port name space – An indexed collection of port names each of which names a particular port right.

- <u>message</u> – A collection of data, memory regions and port rights passed between two tasks.

- message queue – A queue of messages associated with a single port.

- virtual address space – A sparsely populated, indexed set of memory pages that may be referenced by the threads within a task. Ranges of pages may have arbitrary attributes and semantics associated with them via mechanisms implemented by the kernel and memory managers external to the kernel.

- <u>abstract memory object</u> – An abstract object that represents the non-resident state of the memory ranges backed by this object. The task that implements this object is called a memory manager. The abstract memory object port is the port through which the kernel requests action of the memory manager.

- <u>memory object representative</u> – The abstract representation of a memory object provided by the memory manager to clients of the memory object. The representative names the associated abstract memory object and limits the potential access modes permitted to the client.

- memory cache object – A kernel object that contains the resident state of the memory ranges backed by an abstract memory object. It is through this object that the memory manager manipulates the clients' visible memory image.

- processor – A physical processor capable of executing threads

- processor set – A set of processors, each of which can be used to execute the threads assigned to the processor set.

- host – The multiprocessor as a whole.

- node – An individual multiprocessor within a multicomputer.

- clock – A representation of the passage of time (a time value incremented at a constant frequency).

- kernel device – Physical device accessible by user mode tasks.

Note: Most of these elements are kernel implemented resources that can be directly manipulated by threads. The remaining three elements (message, abstract memory object, and memory object representative) are not; their names are underlined in the text above.)

Each of these notions will be discussed in detail. However, since some of their definitions depend on the definitions of others, some of the key notions will be discussed in simplified form so that a full discussion can be understood.

A *thread* is the basic computational entity. A thread belongs to one and only one *task* that defines its virtual address space. To affect the structure of the address space, or to reference any resource other than the address space, the thread must execute a special trap instruction which causes the kernel to perform operations on behalf of the thread, or to send a message to some agent on behalf of the thread. In general, these traps manipulate resources associated with the task containing the thread. Requests can be made of the kernel to manipulate these entities: to create them, delete them and affect their state.

The kernel is just one manager that can provide resources (those listed above) and provide services. Tasks may also provide services, and implement abstract resources themselves. The kernel provides communication methods that allow a client task to request that a server task (actually, a thread executing within it) provide a service. In this way, a task has a dual identity; one identity is that of a resource managed by the kernel, whose resource manager executes within the kernel; the second is that of a supplier of resources for whom the resource manager is the task itself.

With the exception of the task's virtual address space, all other system resources are accessed through a level of indirection known as a *port*. A port is a unidirectional communication channel between a client who requests a service and a server who provides the service. (If a reply is to be provided to such a service request, a second port must be used.) The service to be provided is determined by the manager that receives the message sent over the port. It follows that the receiver for ports associated with kernel provided entities is the kernel and the receiver for ports associated with task provided entities is the task providing that entity. For ports that name task provided entities, it is possible to change the receiver of messages for that port to be a different task. A single task may have multiple ports that refer to resources it supports. For that matter, any given entity can have multiple ports that represent it, each implying different sets of permissible operations. For example, many entities have a *name* port and a *control* port (sometimes called the privileged port). Access to the control port allows the entity to be manipulated; access to the name port simply names the entity, for example, to return information.

There is no system-wide name space for ports. A thread can access only the ports known to its containing task. A task holds a set of *port rights*, each of which names a (not necessarily distinct) port and which specifies the rights permitted for that port. Port rights can be transmitted in messages; this is how a task gets port rights. A port right is named with a port name, which is an integer chosen by the kernel that is meaningful only within the context (port name space) of the task holding that right.

Most operations in the system consist of sending a message to a port that names some manager for the object being manipulated. In this document, this will be shown in the form:

object → **function**

which means that the **function** is to be invoked by sending an appropriate message to a port that names the *object*. Since a message must be sent to some port (right), this operation has an object basis. Some operations require two objects (such as binding a thread to a processor set); these operations show the objects separated by commas. Not all entities are named by ports and so this is not a pure object model. The two main non-port-right named entities are port names/rights themselves, and ranges of memory. To manipulate a memory range, a message is sent to the containing virtual address space (named by the owning task). To manipulate a port name/right (and, often, the associated port), a message is sent to the containing port name space (named by the owning task). A subscript notation,

object [*id*] → **function**

is here used to show that an *id* is required as a parameter in the message to indicate which range or element of *object* is to be manipulated. The parenthesized notion,

> *object* (*port*) → **function**

is here used to show that a (privileged) *port* (such as the host control port) is required as a parameter in the message to indicate sufficient privilege to manipulate the object in the particular way.

Threads

A *thread* is the basic computational entity. A thread belongs to one and only one *task* that defines its virtual address space. A thread has the following state:

- Its machine state (registers and the like), which change as the thread executes and which can also be changed by a holder of the kernel thread port.

- A (small) set of thread specific port rights, identifying the thread's kernel port and ports used to send exception messages on behalf of the thread.

- A suspend count, non-zero if the thread is not to execute instructions.

- Resource (scheduling) parameters.

- Various statistics, including statistical PC (Program Counter) samples.

A thread operates by executing instructions in the usual way. Various special instructions trap to the kernel, to perform operations on behalf of the thread. The most important of these kernel traps is the **mach_msg_overwrite_trap**, which allows the thread to send messages to kernel and other servers to operate upon resources for it. (This trap is almost never directly called; it is invoked via the **mach_msg** library routine.)

Exceptional conditions arising during the thread's execution (floating point overflow, page not resident, etc.) are handled by sending messages to some port. The port used depends on the nature of the condition. The outcome of the exceptional condition depends on setting the thread's state and/or responding to the exception message.

The operations that can be performed upon a thread are:

- Creation and destruction.

- Suspension and resumption (manipulating the suspend count).

- Machine state manipulation.

- Special port (such as exception port) manipulation.

- Resource (scheduling) control.

- Statistical PC sampling.

Tasks

A task can be viewed as a container that holds a set of threads. It contains default values to be applied to its containing threads. Most importantly, it contains those elements that its containing threads need to execute, namely, a port name space and a virtual address space. The state associated with a task is:

- The set of contained threads.

- The associated virtual address space.

- The associated port name space, naming a set of port rights, and a related set of port notification requests.

- A security ID to be sent with messages from the task.

- A (small) set of task specific ports, identifying the task's kernel port, the task's ledger, default ports to use for exception handling for contained threads and bootstrap ports to name other services.

- System call emulation routine addresses for routines that can be set to gain control upon the attempted execution of certain system call instructions.

- A suspend count, non-zero if no contained threads are to execute instructions.

- Default scheduling parameters for threads.

- Various statistics, including statistical PC samples.

Tasks are created by specifying a prototype task which specifies the host on which the new task is created, and which can supply (by inheritance) various portions of its address space.

The operations that can be performed upon a task are:

- Creation and destruction.

- Setting the security ID.

- Suspension and resumption.

- Special port manipulation.

- Manipulation of contained threads.

- Statistical PC sampling of the contained threads.

- Manipulation of the scheduling parameters.

Security Port

All tasks are tagged with a security ID, an opaque (from the kernel's point of view) identifier that encodes in some way the identity and other security attributes of the task. This security ID is included as an implicit value in all messages sent by the task. Servers can use this sent ID as an indication of the sender's identity for use in making access mediation decisions.

A task inherits the security ID of its parent. Since this ID is to be used as an unforgeable indication of identity, privilege is required to change this ID. This privilege is indicated by presenting the host *security* port.

The reserved value of KERNEL_SECURITY_ID indicates the kernel's identity. All messages from the kernel carry the kernel identity.

Ledgers

A ledger is a resource accounting device that counts and limits the various kernel resources consumed by an object. All first-class (port named) dynamically created kernel objects (with the exception of threads since they are bound to a task) are associated with a ledger which represents a pool of kernel resources from which that object's resources are drawn.

The operations meaningful for ledgers are:

- Creation of a subordinate ledger. The new ledger draws its resources from the parent.

- Use of the ledger as the source of resources for the creation of a kernel object.

- Transfer of resource (limits) between a parent and child ledger.

- Destruction. This act also destroys all kernel objects drawn from the ledger.

Ports

A port is a unidirectional communication channel between a client who requests a service and a server who provides the service. A port has a single receiver and (potentially) multiple senders.

The state associated with a port is:

- Its associated message queue.

- A count of references (rights) to it.

- Settable limits on the amount of virtual copy memory, port rights and data that can be sent in a message through the port.

Kernel services exist to allocate ports. Every system entity (other than virtual memory ranges) is named by a port, so ports are also created implicitly when these entities are created.

The kernel will provide notification messages upon the death of a port upon request.

Messages

A message is a collection of data, memory regions and port rights passed between two entities. A message is not a system object in its own right. However, since messages are queued, they are significant because they can hold state between the time a message is sent and when it is received. This state consists of:

- Pure data

- Copies of memory ranges

- Port rights

- Kernel implicit attributes, such as the sender's security ID

Message Queues

A port basically consists of a queue of messages. This queue is manipulated only via message operations (**mach_msg**) that transmit messages. The state associated with a queue is the ordered set of messages queued, and a settable limit on the number of messages.

Port Rights

A port can only be accessed via a port *right*. A port right is an entity that indicates the right to access a specific port in a specific way. In this context, there are three types of port rights:

- receive right – Allows the holder to receive messages from the associated port.

- send right – Allows the holder to send messages to the associated port.

- send-once right – Allows the holder to send a single message to the associated port. The right self-destructs after the message is sent.

Port rights can be copied and moved between tasks via various options in the **mach_msg** call, and also by explicit command. Other than message operations, port rights can be manipulated only as members of a port name space.

Port rights are created implicitly when any other system entity is created and explicitly via explicit port creation.

The kernel will, upon request, provide notification (to a port of one's choosing) when there are no more send rights to a port. Also, the destruction of a send-once right (other than by using it to send a message) generates a send-once notification sent to the corresponding port.

Port Name Space

Ports and port rights do not have system-wide names that allow arbitrary ports or rights to be manipulated directly. Ports can be manipulated only via port rights, and port rights can be manipulated only when they are contained within a port *name space*. A port right is specified by a port *name* which is an index into a port name space. Each task has associated with it a single port name space.

An entry in a port name space can have four possible values:

- MACH_PORT_NULL – No associated port right.

- MACH_PORT_DEAD – A right was associated with this name, but the port to which the right referred has been destroyed.

- a port right – A send-once, send or receive right for a port.

- a port set name – A name which acts like a receive right, but that allows receiving from multiple ports.

All send and receive rights to a given port in a given port name space will have the same port name. Each send-once right to a given port will have a different port name from each other and from the port name used for any send or receive rights held. As port rights are manipulated (by referring to their port names) the port names are sometimes themselves manipulated.

Operations supported for port names include:

- Creation (via creation of a right) and deletion.

- Query of the associated type.

- Rename.

The kernel will provide notification of a name becoming unusable upon request.

Since port name spaces are bound to tasks, they are created and destroyed with their owning task.

Port Sets

A port set is a set of ports which can be treated as a single unit when receiving a message. A **mach_msg** receive operation is allowed against a port name that either names a receive right, or a port set. A port set contains a collection of receive rights. When a receive operation is performed against a port set, a message will be received from one of the ports in the set. The received message will indicate from which member port it was received. It is not allowed to directly receive a message from a port that is a member of a port set. There is no notion of priority for the ports in a port set; there is no control provided over the kernel's choice of the port within the port set from which any given message is received.

Operations supported for port sets include:

- Creation and deletion.

- Membership changes and membership queries.

Virtual Address Spaces

A virtual address space defines the set of valid virtual addresses that a thread executing within the task owning the virtual address space is allowed to reference. A virtual address space is named by its owning task.

A virtual address space consists of a sparsely populated indexed set of pages. The attributes of individual pages may be set at will. For efficiency, the kernel groups virtually contiguous sets of pages that have the same attributes into internal memory regions. The kernel is free to split or merge memory regions at will. System mechanisms are sensitive to the identities of memory regions, but most user accesses are not so affected, and can span memory regions freely.

A given memory range can have distinct semantics associated with it through the actions of a memory manager. When a new memory range is established in a virtual address space, an abstract memory object is specified (possibly by default) that represents the semantics of the memory range, by being associated with a task (a memory manager) that provides those semantics.

A virtual address space is created when a task is created, and destroyed when the task is destroyed. The initial contents of the address space is determined from various options to the **task_create** call, as well as the inheritance properties of the memory ranges of the prototype task used in that call.

Most operations upon a virtual address space name a memory range within the address space. These operations include:

- Creating (allocating) and de-allocating a range.

- Copying a range.

- Setting special attributes, including "wiring" the page into physical memory to prevent eviction.

- Setting memory protection attributes.

- Setting inheritance properties.

- Directly reading and writing ranges.

- Force update a range to backing storage.

- Reserving a range (preventing random allocation within the range).

Abstract Memory Objects

The Mach kernel allows user mode tasks to provide the semantics associated with referencing portions of a virtual address space. It does this by allowing the specification of an abstract *memory object* that represents the non-resident state of the memory ranges backed by this memory object. The task that implements this memory object (that responds to messages sent to the port that names the memory object) is called a *memory manager*.

The kernel should be viewed as using main memory as a (directly accessible) cache for the contents of the various memory objects. The kernel is involved in an asynchronous dialog with the various memory managers to maintain this cache, filling and flushing this cache as the kernel sees fit, by sending messages to the abstract memory object ports.

The operations upon abstract memory objects include:

- Initialization.

- Page reads.

- Page writes.

- Synchronization with force update operations.

- Requests for permission to access pages.

- Termination.

Memory Object Representatives

The abstract memory object port is used by the kernel to request access to the backing storage for a memory object. Because of the protected nature of this dialog, memory managers do not typically give access to the abstract memory object port to clients. Instead, clients are given access to *memory object representatives*. A memory object representative is the client's representation of a memory object. There is only one operation permitted against such a port and that is to *map* the associated memory object into a task's address space. Making such a request initiates a protocol between the mapping kernel and the memory manager to initialize the underlying abstract memory object. It is through this special protocol that the kernel is informed of the abstract memory object represented by the representative, as well as the set of access modes permitted by the representative.

Memory Cache Objects

The portion of the kernel's main memory cache that contains the resident pages associated with a given abstract memory object is referred to as the *memory cache* object. The memory manager for a memory object holds send rights to the kernel's memory cache object. The memory manager is involved in an asynchronous dialog with the kernel to provide the abstraction of its abstract memory object by sending messages to the associated memory cache object.

The operations upon memory cache objects include:

- Set operational attributes.

- Return attributes.

- Supply pages to the kernel.

- Indicate that pages requested by the kernel are not available.

- Indicate that pages requested by the kernel should be filled by the kernel's default rules.

- Force delayed copies of the object to be really copied.

- Indicate that pages sent to the memory manager have been disposed.

- Restrict access to memory pages.

- Termination.

Processors

Each physical processor (that is capable of executing threads) is named by a processor control port. Although significant in that they perform the real work, processors are not very significant in the Mach scheme of things other than as members of a processor set. It is a processor set that forms the basis for the pool of processors used to schedule a set of threads, and that has scheduling attributes associated with it.

The operations supported for processors include:

- Assignment to a processor set.

- Machine control, such as start and stop.

Processor Sets

Processors are grouped into processor sets. A processor set forms a pool of processors used to schedule the threads assigned to that processor set. A processor set exists as a basis to uniformly control the schedulability of a set of threads. The notion also provides a way to perform coarse allocation of processors to given activities in the system.

The operations supported upon processor sets include:

- Creation and deletion.

- Assignment of processors.

- Assignment of threads and tasks.

- Scheduling control.

Hosts

Each machine (uni-processor or multi-processor) in a networked Mach system runs its own instantiation of the Mach kernel. The *host* multiprocessor is not generally manipulated by client tasks. But, since each host does carry its own Mach kernel, each with its own port space, physical memory and other resources, the executing host is visible and sometimes manipulated directly. Also, each host generates its own statistics.

Hosts are named by a name port which is freely distributed and which can be used to obtain information about the host and a control port which is closely held and which can be used to manipulate the host. Operations supported by hosts include:

- Obtaining clock ports.

- Statistics gathering.

- Re-booting.

- Setting the default memory manager.

- Obtaining lists of processors and processor sets.

Nodes

In general, the Mach kernel executes on a single machine, possibly a multiprocessor. Multiple such machines may be connected together in various ways, but this is the province of user space tasks. However, optional (and experimental) support is provided within the kernel for *multicomputers*, "machines" consisting of multiple multiprocessors (without shared memory between multiprocessors). Each uniprocessor or multiprocessor host in such a multicomputer is called a *node* and referenced by a node ID (a number).

Mach's multicomputer support provides transparently distributed shared memory between nodes and transparently distributed Mach IPC between nodes. The only direct operations supported by nodes are the setting and retrieving of a small set of node specific ports.

Clocks

A clock provides a representation of the passage of time by incrementing a time value counter at a constant frequency. Each host (or each node in a multicomputer) implements its own set of clocks based upon the various clocks and timers supported by the hardware as well as abstract clocks built upon these timers. The set of clocks implemented by a given system is set at configuration time.

Each clock is named by both a name and a control (privileged) port. The control port allows the time and resolution of the clock to be set. Given the name port, a task can:

- Determine the time and resolution of the clock.

- Generate a memory object that maps the time value.

- Sleep (delay) until a given time.

- Request a notification (alarm) at a given time.

Kernel Devices

The Mach kernel exports a very simple interface to its kernel device drivers. When initialized, the Mach kernel builds an internal table that lists each device. It exports a single port, the *device master* port, which is responsible for allocating devices. A task that holds send rights to the device master port may request the kernel to *open* a device, returning a port that provides access to that device. Operations on that port then manipulate the device, until it is *closed*.

Operations on devices include:

- Read and write.

- Status return and setting.

- Special purpose operations.

- Mapping a shared memory window between a user space task and the device/device driver.

Chapter 10:

MkLinux Overview

The paper below was given at the Conference on Freely Redistributable Software Conference (February 1995, Cambridge, MA), sponsored by the Free Software Foundation. Although some details may have changed during the intervening months, the historical overview is interesting and the description of the basic porting approach is still accurate.

Linux on the OSF Mach 3 Microkernel

François Barbou des Places
Nick Stephen
OSF Research Institute, Grenoble

Franklin D. Reynolds
OSF Research Institute, Cambridge

Abstract

Ever since the selection of Mach 2.5 as the basis of the OSF/1 operating system, OSF intended to base its OS developments on the Mach 3.0 microkernel, which provides a scalable, extensible, OS-neutral set of abstractions. The OSF Research Institute has made significant improvements and extensions to the original CMU Mach 3.0 microkernel, and the result, named OSF MK, is still available for free. The latest versions of OSF/1 are based on OSF MK but are encumbered by commercial licenses. We decided to produce an unencumbered UNIX-like server on top of OSF MK, providing our members and the research community with a fully unencumbered development environment for their microkernel developments.

In this paper, we first describe the functionalities that were added to OSF MK by the OSF Research Institute and some performance improvements. We describe the architecture of the Linux server, emphasizing the areas requiring interaction between the Linux code and the microkernel. We present some performance figures for the Intel x86 platform and introduce the port of OSF MK and the Linux server on the Apple Power Mac platform.

OSF MK and the Linux server are or will shortly be available for free from the OSF Research Institute for both the Intel x86 and Apple Power Mac platforms.

Introduction

In 1989, OSF chose the Mach 2.5 kernel [Ace86a] to be the basis of the OSF/1 operating system. Mach is a modern, message passing, operating system microkernel. It is a scalable kernel intended for systems ranging from desktop workstations to multiprocessing supercomputers. As a microkernel, Mach provides a subset of the functionality found in the typical operating system. File systems, network protocol services such as sockets, administration tools such as quota services, and security policies are not provided. Instead, Mach strives to provide a core collection of powerful OS-neutral abstractions upon which can be built operating system servers. These abstractions (tasks, threads, memory objects, messages and ports), provide mechanisms to manage and manipulate virtual memory (VM), scheduling, and inter-process communication (IPC).

In addition to the advanced features already present in the Mach microkernel, such as SMP support, network-transparent IPC, and support for application-specific paging policies, the promise of a microkernel architecture was very appealing. OSF's customers have interests in many different operating systems. We needed a way to pursue a program of operating systems research that was not unduly operating system specific. Operating system-specific behavior needed to be separated from OS independent functionality. Our hope was that a microkernel-based architecture would prove to be more portable and modular than the monolithic systems that were prevalent at the time.

Currently OSF provides two versions of OSF/1. Each version of OSF/1 is hosted on top of the microkernel. OSF/1 1.3 is a system suitable for work-stations and minicomputers. Its performance is very competitive with other versions of UNIX [Vaha]. OSF/1 AD, available to OSF RI customers, is a system intended for massively parallel processing supercomputers and clus-ters [Roy93a].

We are interested in promoting the use of our systems technology within the industrial and research communities. The OSF MK kernel is freely avail-able but the OSF/1 server is encumbered by commercial licenses including the SVR2 UNIX license. For many organizations this is not a problem because they already have a SVR2 license but for others the licenses have proved to be serious obstacles. In an effort to remove these obstacles we decided to produce a free UNIX-like server that would suit the needs of Mach developers. We chose Linux for several reasons. It is one of the most popular free implementations of UNIX. Some of our members had expressed an interest in a Linux server. Linux is efficient and has very competitive performance. It provides a very attractive and effective development envi-ronment (GNU tools). There are several research projects based on Linux that could potentially benefit from a microkernel. Finally, it was an oppor-tunity to create and experiment with an operating system server that was not derived from BSD. CMU's UX, BSD-Lites and OSF/1 are all descended from BSD.

In 1995, we began a project to port OSF MK to the Apple Power Mac and to create a Linux server that could run on top of OSF MK. The server was hosted on both Intel x86 and Power Mac platforms. Our goal is to produce a free system that has competitive performance, is usable on multiple, inex-pensive hardware platforms, and is of interest to both our members and the research community. In this paper we will describe the project in detail and some of our future plans. We will also describe some of the important differences between OSF MK and Mach 3.0.

OSF MK, The OSF Microkernel

Our original interest in Mach was due to the powerful abstractions pro-vided by the kernel, its operating system neutrality, and the promise of greater portability and modularity. To a large extent, the microkernel has lived up to our expectations. OSF and some of our customers have ported the kernel to several platforms without undue difficulty. We and our collaborators have hosted different operating system personalities on top of the kernel. And for the last few years we have had an active research program that exploits and extends the abstractions provided by the microkernel.

Portability

The kernel itself is somewhat complex, yet the task of porting it to a new hardware platform is fairly straightforward. We support our version of the microkernel on several different hardware platforms. These include the Intel x86 family, the Intel i860, the DEC Alpha, the HP PA-RISC, and the Apple/IBM/Motorola PowerPC. The microkernel has a clean separation of hardware-dependent and hardware-independent functionality. Writing the hardware-dependent code for the microkernel usually requires approximately four to six months. The difficulty in creating an adequate suite of device drivers can easily exceed the effort necessary to port the rest of the kernel. In some cases the effort can be reduced by converting pre-existing drivers. We will discuss the effort to port the kernel to the Power Mac later in the paper.

Server Performance

In addition to different versions of UNIX, Mac OS and MS/DOS have been hosted on Mach. IBM has hosted OS/2 on their own version of the Mach microkernel. Early efforts to layer OS personality servers on top of the microkernel have had disappointing performance, due to the extra message-based communication between the system components. Often, as much as a 40% performance cost has been reported.

Our recent experience has led us to believe that most of the problems are due to a lack of attention to performance-related issues. After creating the OSF/1 server and noting its disappointing performance, we embarked on an effort to improve its performance.

Thread Migration

Thread migration was derived from work done on Mach 4.0 at the University of Utah [Fora]. It aims at reducing the cost of switching context between the sender and the receiver of an RPC.

The **thread** abstraction has been split into two new entities:

- the **activation**, which controls the resources associated with the thread

- the **shuttle**, which controls the flow of execution.

During an RPC, the shuttle part of the thread migrates to an empty (with no shuttle) activation in the receiver's task.

Short-Circuited RPC

We can optimize the RPC further by avoiding the construction of the Mach message and the marshalling and un-marshalling of the RPC arguments. This is only possible under certain circumstances. It requires thread migration: the sender's shuttle can migrate into an empty activation in the receiver's task and start executing the remote procedure directly.

In the current implementation, it also requires that the sender and the receiver are collocated (see below), i.e. that they are in the same address space.

Collocation

A collocatable server can be dynamically instantiated as a user task or as a kernel task. When a server runs as a kernel task, it has direct access to the kernel's address space and can use the kernel interfaces with little more code than a simple procedure call.

Modularity is preserved because all interactions between the kernel and the server are still done through MIG (Mach Interface Generator) interfaces at the source level, but the generated code can dynamically detect if the sender and the receiver are in the same address space and avoid unnecessary data copying.

Collocating a server as a kernel task should not be done lightly because an incorrect or malicious collocated server could corrupt the kernel. But once a server has been debugged in user mode, it can be loaded into the microkernel for best performance.

The collocatable servers of OSF MK are similar in spirit to the **system actors** found in Chorus [Roz88a], another microkernel-based system developed originally at INRIA.

Combined Effects

Used together, thread migration, short-circuited RPC, and collocation can almost reduce an RPC to a simple procedure call. The kernel to server system call exception RPC and the server to kernel system calls benefit from this optimization, greatly improving the overall system performance.

The performance of OSF/1 as a kernel task is very competitive with other UNIX systems, including the original OSF/1.

In a subsequent experiment we ported OSF/1 1.3 and the microkernel to an HP PA-RISC workstation. Then we layered an HP-UX (HP's version of UNIX) emulation library on top of OSF/1. This allows us to run HP-UX applications unchanged on our system. We then performed a variety of performance tests including AIM III (a common multi-user UNIX benchmark), TTCP, and others. Most of the tests indicate that OSF/1 using HP-UX emulation libraries has equal or superior performance to HP-UX [Ber95a]. This result came as a pleasant surprise and is generally considered a vindication of our performance efforts.

A Real-Time Microkernel

In addition to its portability and its operating-system neutrality, we were interested in the microkernel as a foundation for research into real-time and distributed computing issues. Mach was not designed as a real-time operating system. The original design focus was for scalable, multiprocessing timesharing systems. Extensive use of lazy evaluation techniques were used in the design of the VM and scheduling subsystems. In order for OSF MK to be a suitable foundation for real-time application we had to make enhancements to the microkernel ranging from the prosaic, such as preemption, clocks, and alarms to the innovative, such as real-time RPC, the CORDS framework for network protocols, and **paths**.

Pre-emption

Before the microkernel can be suitable for real-time applications, it must provide reasonable, predictable behavior. Complex real-time operating systems, like the various real-time UNIX systems and the OSF microkernel all use pre-emption to avoid indeterminate event latencies because there are certain features that, though desirable, are inherently unpredictable. Our pre-emption strategy exploits the fine-grained locks already in the kernel to provide Symmetric Multi-Processing (SMP) support. This naturally led to a fully pre-emptible system [Swa94a].

Mach 3.0 had simple and complex locks [Tra93a]. Simple locks provided mutual exclusion and complex locks provided multiple-reader, single-writer semantics. In OSF MK, simple locks were enhanced to prevent pre-emption. This resulted in a working system but because of the original code's extensive use of simple locks the resulting system had unacceptable event latencies. To deal with this problem, we added a new type of lock: a mutex lock. A mutex lock is an inexpensive, mutual-exclusion blocking lock. The difference between a simple lock and a mutex lock is that a kernel thread can be pre-empted while holding a mutex. Most of the algorithms that used simple locks were converted to the new mutex locks.

In the initial version of the system, it was possible to have unwarranted context switching between timesharing threads due to pre-emption. This problem was corrected by a simple modification to the pre-emption code. Pre-emption only occurred if the higher priority thread was a fixed priority thread. With this change, the cost of enabling pre-emption in an SMP environment was negligible when measured by a standard benchmark like AIM III. In a uni-processor environment, the cost of pre-emption is identical to the cost of enabling SMP locks, i.e., approximately 10%. Since our pre-emption mechanisms are integrated so closely with the SMP locking mechanisms, this is not surprising.

Priority Inversion

Kernel pre-emption created a new problem - a type of scheduling anomaly sometimes referred to as a priority inversion [Vaha]. Priority inversions can occur when a high priority thread becomes dependent on or blocked by a lower priority, preempted thread. We designed a straightforward priority-boosting protocol inside the kernel to deal with priority inversions. Priority boosting propagates across dependencies, not just locks. If a thread blocks and becomes dependent on another thread, then the thread controlling the dependency is boosted. If the boosted thread is blocked by another dependency, then the boosting propagates down the dependency chain. A thread remains boosted until it releases its last dependency.

This algorithm is not perfect in that some threads remain boosted longer than absolutely necessary. But it is very simple and inexpensive.

Real-time RPC

The Real-Time RPC [Bur94a] is not layered on top of message-based IPC. Implementing RT-RPC as a new kernel service had important advantages:

RPC-specific optimizations can be made along the entire RPC path (our RPC is twice as fast as the Mach 3.0 RPC optimizations). Real-time RPC-specific behaviors, such as alerts, orphan detection, predictable delivery, and nested time constraint propagation are possible. An efficient, unified programming model for invoking operations across module boundaries within a task, across the task/kernel boundary, or across task boundaries is possible.

The client side of a RT RPC is very similar to a message based RPC. In both cases, threads invoke RPCs using ports and the client thread waits for the server to process the request and reply. The server side is somewhat different. Instead of a pool of threads waiting in a message receive loop, a server creates a pool of empty threads. These threads have no scheduling state. When a client invokes a server and a server thread is available, the kernel chains the client and server threads together and upcalls the server immediately. Many client thread attributes, such as scheduling attributes, are propagated as well as the normal RPC parameters associated with the server's operational interface. When the server completes the service requested by the RPC and replies, the server thread becomes empty and a candidate for future upcalls. The reply parameters are propagated back to the client which returns from the invoke and resumes execution.

If no server threads are available, then the client thread is blocked. When a server thread eventually becomes available, the scheduling policy selects the appropriate client thread based on its scheduling attributes and chains it to the server thread. In this way, client threads are serviced in the correct order. This avoids the scheduling anomalies introduced by Mach IPCs port queues and ordered message delivery guarantees, making it possible for servers to provide service according to client-specified time constraints.

Alerts

Sometimes it is important to signal or generate an exception at the head of an RPC chain rather than a thread somewhere in the middle. One reason for doing this could be the elapsing of a deadline specified by one of the threads in the chain. Alerts are the mechanism used, by either the kernel or an application, to generate a timely exception at the head of an RPC chain.

When an alert is posted to thread A, which is not the head of a chain (suppose a A->B->C->D RPC chain), the kernel propagates the alert towards the head. When the thread that is the current head of the chain is located, in this case thread D, it is suspended and an alert exception upcall is made to the thread's exception port. This gives the task with thread D a chance to respond in a timely fashion to the event that triggered the alert. By using upcalls instead of messages, the time constraints of the target thread can be propagated to the exception handler. In this way, the exception processing can proceed without risk of a scheduling anomaly. The return value in the reply from the exception upcall indicates to the kernel whether the alert was successfully handled or not. If it was not handled, then thread D is terminated (just as with any unsuccessfully handled exception) and the alert is raised on thread C, the new head of the chain. Alerts will be back propagated up the chain until the thread originally alerted is reached.

Orphans

Node failures or other events such as task or thread termination can result in broken chains. Detecting and eliminating the orphaned chain fragment in a timely fashion is important in real-time systems. Responding to whatever failure or event caused the chain to break is as important as responding to any other external event. In some systems, timely response to failures is more important than the processing of ordinary events.

When a chain is broken, the rooted portion of the chain is immediately restarted. It returns from the RPC invocation with an error indicating the chain was broken, taking whatever action is deemed appropriate by the application.

An orphan alert is posted to the head of the orphaned chain. The alert is propagated to the head of the chain where an orphaned exception is generated. This is a fatal alert that cannot be handled correctly, i.e., when the orphaned exception handler returns, the thread is terminated and the alert is raised on the next thread up the chain. This gives each thread on the chain a chance to clean-up (release locks, undo, or perform compensating actions) before being terminated.

Characterization Tools (ETAP)

ETAP (Event Trace Analysis Package) [Car95a] is a tool for characterizing the performance and behavior of real-time applications as well as the system software. ETAP is straightforward in design. The kernel reserves a block of memory as a circular message buffer. The size of the buffer is configurable. The kernel has been instrumented with a variety of probes. When activated, these probes create entries in the circular buffer. Probe entries contain a type field, a time-stamp, a thread ID tuple, and probe specific information. Probes can be used to capture a wide range of information such as context switching events, system calls, lock events, device events, etc. There are global and per-thread probes. Any subset of the probes can be dynamically activated or deactivated. Applications with probes write to the buffer. There is a second task that reads the buffer and records it on disk where the information can be subsequently analyzed using different report generation programs. When configured into the kernel, inactive probes incur an insignificant overhead (approximately 1 percent when running AIM III).

The thread ID tuple identifies the thread and its shuttle or RPC chain. The RPC chain identifier allows us to determine which client thread a server is acting for. This is an invaluable tool for tracking the causal dependency of events in a client/server system. It has also become a valuable tool for debugging the kernel and applications.

Miscellaneous

In addition to the work already described, we have made a variety of relatively small changes and additions to the microkernel. These include:

- POSIX compatible fixed priority scheduling policies (FIFO and RoundRobin)

- Configurable number of priorities (32 to 1024)

- Support for multiple clocks and an alarm (time-out) service.

- Counting Semaphores and Locks for inter-task synchronization

- Real-time threads library (cthreads assumes a timeshare scheduling policy)

- Extensions to IPC to provide control over the lazy evaluation of buffer copies.

We are currently experimenting with a scheduling framework [Hay94a]. This framework both simplifies the task of creating a new scheduling policy, such as Earliest Deadline First or Best Effort and coordinates the scheduling of threads and synchronizers. Including the synchronizers in the framework enables the development of scheduling policies that can deal with scheduling anomalies such as priority inversion.

Networking With CORDS

The support for networks in Mach 3.0 was limited to the packet filter. Protocols and network transparent IPC were expected to be implemented as user-space servers. This had a negative effect on the performance of most uses of the network. The architecture also presented significant obstacles to a correct implementation of network IPC. In OSF MK, we have added an object-oriented framework for network protocols, Communication Objects for Reliable, Distributed Systems (CORDS) [Tra94a]. CORDS is derived from the xkernel, developed by the University of Arizona [Hut91a].

The CORDS framework has many features to simplify the task of implementing network protocols. Complex protocols can be decomposed into a graph of **micro-protocols**. A protocol graph can be extended across protection boundaries, permitting portions of a protocol graph to exist in a task while other parts exist in the kernel.

There is a notion of a **path** that describes the route a message will take through the protocol graph. Resources such as message buffers and threads can be attached to paths, allowing the protocol designer to manage the resources needed to guarantee the end-to-end quality of service needed by the application. Paths also provide a natural means for the treatment of protocol parallelism. We have used the framework to develop a real-time distributed clock protocol based on the Cristian algorithms, node-alive protocol, ordered reliable broadcast protocols, Mach IPC, and RPC protocols among others.

Multi-Computers And Clusters

DIPC (Distributed IPC) and XMM (eXtended Memory Management) [Bry94a] provide transparent internode communication and shared memory on NORMA (No Remote Memory Access) architectures.

DIPC extends Mach IPC in a way that permits applications running on any node to view Mach abstractions such as tasks, threads, memory objects, and ports in a transparent way. XMM supports distributed shared memory.

The OSF/1 AD system uses these two Mach subsystems to provide a scalable, single-system image of UNIX. It is intended for massively parallel processing environments, such as the MPP Intel Paragon, but also for clusters of interconnected workstations.

Configurable Kernel

With all these extensions, the microkernel has grown to become unacceptably large. We want the microkernel to run on low-end machines and we also want to target embedded systems, so we embarked on a program to make most of the microkernel's features configurable [Bla95a]. The target is a minimal microkernel that could run on a compute-only node and would only perform basic scheduling and IPC.

Miscellaneous

We are developing or planning other projects on OSF MK, which are less relevant to the Linux server project because they are not integrated in the mainline microkernel or not freely available. These projects include:

- fault tolerance (still in the design phase),

- high trust: this implies a complete re-implementation of

- OSF MK in C++ with strict layering for even better modularity [Loe95a].

Port Of Mach To Power Mac

Introduction

The OSF MK microkernel is a mature technology on various machine types and processor architectures. Apple Computer Inc. asked the OSF to make available a free, microkernel-based operating system on their Power Macintosh series of computers. The major part of the port to Power Macintosh was that of porting the OSF MK microkernel.

The range of Power Macintosh machines use various different PowerPC processors, together with very different machine architectures, ranging from a board architecture very close to that of the 68000-based Macs through to the latest CHRP machines. We initially targeted the Power Mac 8100/80 machines, which contain the PowerPC 601 microprocessor and a board architecture similar to that in the 68000 Macs.

To illustrate the clean separation between machine-dependent and machine-independent code, we note that in porting OSF MK to the Power Mac, the modifications to the generic parts of OSF MK consisted of two minor source file additions to preprocessor options.

The Early Stages Of A Kernel's Life

When porting an operating system to any new processor, the development environment and compiler tool chain is the first thing which needs to be in place. Since the Power Mac did not have any UNIX-like environment available, we set up a cross-compiling environment to build both Mach and, later, the Linux server. The host machines used for the development were x86 machines running Linux and HP700 machines running OSF/1. Midway through the development, the x86 machines were switched from the monolithic Linux to running the Linux server, in order to provide a self-hosting alpha test site.

The compiler tool chain chosen was GCC 2.7.1, which supports the cross-compilation of PowerPC code using the elf binary format. We also used a crossed version of GDB for remote debugging via a serial line, allowing symbolic debugging of the kernel from an extremely early stage.

Once the tool chain is in place, work can begin on porting the kernel. Initially, the only machine-dependent requirements are a means of I/O, traditionally done via a serial port connected to the development machine. Below is a list of the steps taken in the kernel port:

- simple program cross-compiles and links.

- program loads and performs minimal polled I/O on the serial line

- `printf` works

- remote debugging stubs work

- kernel code linked in to remote debugger stubs

- kernel VM initializes

- traps and exception handlers (first VM fault)

- building user libraries and first user process

- bootstrapping first user process

- first system call from user process works

- clock interrupts implemented

- interrupt driven console device runs

- testing and debugging

The first user task that was executed was a kernel benchmarking and testing suite called MPTS (Microkernel Performance Test Suite) [Ber93a]. It took approximately five engineer-months to have a booting system which correctly executed the full benchmarking suite.

Once the minimal kernel functionality is complete, there remains the issue of device drivers. Device drivers are more platform dependent than they are processor dependent, and on many platforms device drivers may be reused or easily adapted from those written for previous ports. This was the case for both the serial line driver and for the SCSI controller on the Power Macs. Writing a small stub of Power Mac-dependent DMA code meant that the original drivers could be used with little modification.

Trade-offs

In any first implementation of an operating system, the trade-off of simplicity and debuggability is made against those of performance and functionality.

Once an initial version of the kernel is working, more time can be spent padding out stub routines and in optimizing those routines which were written for simplicity instead of performance (routines such as `bcopy` plus bit testing and setting routines start out written in C, before being optimized into hand-coded assembler).

Another trade-off made was to concentrate on obtaining functionality on the available test hardware. Minimal effort was made to cater to other processors in the PowerPC family or to other Power Mac machine architectures, since testing on these other machines was not possible. However, the assembly code and low-level exception handlers have been written so that it should be simple to incorporate the behavior of the other PowerPC processors (the 603 and 604 in particular). Additional device drivers and interrupt-handling code will have to be written for the other machine architectures when porting to those machines.

Linux Server Architecture

A Single Server

Our Linux server is a **single server**, meaning that the entire Linux functionality resides in one single Mach task. The alternative to this design is the **multi-server** design, where functionality is split between smaller specialized tasks communicating though Mach RPC.

The multi-server design takes better advantage of the Mach architecture and allows one to re-use more code between different OS personalities: a generic terminal server could be shared by most OS servers, for example. The drawbacks lie in the areas of performance and complexity. Performance is reduced by the cost of the extra communication between the various servers. Because servers can call each other in random ways, complex RPC chains are created, making it hard to implement some aspects of the OS functionality, like interrupting a system call for example. One has to implement potentially complex mechanisms to chase the system call through the various servers and abort it in a sensible way.

Although we are convinced that multi-servers are the way to go to produce high-quality operating systems on top of Mach, this strategy was not applicable in our case because we started from an existing monolithic kernel and we wanted to maximize the code reuse ratio to make it easier to track new releases of Linux and leverage the Linux community effort.

A Multi-Threaded Server

A server on top of Mach simply receives and replies to requests from user tasks or from the microkernel. It has no explicit control on scheduling nor hardware interrupts, so it cannot decide what it needs or wants to do at a given time. We do not want to add code everywhere to check if there is something more important to do (like receive an incoming network packet or disk block) or to manage explicit context switches when we can rely on Mach threads and the user-mode **cthreads** library. This library offers various synchronization primitives (simple locks, mutexes and condition variables) and hides most of the necessary synchronization of the underlying Mach kernel threads.

The Linux server has dedicated threads to handle the following tasks:

- keep track of time (**jiffies**)

- process replies to asynchronous device requests

- process incoming network packets

- process pager requests

- dispatch fake interrupts

- idle thread, to wake up timed out tasks and tasks with pending signals

- process system call and exception messages from user tasks.

Most of these threads wait on a dedicated Mach port to receive a messages. The system call threads are managed as a pool and wait on a port set regrouping all the user tasks' exception ports. A system call thread is not dedicated to a given user task.

The system is serialized by a global mutex. Server threads must acquire it before doing anything sensible and release it when about to block.

System Call Redirection

As we mentioned earlier, communication between the user applications and the server is a critical issue for performance. Mach 3 offers a system call emulation facility based on the redirection of the control flow to an emulation library, a piece of code that resides in the user address space and is able to communicate with the server via Mach RPC. For performance reasons, this library can implement some system calls (`getpid,` signal mask operations, etc...) locally without any interaction with the server [Gol90a].

Although this provides excellent performance, it means that the server functionality is shared between this emulation library and the server itself, leading to extra complexity and consistency problems; the server cannot really consider the emulation library like the rest of the user code, especially with respect to signal handling. The emulation library is not protected from user access and is therefore a potential Trojan horse for a malicious user. It is extremely complex (and inefficient) to protect the server against malicious usage of the emulation library's privileged communication to the server. Furthermore, multi-threaded applications imply even more complexity for the emulation library, which has to be fully-reentrant and has to identify the user threads.

For these reasons, we decided against the use of such an emulation in our servers. We extended the Mach exception mechanism to be more flexible and efficient [Pat93a]. With OSF MK, a system call from a user task raises an exception and enters the microkernel, which sends an exception RPC to the server, providing the user thread's state. This is similar to the way a system call enters a traditional UNIX system.

Combined with the collocation, thread migration, and short-circuited RPC microkernel improvements, this method has proved to have competitive performance.

User Memory Access

Having the Linux server running as a regular user task makes it harder for it to access the memory of its user processes. The monolithic Linux kernel just uses segment registers to get inexpensive access to the user address space, but the Linux server has to use the Mach VM interfaces. This is also a critical aspect for the overall system performance. We cannot afford to suffer the overhead of switching to the microkernel for each access to user memory. We map the necessary user memory areas into the server's address space, using Mach VM services. Once the mapping is done, the server can access the memory without any performance penalty.

When the Linux server is collocated in the microkernel's address space, it can even avoid to setting up the mapping and use the microkernel's `copyin` and `copyout` mechanisms, which are similar to the monolithic Linux `memcpy_fromfs` and `memcpy_tofs` interfaces. There is still an extra cost because the server does not have direct access to the microkernel routines (it is a separately linked task) and has to go through short-circuited-RPC-like interfaces. This overhead is not a problem in itself, but is emphasized by Linux's habit of doing lots of very small (byte or word) copies at a time. By re-organizing some pieces of code in critical places (mainly in the exec path), we managed to get reasonable performance.

Device Access

The device drivers are in the microkernel, but the server has to access them and let its processes use them. Linux handles device numbers and uses its own device operation routines. Mach names its devices with regular names ("console", "hd0a", "fd0a", "sd0a", etc...) and offers its own device interfaces. In the Linux server, we just added a generic emulation layer, replacing the bottom half of most Linux device drivers.

The device emulation code fulfills two tasks:

- translate a Linux device (major, minor) into a Mach device name

- translate Linux device operations (open, read, write, etc...) into the appropriate Mach device requests.

Just as Linux devices get registered when they are detected, we register some additional information, for instance a couple of routines to translate a Linux device number into the equivalent Mach device name and the reverse. The **device operations** structure is replaced with more or less generic routines (we have a set of routines for block devices and another for character devices): accessing an IDE disk, a SCSI disk or a floppy does not make any difference for the Linux server once it has found which Mach device to use.

The device-specific code is therefore reduced to the initialization routine; most of these routines only differ by the Mach device name they register.

Scheduling

Scheduling is another of the microkernel's duties. The Linux `schedule` routine is still used to scan the task list for newly runnable tasks, but no actual context switching between user processes is done in the Linux server.

User tasks **block** when running in one of the server threads, using some Mach synchronization primitives provided by the **cthreads** library.

`schedule` calls **condition_wait** when the current task's state is no longer **TASK_RUNNABLE** and we call **condition_signal** whenever the task becomes runnable again.

Fake Interrupts

In monolithic Linux, like in most UNIX systems, pending signals are delivered to a user process when it returns from kernel mode to user mode. A user process can enter kernel mode when issuing a system call, when causing an exception (page fault, arithmetic error, etc...), or when interrupted by a hardware interrupt (like a clock interrupt). The Linux server follows this scheme, but will never be interrupted by the hardware since interrupts are handled by the microkernel. This means that a user process looping in user-mode without doing any system calls or exceptions is virtually unkillable because signals will never be delivered to it.

This problem has affected all UNIX servers on top of Mach 3. Some decided to solve this issue by adding an extra thread in the emulation library, to listen for messages from the server, and forcing the real user thread to check for signals when required. Despite the fact that it adds even more complexity to the emulation library, this could not be applied to the Linux server because we rejected the emulation library solution in the first place.

Our solution was to implement **fake interrupts** to allow the Linux server to regain control of a user process even if does not cooperate. The server takes control of the user thread, gets its state, and jumps to the system call return code where signals will be processed. Race conditions with a possibly incoming or returning system call are avoided by suspending the user thread and making sure that it's suspended in a safe place, using the **thread_abort_safely** Mach service. Of course, `thread_abort_safely` will fail if there's an exception message on its way to or from the server.

Linux Jiffies Emulation

In monolithic Linux, the `jiffies` global variable counts clock ticks since the system start-up time. It is incremented in the clock interrupt handler and is widely used throughout the rest of the system.

The Linux server does not receive clock interrupts; the only way for it to count time is to use the Mach alarm services, which are obviously more expensive than a simple increment every 10 milliseconds. The OSF/1 server does not manage its own idea of the time and relies on the microkernel for that. It has a time-out thread which keeps on blocking and requesting to be woken up by Mach when the next OSF/1 time-out expires. Unfortunately, the wide usage of `jiffies` and our desire to maximize code-reuse forced us into emulating the Linux kernel's behavior.

A jiffies thread is woken up at regular intervals by the microkernel and increments `jiffies` by the amount of clock ticks that have passed during its sleep. The interval could be set to exactly one clock tick, in which case we would have the same clock precision as the monolithic Linux, at the expense of a context switch and some overhead every 10 ms. Although we have not measured the impact of this overhead yet, we currently use a 100ms interval.

The real time itself can be obtained more accurately from the microkernel by mapping it in the server's address space, and updating the Linux **xtime** global variable before sensitive uses.

Linux VM Emulation

The Mach VM interfaces allow a user task to create memory objects and map them in an address space. Page management is totally hidden by the micro-kernel. The obvious place to connect Linux VM with Mach VM is therefore the **vm_area** structure management, which is roughly the equivalent of the **vm_map** structure in Mach.

The Linux page table management code could be discarded if Linux did not reference the page tables so widely. To minimize changes to the original Linux code, we chose to provide a machine-independent dumb emulation of the page table macros and routines. The Linux server does not make any sensible use of these page tables and they are mostly empty, but it allows more Linux code to compile and run unchanged.

VM Mappings

When Linux establishes a VM area, the Linux server has to use the Mach VM interfaces to perform the equivalent operation. We do that in the Linux **insert_vm_struct** and **remove_shared_vm_struct** routines.

Mapping a file is done by creating a memory object associated with the file and establishing the mapping with the vm_map Mach interface. Allocating zero-filled memory (for the **brk** system call for example) is done with the **vm_allocate** Mach interface. When removing a **vm_deallocate** mapping, we use the Mach interface.

This simple emulation has minimal impact on the original Linux code and covers the vast majority of the Linux VM operations. Unfortunately, we had to rewrite some Linux code to make it more Mach-friendly. For example, the brk system call shrinks a VM area by removing the old mapping and establishing a smaller one. This works in Linux because the page tables are not touched so the old memory is still there when the new mapping comes in place. Our emulation code discards the memory when removing the old mapping and cannot resuscitate it when establishing the new mapping. We just re-arranged the Linux code to avoid the "remove and replace" trick.

Memory Map

The **mem_map** array contains an entry for each physical memory page. Since it is widely used throughout the Linux code, we also chose to emulate this array and use the Linux page allocator. The server allocates a virtual memory area as big as the physical memory and uses this pool of pages when it needs memory, using the Linux **get_free_page** and **free_page** routines.

This is unnecessarily inefficient and restrictive; we would like to get rid of this implementation in a future release. If the original Linux code did not use the mem_map array explicitly, but hid it under macros or in-line routines, it would have given us freedom to implement whatever page allocation algorithm suits our architecture. This problem is an illustration of the advantages of modularity, which allows wider choices of implementation by reducing the interdependencies between system components.

External Inode Pager

As mentioned in the previous paragraph, mapped files are implemented by creating a memory object associated with the file and mapping this memory object. The Linux server then has to serve paging requests from the microkernel for this memory object. This is done by an external memory manager that we called the **inode pager**.

The inode pager is currently a single thread running in the Linux server task. It manages the relation between a Mach memory object and a Linux inode, and replies to microkernel paging requests.

When a page-in request comes in, the inode pager reads the required data from the disk and sends it back. For a page-out request, the microkernel sends the page inside the page-out message and the inode pager writes it back to disk. Of course, the microkernel only sends back dirty pages and silently discards clean ones, so the inode pager never has to write back text pages, for example.

The inode pager is also responsible for flushing a memory object from the microkernel cache when needed, for example when a mapped binary is recompiled.

Dynamic Buffer Cache

The dynamic buffer cache was a decisive point when we chose Linux as the free UNIX to port on OSF MK. We had already tried a dynamic buffer cache on the OSF/1 server with excellent results, but with some problems related to the OSF/1 file system design (it derived from BSD and is parallelized). We looked forward to making an easier experimentation with Linux, where everything was already in place.

The challenging part of a dynamic buffer cache for a Mach-based OS is that the buffer cache (in the Linux server) and the VM (in the microkernel) need to interact to let the system make the best use of the available mem-ory.

Letting the buffer cache grow is the easy part: the Linux server manages only virtual memory and can therefore provide the buffer cache with more pages than there are in the physical memory. The tricky part is to get the buffer cache to shrink when the system is short on memory and before it starts paging.

Advisory Page Out

The microkernel doe not report memory shortage. When it really needs a page, it selects a physical page and sends a page-out request to the appropriate memory manager. The Linux server had no way to know that the system was short on memory before paging was already started.

OSF extended the external memory manager to offer **advisory page out**. That is, instead of un-mapping a page and sending it to the memory manager, the microkernel can now leave the page in place, send a discard request to the memory manager, and let it take any appropriate action. The Linux server can then use the `try_to_free_page` routine and free a page other than the one selected by the microkernel. Of course, the microkernel cannot be made to rely on an external memory manager to eventually free a page. If the memory manager does not free a page in time, the microkernel will send the data to the default pager, a privileged and trusted memory manager.

On the Linux server side, the only major change required is to allocate the buffer cache pages from a separate memory object, the size of the physical memory, and backed by another external memory manager.

<u>Avoiding Double Paging</u>

Apart from making the best use of the available memory, a dynamic buffer cache also fixes a classic problem of Mach servers: double paging. The memory in the buffer cache comes from the disk and will eventually go back to the disk. There is some space reserved on disk for this data. Without a dedicated memory manager, buffer cache pages could be paged-out to the default pager's paging space when the microkernel decides to discard a buffer's memory. And, when the Linux server decides to re-use this buffer (either to write it back to disk if it's dirty, or to overwrite it with another disk block), the page fault will cause the page to be read from the paging space. With a dynamic buffer cache, we get the opportunity to write the buffer back to disk (if dirty) or just discard it without any useless paging activity.

Linux Server On The Power Mac

Once the Linux server was robust on the Intel platform, and the Mach microkernel was ready on the Power Mac, the two needed to be wed. Because Linux has already been ported to some other PowerPC machines, we aimed to re-use as much of the code from the native Linux port as possible, with the goal of offering complete source and binary compatibility with this port of Linux on other PowerPC machines, in a similar way to that already done on Intel machines.

The major part of porting the Linux server was to adapt the necessary header files for the Mach server. This took approximately one week to do; once this was done, the server was able to start to boot on the Power Mac.

Being able to use the Linux server on Power Mac machines was not simply a question of porting the server; commands and libraries were also needed, together with a file-system from which Linux could boot. We added some code to the Mach kernel to recognize the disk label and partition tables on a Macintosh disk, and ported the tool from the Minix distribution to create an initial populated file-system. As for commands and libraries, we were able both to build them ourselves and also to recover commands and libraries from an early binary distribution of native Linux on the PowerPC. Below is a list of steps taken in porting the Linux Server to the Power Mac:

- porting the include files

- porting the server's processor-dependent state

- recognizing Mac disk labels and partitions

- creating a file-system

- booting the Linux server from the file-system

- running `init` (first server system call)

- paging file found

- running `/etc/rc.S` (first signal taken)

- single user # prompt

- multi-user

- networking

- self-hosting

The work to generate a minix file system on a Mac disk was done in parallel to the port of the Linux server, using `mach_perf` as the server to boot from the file system. Reaching the multi-user # prompt took less than three engineer-weeks from the start of the port to the Power Mac.

Differences With The Native Linux

It is still a little early to give a complete listing of functional differences between native Linux on other PowerPC platforms and the Linux server on Power Macs, especially since both projects are under constant development. One current difference is that the Linux server offers the full 32-bit address space to user processes, rather than the restricted 31-bit address space offered by native Linux.

Performance

We have not had time to make extensive performance measurements and analysis for the Linux server, but we ran a few benchmarks to get an idea of the critical areas. We used the NONAIM benchmark, derived from the AIM III benchmark, which measures the behavior of the system under an increasing workload, trying to simulate real life user behavior.

We also ran the Byte benchmarks, which give finer results on the relative performance of more specific parts of the system.

The benchmarks were run on a DEC PC450, with a 50MHz i486 and SCSI disks, running a Slackware 3.0 ELF distribution. The benchmarks themselves were in a.out format and were run on a 1kB-block ext2 file-system.

We profiled the microkernel and Linux server during those benchmarks and performed quick optimizations in two areas:

- system call path,

- access to user memory.

These optimizations improved some benchmarks and we now have reasonable performance for AIM III throughput when the system is not I/O-bound. The Linux server reaches 93% of the AIM III performance of the native Linux kernel.

Next, we started investigating disk I/O performance. The default file-system block size is one kilobyte on Linux. The Linux kernel is able to group disk requests into larger requests and doesn't suffer from the small block size. Neither the Linux server nor the micro-kernel perform such an optimization currently, and the penalty is made even worse by the extra overhead of Mach device interfaces. The result is that we read only one block per disk revolution.

Conclusion

Although the Byte results show there is still room for performance improvement, the AIM results are encouraging. Even with the huge system call overhead penalty and the currently poor disk I/O performance, we are still within arm's reach of the native Linux kernel.

We plan to do more exhaustive performance measurements and analysis in the future and to extend our tests to multi-processor platforms.

Status And Future Work

Portability

It took approximately five engineer-months to convert Linux into a Linux server on the Intel x86 platform and two more engineer-weeks to port the Linux server to the Power Mac.

Admittedly, this port was able to re-use some of the machine-dependent files from the Linux/PowerPC project, but it is a fact that the code that requires a lot of work when porting is not used by the Linux server. Boot-strap issues, device drivers, context switching, trap handling, and, last but not least, virtual memory management are all handled by the microkernel and what is left of these components in the Linux server is mostly machine independent.

What is left to port is:

- a few header files describing some VM constants, like page size and mask

- the system call and exception handling routine, which has to fill the Linux registers structure from the Mach thread state structure

- the `copy_thread` routine, to initialize the state of the new Mach thread during a fork system call

- the signal delivery routine, which pushes the signal handler stack frame on the user stack.

Status On The Intel Platform

The two main missing pieces of functionality are virtual consoles, which seem necessary for X11 support, and the dynamic buffer cache support (the shrinking part). The performance is reasonable, although there is plenty of room for improvements.

We will address both the functionality and performance issues as soon as possible.

Status On The Power Mac Platform

At the time we write this paper, the Power Mac has just started booting Linux with a minimal file-system. It reaches the "login" prompt and is able to run most of the commands we have. We have a minimal set of drivers; we use a serial line as console and can access the SCSI disks. No floppy, CD-ROM, graphics, or network drivers are available for the moment, but work is in progress on these.

Linux Code Base

The Linux server is currently based on the 1.2.13 Linux kernel version. It can be seen as a port of the Linux kernel to new architectures: osfmach3_i386 and osfmach3_ppc.

Because we have always taken care to minimize the changes to Linux code, it is fairly easy to upgrade to new Linux kernel releases. We will provide a Linux server based on the latest 1.3 kernel (or maybe 1.4) as soon as possible, but our current priority is to complete the ports to the Power Mac.

Linux Device Drivers

A team at Columbia University has developed a framework to include Linux device drivers into Mach with virtually no changes. This work was done on Mach 4, but should be fairly easy to adapt to OSF MK. This would greatly improve the supported hardware list of the microkernel for the Intel x86 platform.

Development Environment

The OSF uses its own development environment, called ODE (OSF Development Environment). ODE is available for free from the OSF, and is currently required for building OSF MK. Although this still requires more work, OSF MK should compile for the x86 and Power Mac platforms from an Intel x86 system running Linux (server or monolithic), using a GCC compiler.

The Linux server is built using the same method and tools as the regular Linux kernel.

Being isolated from the hardware by the microkernel, the Linux server can share the machine with other operating system servers. In fact, it was developed as a regular OSF/1 process, started from a shell and debugged with a Mach-aware version of GDB (which can handle multi-threaded applications). This is a very powerful way to debug the system. There is no need to reboot the machine before each test and it provides full user mode debugging possibilities; is possible to debug the Linux server with GDB from its very first instruction.

Although Linux does not support multi-threaded tasks (at least not in the way we would like it to), we were able to start a Linux server from another Linux server. And, more generally, one could run any desired system person-alities in parallel on a single machine.

The microkernel can be debugged using the powerful (although afflicted with a weird syntax) kernel debugger on the Intel x86 platform, or using a remote GDB for the Power Mac.

Availability

The OSF MK microkernel and the ODE development environment are pro-tected by the OSF Free Copyright, allowing free usage of sources and bina-ries, copying and distribution under certain conditions, and some restrictions on commercial use. The Linux server is protected by the GNU General Public License.

They are both freely available from the OSF Open Software Mall (`www.osf.org/mall/`).

Related Work

BSD-Lite Server

Johannes Helander, Jukka Virtanen and others in Finland developed a BSD-Lite server based on the 4.4BSD sources. This server has an architecture similar to the 4.3BSD UX server from CMU: it uses an emulation library mapped into the user task's address space and uses similar code to manage its threads (CMU c-threads).

They partially ported their server to OSF MK in March 1995, but their server architecture did not allow them to take advantage of OSF MK's performance improvements. The Lites server may be ported to the latest OSF MK free release, sometime in 1996.

We could have used their work as a basis for our free UNIX server, but, because we do not use emulation libraries and have rather different server architecture designs, we preferred to start from scratch. We also wanted to demonstrate that a non-BSD UNIX could be implemented on Mach. OSF/1 and 4.4BSD have similar VM implementations, derived from Mach's VM, making it fairly straightforward to emulate with Mach interfaces.

GNU Hurd

The GNU Hurd has a very innovative and interesting design and might well be the first complete multi-server OS to run on top of Mach. Several multi-server projects have been started at CMU and OSF, but they never quite reached product-quality, due to design flaws and a relative lack of interest for such complex software.

The GNU Hurd is not yet available and we wanted to offer a develop-ment environment to our members and the research community as early as possible, so we produced yet another single server.

Conclusions

We have demonstrated that OSF MK could support a Linux personality server with reasonable performance and that the combination could be painlessly ported to a new hardware platform: the Power Mac.

We are now able to offer a completely free and unencumbered development environment based on the microkernel. We hope that the research community will find this environment attractive for their microkernel related projects.

Acknowledgments

We would like to thank Brett Halle, Michael Burg, and others at Apple Computer, Inc. for the valuable Power Mac expertise they have offered during the port of the microkernel.

Thanks to Philippe Bernadat for helping us in measuring and analyzing the system's performance. Philippe Bernadat also helped with microkernel enhancements for the Linux server support on the Intel x86.

We also want to acknowledge the work of the team who has been porting native Linux to the PowerPC and especially Joseph Brothers, Daniel Puertas, and Gary Thomas.

References

[Ace86a]

Mike Accetta, Robert Baron, William Bolosky, David Golub, Richard Rashid, Avadis Tevanian, and Michael Young, *Mach: A New Kernel Foundation For UNIX Development*, USENIX Proceedings, pp. 93-112, Atlanta, Summer 1986.

[Ber93a]

Philippe Bernadat, *Microkernel benchmarking techniques*, OSF RI Symposium '93, 1993. Slides

[Ber95a]

Philippe Bernadat, Christian Bruel, James Loveluck Eamonn McManus, and Jose Rogado, *A Performant Microkernel based OS for the HP PA-RISC*, OSF RI Collected Papers, vol. 4, 1995.

[Bla95a]

David Black and Philippe Bernadat, *Configurable Kernel Project Overview*, OSF RI Collected Papers, vol. 4, 1995.

[Bry94a]

Bill Bryant, Steve Sears, David Black, and Alan Langerman, *An Introduction to Mach 3.0's XMM system*, OSF RI Collected Papers, vol. 2, 1994.

[Bur94a]

Peter Watkins, and Bill Willcox, Ed Burke, Michael Condict, David Mitchell, Franklin Reynolds, *RPC Design for Real-Time MACH*, OSF RI Collected Papers, vol. 3, 1994.

[Car95a]

Joseph Caradonna, *The Event Trace Analysis Package Design Specifications*, OSF RI Collected Papers, vol. 4, 1995.

[Fora]

Bryan Ford and Jay Lepreau, *Evolving Mach 3.0 to use Migrating Threads*, UUCS-93-022.

[Gol90a]

David Golub, Randall Dean, Alessandro Forin, and Richard Rashid, *UNIX as an Application Program*, Usenix Conference Proceedings, Summer 1990.

[Hay94a]

Robert Haydt, Joseph Caradonna, and Franklin Reynolds, *Mach Scheduling Framework*, OSF RI Collected Papers, vol. 3, 1994.

[Hut91a]

N. C. Hutchinson and L. L. Peterson, *The x-kernel: an Architecture for Implementing Network Protocols*, IEEE Trans. on Software Eng., vol. 17, no. 1, pp. 64-76, Jan 1991.

[Loe95a]

Keith Loepere et al., *MK++ Kernel High Level Design*, 1995.

[Pat93a]

Simon Patience, *Redirecting System Calls in Mach 3.0: An alternative to the emulator*, OSF RI Collected Papers, vol. 1, 1993.

[Roy93a]

Paul Roy, David Black, Paulo Guedes, John Lo Verso, Durriya Netterwala, Faramarz Rabii from OSF RI, and, Michael Barnett, Bradford Kemp, Michael Leibensperger, Chris Peak, and Roman Zajcew from Locus Computing Corporation, *An OSF/1 UNIX for Massively Parallel Multi-computers*, OSF RI Collected Papers, vol. 2, 1993.

[Roz88a]

M. Rozier et al., *CHORUS Distributed Operating Systems*, Computing Systems, vol. 1, no. 4, December, 1988.

[Swa94a]

Dan Swartzendruber, *A preemptible MACH kernel*, OSF RI Collected Papers, vol. 3, 1994.

[Tra93a]

Franco Travostino, *MACH 3 Locking Protocol*, OSF RI Collected Papers, vol. 2, 1993.

[Tra94a]

Franco Travostino and Franklin Reynolds, *An O-O Communication Subsystem for Real-time Distributed Mach*, IEEE Proceedings of the Workshop on Object-Oriented Real-Time Dependable Systems (WORDS), 1994.

[Vaha]

Uresh Vahalia, *UNIX Internals: The New Frontiers*, Prentice-Hall.

The OSF RI Collected Papers are accessible on the WWW at `www.osf.org/os/os.coll.papers/`.

Biography

François Barbou des Places received the MSc. in Computer Science from the University of Paris XI, Orsay, France in 1987 and a Diplome d'Etudes Approfondies from the University of Grenoble, France in 1989. He also graduated from the Ecole Nationale Superieure d'Informatique et de Mathematiques Appliques in Grenoble in 1989. He is currently a Research Engineer at the OSF Research Institute in Grenoble.

Nick Stephen received a first class honours BSc. in Computer Science from the University of Southampton, England in 1990. He is currently a Research Engineer at the OSF Research Institute in Grenoble, France. His research interests include microkernel operating systems and distributed systems.

Franklin Reynolds has been involved in the computer industry for over twenty years. For the last six years he has been employed at the Open Software Foundation's Research Institute in Cambridge, MA. His current research interests include real-time and highly available distributed systems and active networks.

The work described in this paper (the Linux server and the port of the microkernel to the Power Mac) was partly supported by Apple Computer, Inc., who also provided useful technical information on the Power Mac.

Chapter 11:

- *Compatibility Issues*
- *Come Help!*
- *Hardware Information*

Hardware Overview

Many Mac OS users have no interest whatsoever in the hardware that lies beneath their operating system and applications. If you wish to approach MkLinux in the same manner, we have no objections whatsoever. We are, in fact, very happy that MkLinux allows this kind of usage!

Some MkLinux users, however, may want to peek under the covers a bit. If you are in this camp, you should find the next few chapters very useful and interesting. We cover a spectrum of hardware issues, ranging from devices and controls through interfaces to processor descriptions and chip use.

In addition, the PTF Reference disc contains a number of Apple documents that have useful hardware information. If you are willing to skip past the Mac OS-specific sections, you may find exactly the information you need.

Compatibility Issues

Apple's engineers work very hard (and quite successfully!) at hiding the differences among different Macintosh processors. Nonetheless, there are quite significant differences between the different models. Both the Mac OS and MkLinux programming staff need to address these issues very carefully, lest their users (and third-party programmers) fall into the gaps.

Because the Power Macintosh has been available for several years, the Apple MkLinux Team has quite a lot of catching up to do. Nonetheless, we expect that they will make good on their promise to support the entire range of Power Macintosh systems. To understand how much work is involved, it may be useful to review a bit of personal computer history.

The initial "IBM PC" computers were in fact manufactured by International Business Machines (IBM). And, for much of the PC's history, IBM was the *de facto* defining authority. No official standards bodies existed; indeed, IBM was not all that eager to publish its specifications.

Consequently, as various vendors attempted to market "PC-compatible" machines, users settled on a simple, if somewhat brutal test: "All my software must work the same way on this machine as it does on a 'real' IBM PC." If a computer passed this test, it was compatible; if not, it was sent back to the vendor as defective.

Two results emerged from this testing process. First, PC hardware engineers learned to design "bug-for-bug compatible" motherboards and interface cards. This was not a totally desirable result, but it did serve the PC users' immediate need for cheap, functional, and reliable machines.

The other result, which plagues operating system writers to this day, is that hardware vendors *only* felt it necessary to test their hardware on the most popular software: MS-DOS and a small suite of applications. If any other operating system could not deal with the vagaries of a particular PROM set, that was just too bad!

Meanwhile, engineers at companies like Apple and Sun faced a totally different set of constraints: pack the maximum capability into the smallest (read, cheapest) number of chips and devices. If a software interface got changed in the process, no problem. The operating system code can always be modified to deal with hardware changes (It's just a simple matter of software! :-).

Given the variety of machine architectures produced by these vendors, it's rather amazing that the system software was capable of dealing with all the hardware combinations, let alone handling new hardware features and (Oh, yeah!) adding new software (e.g., user interface) bells and whistles.

Now, however, we move to the present. A small band of programmers at Apple Computer and the Open Group Research Institute are tasked with making a Mach-based Linux variant work on the entire range of PowerPC-based Macintosh systems. Said systems collectively use more than three dozen special-purpose chips, in addition to several CPU implementations and a varying complement of off-the-shelf support chips.

Clearly, the MkLinux porting team has a lot of work to do. Equally clearly, members of the MkLinux user community will have to help with some of the more esoteric issues (e.g., audio support on a particular Performa model) if they are not willing to wait *quite* a while for a solution.

The Apple MkLinux Team is miniscule; just a few engineers. Consequently, the MkLinux community is expected to test releases, report bugs, and (if possible) suggest solutions. By actively employing the services of several thousand testers, we can help the Team to ferret out bugs, hardware design peculiarities, etc. Once this is done, we can get on with porting application software and even (gasp!) using the system...

Come Help!

If you are interested in getting involved in the porting effort, visit the MkLinux Web site. It has an area devoted to projects that are currently being done, as well as projects that have not yet been taken on.

If a project sounds interesting to you, contact the appropriate parties, telling them of your background, interests, etc. If there seems to be a match, you will be given a task to perform. Do a good job and your name will go up in lights. Fail, and you will languish in well-deserved obscurity (:-).

Seriously, there is an immense amount of room for interested programmers (both kernel and application) to help make MkLinux a better system. Many kinds of drivers are needed, hundreds of application packages need to be ported, and a zillion useful HOWTOs have yet to be written. Come help!

Hardware Information

The next several chapters contain information on computer hardware, with particular emphasis on Power Macintosh systems. Much of this material was adapted from Apple documentation, including the *Inside Macintosh* and *Reference Library* (Developer CD Series) CD-ROMs.

For the original versions of these documents, see the PTF Reference disc and /or the Apple publications themselves. Please note, however, that the original versions contain a large amount of Mac OS-specific information and that you will need to search carefully (as we did) to find the nuggets of hardware-specific information.

Chapter 12:

- *CD-ROM Drive*
- *Floppy Disk Drive*
- *Hard Disk Drive*
- *Interrupt Button*
- *Keyboard*
- *Monitor*
- *Mouse*
- *Power Switch*
- *Power-on Light*
- *Reset Button*

Controls And Devices

Power Macintosh systems, unlike conventional PCs, are equipped by default with a substantial number of standard controls and devices. At this writing, MkLinux does not support all of these items. We expect, however, that they will be supported in the relatively near future.

This chapter, in any event, is a high-level summary of these items, with some emphasis on their technical characteristics. The exact complement of controls and devices on a Power Macintosh system may vary. Nonetheless, any Power Macintosh system will have most of the controls and devices covered in this chapter.

Note: For specific information on the exact complement and placement of devices and controls on your system, review the descriptions and drawings in the User's Guide (or equivalent document) that came with your system.

CD-ROM Drive

Apple's built-in CD-ROM drive is capable of reading both CD-ROMs and Audio CDs. The control and status functions of the drive are accessed via the SCSI bus. Digital data is read over the SCSI bus; audio signals are fed through the computer's audio input subsystem.

Note: Some CD-ROM drives (e.g., the **Apple CD300**) are capable of sending audio data blocks over the SCSI bus. This is not particularly useful as a playback method, but it is very handy if you are trying to make copies or edited collages of audio CDs for personal use, etc. (Just be sure to comply with any relevant copyright laws.)

To use the CD-ROM drive, press firmly on the eject button, located below the right-hand end of the drive. This will send a signal to the operating system software, requesting that the drive be opened for access. The system will then request the drive to open, allowing you to insert a CD-ROM disc.

Center the disc in the CD-ROM drive's access tray, with the printed side up. Be sure the disc is sitting down in the well of the tray; a mis-aligned disc could be damaged when the tray retracts.

Now, press firmly on the eject button, requesting the system to retract the tray. The drive will also interpret a slight inward pressure as a request to retract the tray; be careful, however, not to push too hard, lest you damage the drive mechanism.

Ejecting a CD-ROM

Although the built-in CD-ROM drive has an eject button, it is mostly used to open an empty drive for insertion of a disc. If the drive does not respond to the button, there are two likely problems:

- The operating sytem is not responding to the eject button.

    If you are using Mac OS, and there is already a disc in the drive, this is normal behavior. Mac OS expects you to eject CD-ROMs by dragging their icons to the Trash.

    If you are using MkLinux, it may be that the operating system has **mounted** a disc and will not open the drive until the disc is **unmounted**. You can then use the `eject` command; see the `eject`, `mount`, and `umount` manual pages for details.

- The drive is not responding to the operating system.

If you are doing all the right things and the drive still won't eject, the system might simply be confused. A system reboot is a drastic, but often effective, way to clean up this sort of problem.

If you have rebooted the system (under both Mac OS and MkLinux, in case only one of them is confused) and still cannot get the drive to open, you should have your system inspected by a qualified technician.

Emergency measures

If you need to retrieve a disc from a CD-ROM drive that will not open, you may wish to try the following trick (at your own risk!):

- Unwind and straighten a little more than 2" of a wire paper clip.

- Slide the straightened end into the small hole just to the left of the eject button.

- Hunt around, pressing the wire gently against obstructions. With a bit of patience and luck, you should encounter a mechanical release that reacts to pressure from the end of the paper clip. Press on this until the tray has come out far enough to be gently grasped by your hand. Then, (very gently!) pull the drawer out until it stops.

- Remove the disc, then press firmly on the eject button. If you are lucky, the tray will slide back into the unit, indicating that the drive may once again be working normally. If not, it's time to call in the aforementioned technician.

- If the tray now closes on command, a few open/close cycles might be in order, to make sure the problem has been completely resolved.

Floppy Disk Drive

Apple's floppy disk drive uses an industry-standard 3.5" floppy disk, but it is capable of reading and writing it in a distinctly non-standard manner. For compatibility with **PC floppy disks**, the Apple drive handles DOS-compatible **Modified Frequency Modulation (MFM)** format as well as Apple's **Group Code Recording (GCR)** format.

As a MkLinux user, you will probably not need to worry about the fine points of these recording formats. Just be aware that there are two kinds of disks around, and that they may be physically identical, but act differently.

On most floppy (or, for that matter, hard) disks, there are several levels of data formatting that must be in agreement before the disk can be read:

- **Partitioning.** Disks that contain file systems commonly have a label, or partition map, that tells the operating system which disk blocks are used for what purpose. This labelling is generally unique to particular families of operating systems.

  Note: MkLinux currently uses Mac OS-style partitioning for its hard disks. Intel-based Linux systems, in contrast, use a DOS-based scheme. The Apple MkLinux Team is working on this problem; watch the web site (`www.mklinux.apple.com`) for future developments.

- **File System.** Each file system (e.g., EXT2, HFS) has its own unique way of encoding file names, offset information, etc. In addition, EXT2 file systems from different architectures (e.g., Intel and PowerPC Linux) may be written with incompatible byte ordering. See the installation documentation (on the Apple MkLinux disc) for current information.

  In addition, under Mac OS, a file has multiple (e.g., data and resource) forks. In general, other operating systems will not know how to interpret, let alone create, **resource fork** information.

- **Line Termination.** Mac OS terminates text lines with Carriage Returns (octal 15), UNIX uses Line Feeds (octal 12), and MS-DOS uses a Carriage Return/Line Feed sequence. You may need to change the line termination on a file before you can use it on a different machine.

To use the built-in floppy drive, simply insert the disk into the drive's access slot. Make sure the metal slide goes in first and that the opening for the disk's hub is on the bottom of the disk. If you intend to write on the disk, make sure that the write lock slider (on the upper-right corner of the disk) has been slid downward completely, obscuring the hole.

Ejecting a floppy disk

To eject a floppy disk, use the appropriate operating system command. (On MkLinux, this should be the `eject` command; see the online manual pages for details.) If the disk does not eject, there are two likely problems:

- The operating sytem is not responding to the `eject` command.

  If you are using Mac OS, this is normal behavior. Mac OS expects you to eject floppy disks by dragging their icons to the Trash. If you are using

MkLinux, it may be that the operating system has **mounted** a floppy disk and will not open the drive until the disk is **unmounted**.

- The drive is not responding to the operating system.

The first scenario is far more likely than the second. Try to ascertain why the operating system might be ignoring your request to eject the disk. For instance, it may be that the operating system has **mounted** a disk and will not open the drive until the disk is **unmounted**.

If you are doing all the right things and the drive still won't eject, the system might simply be confused. A system reboot is a drastic, but frequently effective, way to clean up this sort of problem.

If you have rebooted the system (under both Mac OS and MkLinux, in case only one of them is confused) and still cannot get the disk to eject, you should have your system inspected by a qualified technician.

Emergency measures

If you need to retrieve a floppy disk from a drive that will not eject it, you may wish to try the following trick (at your own risk!):

- Unwind and straighten a bit more than 1" of a wire paper clip.

- Slide the straightened end into the small hole just under the right end of the floppy disk access slot.

- Hunt around, pressing the wire gently against obstructions. With a bit of patience and luck, you should encounter a mechanical release that reacts to the pressure of the end of the paper clip. Press on this until the disk has come out far enough to be (gently!) removed by hand. Look over the disk to see if there are any rough or dirty parts that might explain the mechanical problems.

- If you are feeling experimental, take a (spare) disk and insert it back into the drive. If you are lucky, the drive will now accept and release the disk without problems. If not, it's time to call in the technician.

- If the drive now appears to work normally, a few insert/eject cycles might be in order, to make sure the problem has been resolved.

Hard Disk Drive

Power Macintosh hard drives get larger with each new product release. Many current models have drives which are a gigabyte or even larger. (We have seen third-party SCSI drives in excess of 20 GB!) The Apple file system format, however, has not grown to keep pace.

A single partition, formatted for Apple's **Hierarchical File System (HFS)**, holds a maximum of 64 K files. Although this may not seem like a problem, remember that this sets the minimum file size on a 2 GB disk to 32 KB (2 GB /64 K). If your system has very large partitions and lots of small files, you may be wasting a great deal of space.

Consequently, you should consider splitting large hard disk drives into multiple partitions. Just remember to balance convenience against the desire for efficiency. That is, if you have a relatively small number of large files, consider using very large partitions, etc.

And, given that you are reading this book, you will have to split at least one drive into multiple partitions. Apple supplies copies of **Apple HD SC Setup** and/or **Drive Setup** as part of the MkLinux distribution, but you can use **Silverlining** or some other partitioning tool if you desire. Just be sure to create all the partitions needed by MkLinux (See the Preparation chapter and online Installation Notes for up-to-date information.)

Note: If you are considering using a hard disk to transfer data between systems, be sure to read the format-related notes in the section on Floppy Disk Drives, above.

Interrupt Button

The Interrupt button sends a **non-maskable interrupt (NMI)** to the PowerPC CPU. The interpretation of this interrupt is controlled by software:

- On Mac OS, this button typically brings up a debugger (e.g., **MacsBug**).

- On **DEBUG** MkLinux systems, this button starts up the **kernel debugger**.

- On **PRODUCTION** MkLinux systems, this button is ignored.

Unless you are debugging the kernel, you can safely ignore this button.

Keyboard

The Keyboard is connected to the computer by means of the **Apple Desktop Bus** (**ADB**), discussed later in this chapter. Apple keyboards are rather conventional in appearance and function, with a few small exceptions:

- The **Option** and **Command** keys, which can act as modifiers to other keyboard characters.

- The **Power** key, which can be used to power the computer on and off, and (when combined with other keys) send interrupts to the system.

Apple offers several keyboards, ranging from compact ("Apple Keyboard II") through extended ("AppleDesign Keyboard"). Third-party vendors offer a number of variations, including ergonomically contoured keyboards, keyboards with built-in trackballs or touch pads, etc.

You may want to keep an extended keyboard around; function keys can be very handy for applications like Microsoft Word. Otherwise, we don't find most Apple-compatible keyboards well suited for use with MkLinux. The Control, Escape, and Tilde keys are generally awkward to reach, while the Caps Lock is placed where it is almost certain to be hit by accident.

If this annoys you, try to acquire one of Apple's discontinued "UNIX" keyboards (Model M0116, also known as 6610383). Look for a compact keyboard with no function keys and a Caps Lock key in the lower-left-hand corner. We have heard that the Apple IIgs keyboard (also discontinued) is both ADB-compatable and UNIX-friendly. You *may* be able to get one of these keyboards from a used equipment dealer such as Pre-Owned Electronics:

> Pre-Owned Electronics, Inc.   +1 800 274-5343
> 205 Burlington Road   +1 617 275-4848 (fax)
> Bedford, MA 01730

Monitor

Any Power Macintosh system will have at least one monitor, capable of at least medium-resolution graphical display. Many older Apple monitors use fixed syncronization frequencies, making them unsuitable for use with other systems. Recent monitors typically support **multisync** (automatic sync detection), which greatly increases their versatility.

A typical monitor will have a number of controls, most of which can be ignored unless the picture quality needs adjustment. Here are some of the controls you should expect to use fairly frequently:

- The **Brightness** knob, used to adjust the overall brightness of the screen.

- The **Contrast** knob, used to adjust the available range of contrast in the displayed image.

- The **Degaussing** button, used to demagnetize internal metal structures inside the **Cathode Ray Tube** (**CRT**). Try using this if you see distortions of colors or images. (On many monitors, a degaussing cycle is performed automatically on power-up.)

- The **Power** switch, used to power the monitor on and off. If the monitor is plugged into the computer's power output socket or a switched power strip, this switch can be left on.

    Note: Most recently manufactured monitors are **Energy-Star** compliant. When the **horizontal syncronization** signal is removed, they power down most of their circuitry. If you have such a monitor, you can leave it on without worrying about excessive energy usage.

Your monitor may also have a few other controls, possibly hidden behind a hinged or removable panel. If you are having a problem with the size, shape, or position of the image, these controls can be used (typically in concert) to set things right:

- **Horizontal Centering** (left-right position of image)

- **Vertical Centering** (up-down position of image)

- **Horizontal Size** (width of image)

- **Vertical Size** (height of image)

- **Curvature** (straightness of image edges, sometimes referred to as pincushion or barrel distortion)

- **Alignment** (orientation of image edges, sometimes referred to as keystone distortion)

On some Apple monitors, the above controls are adjusted by software (e.g., a Mac OS Control Panel). This functionality may not be present in MkLinux; if necessary, reboot into Mac OS to perform the needed adjustments.

Mouse

The mouse is connected to the computer by means of the Apple Desktop Bus (ADB). The standard Apple mouse, designed for use with Mac OS, only has one button. This is a nuisance under MkLinux, however, because the X Window System expects mice to have (at least) three buttons. (For convenience, Option-2 and -3 are interpreted as mouse buttons 2 and 3.)

Fortunately, several **multi-button mice**, **trackballs**, and other **pick devices** are available for ADB. In general, MkLinux supports all multi-button pick devices that conform to Apple's multi-button mouse protocol. For the latest information on supported pick devices, see the MkLinux Web site.

Power Switch

The power switch is used to control the supply of **AC power** to the computer. It should *not*, in normal circumstances, be used to shut down the computer. (The OS needs to put things away and generally tidy up!) So, shut down the system by means of the appropriate operating system command.

It is quite useful, however, to have a switched power strip dedicated to your entire computer system. Being able to power down all of your peripherals at a single stroke is very convenient and tends to reduce errors. More critically, it gives you a single switch to flip if something in your system starts to smoke!

Power-on Light

The power-on light indicates that the computer is receiving AC power, that the power switch is turned on, and that the appropriate line on the ADB has been momentarily grounded (typically by the power key on the keyboard).

Reset Button

The reset button sends a **hardware reset** signal to the PowerPC CPU. The interpretation of this signal is controlled by hardware; regardless of the operating system or other software being run, the computer will reboot.

Chapter 13:

- *Audio*
- *Television*
- *Video*

Analog I/O

All Power Macintosh systems support audio input and output and video output (i.e., support for a monitor). Some Power Mac systems (especially Performa's) support additional analog facilities, including television input and/or output.

It may be quite a while, however, before these capabilities are available under MkLinux. Several levels of problems must be solved:

- **Real-Time support.** Real-time applications (such as audio input) must be guaranteed a certain amount of CPU time on a controlled and predictable basis. Because Mac OS allows applications to take over the entire machine, it has no problem meeting this requirement.

  MkLinux, in contrast, does **preemptive multi-tasking**, switching the CPU between processes according to constantly changing levels of priority. This gives MkLinux better overall performance than Mac OS, but prevents it from supporting real-time applications. We expect, however, that improvements to the Mach microkernel underlying MkLinux may soon resolve this problem.

- **Drivers.** There is as yet no driver software for any of the audio or video hardware. We expect this to show up over time, but it is not likely to get much attention from the Apple MkLinux Team until the majority of Power Macintosh platforms have been made to work under MkLinux.

- **Applications.** Although Mac OS has a great deal of software to support audio and video, these applications will not function under MkLinux. Thus, we expect that the Linux (and more generally, UNIX) community will be the best source of audio-visual support software.

This software may not be trivial to port, however, due to differences in the underlying hardware. For example, Macintosh sampling rates and data formats may not be the same as those used in the PC community. Still, none of these problems are insuperable. If you want MkLinux to handle a particular audio or video function, sign up as a volunteer!

The current nebulous state of affairs makes it impossible for us to describe how a MkLinux programmer or user might access most of these analog channels. Still, we can present some selected overview and reference material. We hope you will find it useful.

A note on audio terminology

It is quite common for documentation (including some of the text in this book) to specify audio **sampling rates** in terms of **kHz** (**kiloHertz**). This is a convenient (if possibly misleading and technically incorrect) way of saying "thousands of samples per second".

To avoid **aliasing** (generation of spurious frequencies), each audio cycle must be sampled at least twice. So, when you see a number like 44.1 kHz, be careful to consider the context. If it is being presented as a sampling rate, the corresponding **audio bandwidth** can be no more than 22.05 kHz.

Audio

Only a few Power Macintosh systems have built-in microphones, but all of them support **audio input**, generally by means of a **PlainTalk** microphone port. PowerBooks use a **Line in** port; some Workgroup Servers use an **Omni** port. Some Power Macintosh models (e.g., the 7500 and 8500) also have RCA-style phono connectors. Finally, the **HDI-45** connector (described below, under Video) also contains a variety of audio signals.

The **PlainTalk** port uses a unique (3/4" long) variant of the standard 1/8" stereo mini-plug. The computer supplies +5V DC power to the tip, for use by the internal pre-amplifier in the PlainTalk microphone. The ring and sleeve are used, respectively, for line-level audio and a common ground. Standard (1/2" long) mini-plugs are compatible with the port, as long as they provide line-level signals.

The **Line in** port is designed to take a line-level signal, as generated by most comsumer audio pre-amplifiers, etc. The **Omni** port is designed for use with

Apple's Omni (Omni-Directional) microphone, which generates **mic level** (microphone level) signals.

Once the received signal is available to the computer hardware, it can be sampled, digitized, and made available to the operating system. Current Power Macintosh systems are capable of digitizing incoming audio at CD quality: two channels (stereo) at a **resolution** of 16 bits per sample, with **sampling rates** of 22.05 or 44.1 thousand samples per second. Some early systems support only a single channel (mono) and/or 8 bits per sample.

All Power Macintosh systems support **audio output**, if only by means of a built-in speaker. Most systems have a **Speaker Port** and a **Headphone Port**. Some systems are able to control the level of audio output reaching the speaker by means of a **Remote Control**.

Current Power Macintosh systems are capable of reproducing audio at CD quality: two channels (stereo) at a **resolution** of 16 bits per sample, with **sampling rates** of 22.05 or 44.1 thousand samples per second. Some early systems support only a single channel (mono) and/or 8 bits per sample.

Here are some typical specifications for Power Macintosh audio I/O:

- **input** – 8 kΩ impedance, 2 V rms maximum, 82 dB SNR

- **output** – 37 Ω impedance, 0.9 V rms maximum, 85 dB SNR

- **frequency response** – 20 Hz to 20 KHz, ± 2 dB.

- **total harmonic distortion and noise** – less than 0.05% between 20 Hz and 20 KHz, with a 1 V rms sine wave input.

Television

Some Power Macintosh systems (primarily AV systems and Performas) are capable of accepting and displaying television signals, generally by means of an Apple **AV Card**. This card accepts **composite** or **S-video** format signals in the NTSC, PAL, and SECAM formats:

- The **NTSC** (National Television System Committee) video standard is used for television signals in North America. The frame rate is 29.97 frames per second, with two interlaced **fields** making up each frame. NTSC is theoretically capable is displaying 480 horizontal lines, but older and/or inexpensive television sets may not resolve the two fields properly. So, 240 lines is a more realistic limit for general use.

- The **PAL** (Phase-Alternation Line) video standard is used for television signals in Western Europe and Australia. It has higher vertical resolution than NTSC (625 vs 525, not counting the vertical blanking interval), but a slower frame rate (25 frames per second).

- The **SECAM** (Séquentiel Couleur Avec Mémoire) video standard is used for television signals in Eastern Europe and Russia. There are many different versions of SECAM, including SECAM-B and SECAM-L.

A few Power Macintosh systems (primarily Performa's) also contain a television **tuner**, which allows the system to receive **RF** (**radio frequency**) television signals directly from sources such as cable TV or a broadcast signal. If your system does not have a tuner, you will need to demodulate the RF signal by means of an external tuner or VCR.

A note on television formats

Most consumer-grade (e.g., **VHS**) **Video Cassette Recorders** (**VCRs**) accept composite video signals, which contain both **luminance** (brightness) and **chrominance** (hue) information. Because of limitations in the encoding technique, the two kinds of information can interfere with each other, to the detriment of picture quality.

Recognizing this problem, the designers of S-video cassette recorders decided to separate the two kinds of information. Partly as a result of this, S-video equipment is able to reproduce video with significantly higher quality than composite-based systems.

Video

All Power Macintosh systems support **video output**, generally in **RGB** (Red/ Green/Blue) format. Some systems (e.g., Performa's and PowerBooks) have built-in displays. By means of add-on cards, systems can support additional displays. Power Macintosh AV systems are also able to convert computer-generated video for use by a television set or VCR.

A substantial number of video cards are available for **NuBus**-based Power Macintosh systems, despite the fact that the bus was never widely adopted by system vendors other than Apple Computer. The real opportunity, however, is found in the PCI bus arena.

A large number of computer vendors have adopted the **PCI bus**, creating a substantial market for PCI-based video (and other) cards. PCI-based MkLinux systems can use (at least theoretically) a vast amount of cards. Porting any given PCI card to MkLinux, however, may take a bit of work and investigation. In some cases, technical specifications for the card in question may not be available. Before you begin a port, be sure to look for any other (e.g., Intel- or DEC Alpha-based) Linux drivers, interface specifications, etc.

Resolution and bit depth

The **video resolution** is composed of two values. The **horizontal resolution** specifies the number of pixels that can be displayed from left to right on the screen. The **vertical resolution** specifies the number of pixels that can be displayed from top to bottom on the screen.

The **bit depth** controls the number of unique colors (or shades of gray) that can be displayed by a given **pixel** (**picture element**), as:

$$\text{colors} = 2^{\text{depth}}$$

Apple has standardized on certain bit depths and video resolutions, many of which are not used by any other vendors. All Power Macintosh systems support some of the following standardized bit depths:

Depth	Colors	Notes
1	2	Black & White
2	4	Grayscale, usually
4	16	
8	256	
16	32,768	"Thousands"
24	16,777,216	"Millions"

The design of a given piece of display hardware limits both the bit depth and the video resolution. In addition, the bit depth that is available at a given resolution is limited by the amount of **Video RAM** (**VRAM**). A 1024 by 768 display, with a bit depth of 8 bits, needs nearly a megabyte of Video RAM:

1024 * 768 = 786,432 bytes (* 8 = 6,291,456 bits)

All Power Macintosh systems support some of the following standardized video resolution pairs:

Horizontal	Vertical	Notes
512	384	
640	400	
640	480	common
640	870	
800	600	common
832	624	common
1024	768	
1152	870	
1280	1024	

The DB-15 video connector

Most Power Macintosh systems make the video signal available via a DB-15 connector:

Pin Number	Signal Name	Signal Description
1	RED.GND	Red ground
2	RED.VID	Red video signal
3	/CSYNC	Composite synchronization signal
4	SENSE0	Monitor sense signal 0
5	GRN.GND	Green ground
6	GRN.VID	Green video signal
7	SENSE1	Monitor sense signal 1
8	n.c.	Not connected
9	BLU.VID	Blue video signal
10	SENSE2	Monitor sense signal 2
11	C&VSYNC.GND	Ground for CSYNC & VSYNC
12	/VSYNC	Vertical synchronization signal
13	BLU.GND	Blue ground
14	HSYNC.GND	HSYNC ground
15	/HSYNC	Horizontal synchronization signal

The sense lines are used to inform the computer about the desired video resolution for the monitor. If you have a third-party monitor, you may need to obtain an adaptor to set these lines appropriately.

The HDI-45 multipurpose connector

On some systems, a large complement of audio and video signals is made available via an **HDI-45** (45-pin **High-Density Interconnect**) connector:

Pin Number	Signal Description
1-2	Audio shields, output & input
3-4	Audio input signals (microphone), left & right
5-6	Audio output signals (headphone), left & right
8-9	Monitor sense bits 1 & 2
10-11	Green video shield & signal
12-13	Video input ground & power supply
18	Monitor sense bit 3
19-21	Video input shield, luminance, & chrominance
26-27	Red video shield & signal
28-29	Video input controls 1 & 2
33-34	Video synchronization signals, vertical & composite
35-36	ADB power (+5 V DC) & logic ground
37	ADB pin 1: serial data bus
38	ADB pin 2: power on signal
42	Horizontal video synchronization signal
43	Video synchronization return
44-45	Blue video shield & signal

All pins not explicitly listed above are reserved for future use.

Video Cabling

Video signals contain very high frequency information. A 1024 by 768 color display, being refreshed at 70 Hz, is receiving three analog signals, each carrying 55 million samples per second, just for color information:

$$1024 * 768 * 70 = 55,050,240$$

This is further complicated by the fact that the screen does not spend all of its time displaying pixels (up to a third of the time is spent in horizontal and vertical retrace intervals) and by the fact that each sample should be resolvable into one of 256 unique intensity levels.

For proper results, the cables used for high-resolution video must be capable of carrying analog signals having well over 100 MHz of bandwidth. It is not generally possible to create cables of this quality in a home workshop. Nor, sadly, are all commecial cables up to this standard.

If you see **ghosts** (horizontal echoes, to the right of the initial image) or other image problems, you may have a cabling problem. Try using a high-quality video cable to see if your picture quality improves.

Chapter 14:

- *Busses*
- *ADB*
- *Ethernet*
- *IDE*
- *LocalTalk*
- *NuBus*
- *PCI Bus*
- *PCMCIA*
- *SCSI Bus*
- *Serial Port*

Digital I/O

The Power Macintosh has a variety of **digital interfaces** (electrical connections used to carry digital signals). Each of these is standardized in terms of its wiring, signal levels, timing protocols, etc. These standards allow independent vendors to make devices that can attach to the system.

The exact complement of digital interfaces on a Power Macintosh system may vary. Nonetheless, any Power Mac will have some of the following:

- ADB (Apple Desktop Bus)

- Ethernet

- IDE (Integrated Drive Electronics)

- NuBus

- PCI (Peripheral Component Interconnect) bus

- PCMCIA (Personal Computer Memory Card International Association)

- SCSI (Small Computer System Interface) bus

- Serial port (RS-422)

Busses

Before we begin our tour of Power Macintosh digital interfaces, we should discuss a few basic concepts and definitions regarding **busses**. Although any digital interface can be used to link to a single device, most of the interfaces discussed in this chapter can support communication with multiple devices.

This greatly increases their utility; if an interface can handle several devices, far fewer interfaces will be needed. In addition, busses commonly support abstract (as opposed to device-specific) protocols. This allows busses to support many *types* of devices at the same time.

For our purposes, a **bus** is a digital interface that supports multi-way transfers of information. In contrast, a point-to-point interface (such as a serial line connecting a computer to a modem) is not a bus. This definition is very broad. It does not specify the number of wires, speed, or method of arbitration. On the other hand, it does provide a common frame of reference.

A bus may have one or more **lines** (wires), carrying control signals and/or data. Busses which have only a single data line (or one in each direction) are known as **serial** busses, because the data goes serially down a single wire. ADB falls into this category.

Busses which use multiple data lines are known as **parallel** busses, because some amount of data (e.g., the bits in a byte) is transmitted in parallel down a set of wires. The SCSI bus and all internal (system) busses fall into this category.

In most busses, all of the lines pass from device to device until they reach the end. This is commonly called **daisy-chaining**, but see below. Ethernets that use **co-axial cable** (e.g., **10Base-2**) operate in this manner.

A central **hub** is sometimes used, in concert with a set of point-to-point interfaces, to achieve the same result. This is often called a **star** configuration and is commonly seen in **twisted-pair** (e.g., **10Base-T**) Ethernet systems.

The individual lines in a bus may be **shared** or **daisy-chained**. If a line is shared, all devices are connected to it at all times. A daisy-chained line must, in contrast, be allowed past each device to reach the next device.

Most lines are shared; daisy-chaining is used mostly for bus arbitration, signalling lines, etc.

Note: The term daisy-chain originally referred to a flower-arranging technique in which daisies are tied in long sequences by their stems. In the case of devices that are interconnected, it is commonly used to mean that a cable passes by several devices in sequence (e.g., SCSI or **coax**-based Ethernet). In the case of busses and device interface cards, however, it takes on the specific meaning that the signal must be gated through circuitry on each card.

Busses that operate at speeds above one Mbps often require **termination**. In an unterminated (or improperly terminated) line, a signal may go to the end, get reflected back, and cause interference with succeeding data bits. Loosely speaking, termination damps out these reflections. SCSI and coax-based Ethernet require termination, as do some system busses.

Note: Termination is also required for LocalTalk, but the requirement has more to do with the need to have a continuous DC bias on an **RS-485** bus than with any question of reflections.

If all devices on the bus transmit data according to a common, shared **clock** signal, the bus is said to be **synchronous**. If each device controls its own timing, the bus is said to be **asynchronous**.

Asynchronous busses are generally more efficient than synchronous busses. Because asynchronous busses are more likely to exhibit **race conditions** (unpredictable, timing-dependent behavior), however, they can be more difficult to design in a reliable manner.

ADB

The **Apple Desktop Bus** (ADB) is a low-speed (10 kHz), single-master, multiple-slave, asynchronous serial bus. It is used to connect input devices, such as keyboards, mouse devices, and graphics tablets, to Macintosh computers or to other hardware equipment. For information on the number of devices that you can connect to the ADB, see *Guide to the Macintosh Family Hardware*, second edition. Macintosh computers come equipped with one or two ADB connectors, wired in parallel.

The ADB is Apple Computer's standard interface for input devices such as keyboards and mouse devices. Apple provides a mouse with each system, except for models equipped with a trackball or a touchpad. Additionally, Apple provides various keyboard options, such as the Apple Standard keyboard, the Apple Extended keyboard, and the Apple Adjustable keyboard.

The ADB connector is a **4-pin mini-DIN** socket. The drawing below shows the pinout, as seen looking into the connector on the Macintosh:

Pin	Name	Description
1	ADB	Bidirectional data bus (The Macintosh pulls this up to 5 volts. Devices should use open collector outputs.)
2	PSW	Power-on signal (This line is grounded to generate a power-on request. It may also be used, in combination with other keys, for reset and interrupt signalling.)
3	+5 V	Power from the computer to external devices
4	GND	Ground from the computer

Note: The total current available for all devices connected to the +5 V pins on the ADB and the modem port is 500 mA. Each device should use no more than 100 mA.

For more information about the ADB, see *Guide to the Macintosh Family Hardware,* second edition. The software characteristics of the ADB are described in *Inside Macintosh: Devices.*

An **ADB device** is any input device that can connect to the ADB and meets the design requirements described in the *Apple Desktop Bus Specification* (included in the Apple ADB license distribution).

Note: Apple Computer, Inc. owns patents on the Apple Desktop Bus. If you want to manufacture a device that works with the ADB software, you must obtain a license and device handler ID from Apple Computer, Inc. Write to:

Apple Software Licensing
Apple Computer, Inc.
1 Infinite Loop
Cupertino, CA 95014

A properly designed ADB device has the following features:

- the memory in which to store data

- a default ADB device address and device handler ID

- the ability to detect and respond to bus collisions

- the ability to assert a service request signal

ADB devices cannot issue commands. Consequently, the computer must poll the devices to obtain their current status. If the computer detects a service request signal, it polls all the devices on the ADB. In addition, it does a continuous poll of the **active ADB device** (the last device that sent new data after requesting service with a service request signal).

If a device has information for the computer, it asserts a **service request signal**. The computer then polls all of the ADB devices. This polling is accomplished by means of **ADB commands**, described below. The commands access one of four **ADB device registers**. Registers 0 and 3 are defined according to specifications set by Apple. Registers 1 and 2 are device-dependent and can be defined by a device for any purpose. Each register may store between 2 and 8 bytes of data.

Each ADB device has a default address and initially responds to all ADB commands at that address. A **default ADB device address** is a 4-bit bus address that uniquely identifies the general type of device (such as a mouse or keyboard). An **ADB device handler ID** (identification) is an 8-bit value that identifies a more specific classification of the device type (such as the Apple Extended keyboard) or specific mode of operation (such as whether the keyboard differentiates between the Right and Left Shift keys).

An **ADB command** is a 1-byte value that specifies an ADB device address and encodes an action the target device should perform. In some cases, additional data may follow an ADB command. For example, the computer may transmit data to the device or the device may respond to a command by transmitting one or more bytes of data back to the computer. It's important to remember, however, that ADB devices never issue commands to the computer. At most, the device can assert a service request signal, asking that the computer poll the bus for any devices wishing to transmit data.

The computer can send any of four bus commands to an ADB device. Three of these commands, Talk, Listen, and Flush, are addressed to specific registers on a specific device. The fourth command, SendReset, applies to all ADB devices.

- **Talk.** The computer sends a Talk command to a device to fetch user input (or other data) from the device. The Talk command requests that a specified device send the contents of a specified device register across the bus. After the device sends the data from the specified register, the computer places the data into a buffer in RAM, which the computer makes available for use by device drivers or (in rare cases) programs. In the case of a Talk Register 0 command, the ADB device should respond to the computer only if it has new data to send.

- **Listen.** The computer sends a Listen command to a device to instruct it to prepare to receive additional data. The Listen command indicates which data register is to receive the data. After sending a Listen command, the computer then transfers data from a buffer in RAM to the device. The device must overwrite the existing contents of the specified register with the new data.

- **Flush.** The computer sends a Flush command to a device to force it to flush any existing user-input data from a specified device register. The device should prepare itself to receive any further input from the user.

- **SendReset.** The computer uses a SendReset command to force all devices on the bus to reset themselves to their startup states. Each device should clear any of its pending actions and prepare to accept new ADB commands and user input data immediately. Note that the ADB device does not actually receive the SendReset command but recognizes that it should reset itself when the bus is driven low by the (3 ms.) **reset pulse**.

Note: Your application should never send the SendReset command. In point of fact, it appears that this signal is never issued (even by the operating system).

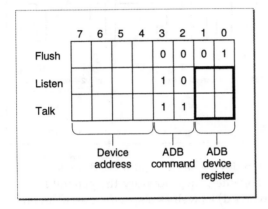

The figure above shows the command formats for the Talk, Listen, and Flush commands. Bits 0-1 specify the ADB device register, bits 2-3 specify the command code, and bits 4-7 specify the device address. (In the Send-Reset command, bits 0-3 are zero; bits 4-7 are ignored.)

An **ADB transaction** is a bus communication between the computer and an ADB device. A transaction consists of a command sent by the computer, followed by a **data packet** of several bytes sent either by the computer or a device. An ADB command consists of four parts:

•   an Attention signal

•   a Sync signal

•   one command byte

•   one stop bit

The figure below shows a typical ADB transaction, consisting of a command followed by a data packet.

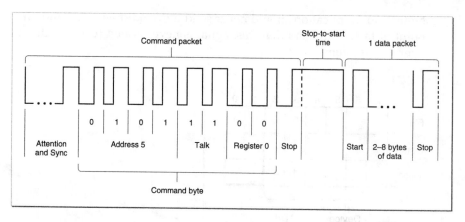

As previously described, each ADB device has a default ADB device address and device handler ID. Together, these identify the general type of device (such as a mouse or keyboard) as well as a specific classification of the device type (such as the Apple Extended keyboard) or specific mode of operation (such as whether the keyboard differentiates between the Right and Left Shift keys).

A default ADB device address is a 4-bit bus address that uniquely identifies devices of the same type. The currently defined default addresses have values between 1 and 7. Though it is not mandatory that a device's default address define the device type, doing so significantly reduces the possibility of multiple devices on the ADB sharing the same default address.

Most default addresses are movable addresses, which means that they can be replaced with a new address. If two ADB devices have the same default address, the computer must move one of the devices to a new address.

The device handler ID is an 8-bit value that further identifies the specific device type or its mode of operation. For example, an Apple Standard keyboard has an ID of 1, while an Apple Extended keyboard has an ID of 2. An ADB device can support several IDs, changing its mode of operation according to its current ID, as set by the computer.

Apple's mice have only one button. MkLinux supports multi-button pick devices (e.g., mice, touch pads, trackballs), however, if their behavior complies with Apple's multi-button mouse protocol.

Ethernet

Ethernet is a 10 Mbps bus used for **Local Area Networks (LANs)**. It is built into most Power Macintosh systems and is available (by means of add-in cards) on the remainder. Ethernet is an asynchronous, serial bus. Coax-based Ethernets share a single daisy-chained data line; 10Base-T Ethernet uses multiple twisted pair lines, wired to a central hub.

Most Power Macintosh systems connect to the Ethernet by means of an **adaptor** (also known as a **transceiver**), which connects to the computer by means of a parallel interface. Some add-in cards for Macintosh systems use a 15-pin **AUI** (Attachment Unit Interface) connector for this purpose. This is a female **DB-15** connector. Add-in cards may also have **BNC** connectors (for direct connection to **thin Ethernet** coax) or 8-pin **modular** connectors (for use with **10Base-T** twisted-pair).

Newer Macintosh models tend to have built-in Ethernet capability. Most use the 14-pin **AAUI** (**Apple AUI**) connector. AAUI and AUI connectors have the following pin assignments:

AAUI Pins	AUI Pin	Signal name	Signal description
1, 7, 8, 14	13	+5 V	Fused +5 volts DC
2	5	DI+	Data in positive
3	12	DI–	Data in negative
4, 11	6	GND	Ground
5	2	CI+	Clock in positive
6	9	CI–	Clock in negative
9	3	DO+	Data out positive
10	10	DO–	Data out negative
n.c.	7	-	Control Out A
n.c.	15	-	Control Out B
n.c.	1	-	signal shields
shell	4, 8, 11, 14	-	signal shields

Note: AUI-based Ethernet transceivers typically require a source of +12V power, which the AAUI may not provide. Thus, in order to drive an AUI-based transceiver from an AAUI, an external power supply may be needed. In general, you are well-advised to use AAUI and AUI adaptors for their designed purpose, rather than attempting to wire from one to the other.

Some Power Macintosh systems support 10Base-T directly, using an internal transceiver. If a machine has both AAUI and 10Base-T interfaces, and both are in use, the latter takes precedence. The 10Base-T connector uses the following pin assignments:

10Base-T Pin	Signal name	Signal description
1	DO+	Data out positive
2	DO-	Data out negative
3	DI+	Data in positive
4	n.c.	No connection
5	n.c.	No connection
6	DI-	Data in negative
7	n.c.	No connection
8	n.c.	No connection

Note: Despite similarities in signal naming, AAUI and AUI connectors do not carry the same electrical signals as the 10Base-T connector. Do *not* attempt to wire an AAUI or AUI connector directly to a 10Base-T circuit!

At most sites, Ethernet cabling will be shared (e.g., 10Base-2) coax or a 10Base-T star configuration, using twisted-pair cable. If you are putting in 10Base-T cable, by the way, be sure to use **Category 5** wire. It costs slightly more, but could more than repay the investment if and when you upgrade to 100Base-T, ATM, or one of the other upcoming standards.

Devices on an Ethernet send and receive **packets** of information, using an access control method known as **CSMA/CD** (Carrier Sense Multiple Access, with Collision Detection). CSMA/CD operates very much like a polite human conversation.

Each Ethernet device listens for an "open space" in the interchange. When it finds a gap, it starts to transmit, listening to the result. If it detects a collision (i.e., simultaneous transmission by another device), it stops and waits a pseudo-random amount of time (**back-off** period) before trying again.

There is no absolute guarantee that a given device will ever get to transmit its data. This may concern real-time designers, causing them to use other (e.g., **token ring**) networks. In practice, however, moderately loaded Ethernets allow all packets to get through with minimal delays.

Somewhat obviously, Ethernets cannot be expected to carry anything like their theoretical bandwidth if more than one device is trying to talk. In practice, Ethernets run best at traffic levels below five Mbps.

Ethernet packets have several mandatory components:

- **Preamble** (62 bits) – a series of alternating ones and zeroes. This is generated by the transmitting chip and is used by the receiving chip to acquire bit synchronization.

- **Start Of Frame Delimiter** (2 bits) – two consecutive one bits. This is generated by the transmitting chip and is used by the receiving chip to acquire byte synchronization.

- **Destination Ethernet Address** (6 bytes) – address of the intended receiver (all ones for **broadcast** packets).

- **Source Ethernet Address** (6 bytes) – address of the transmitting chip.

- **Length or Type field** (2 bytes) – For IEEE 802.3, this is the number of bytes of data. For Ethernet I and II, this is the packet type code. To avoid interpretation as length values, type codes are always greater than 1500.

- **Data** (46 to 1500 bytes) – Short packets must be padded to 46 bytes.

- **Frame Check Sequence** (4 bytes) – a 32 bit **Cyclic Redundancy Code (CRC)** checksum, calculated using the **AUTODIN II polynomial**. The FCS field normally is generated by the transmitting chip.

Aside from the fact that all Ethernet packets must have the same basic format, there is no requirement that the packets sent by one application (or operating system) be meaningful to another. Higher level protocols (e.g., **IP** and **TCP**) are used to provide these levels of compatibility.

IDE

IDE (Integrated Drive Electronics) is a very popular disk interface in the PC arena. It is used by Macintosh PowerBooks for internal and plug-in disk drives. IDE is also found on some desktop systems or can be added by means of interface cards.

The principle benefit of IDE is cost; small IDE disks tend to be noticeably cheaper than their SCSI equivalents. On the other hand, the cost of larger IDE and SCSI drives is essentially the same. The drawbacks of IDE are:

- It is not suitable for external devices.

- It only handles two devices per interface.

- It only handles disks (and things that act like them).

- It involves disk drivers in low-level issues like cylinders, heads, sectors, and tracks.

These limitations make IDE a poor choice for Power Macintosh systems. Its cost advantages are negligable on the larger drives used with either Mac OS or MkLinux. Consequently, we recommend that you use SCSI-based disk drives, where possible.

LocalTalk

LocalTalk is a low-performance (~250 Kbps) version of AppleTalk, transmitted by means of an Apple **serial port**. Suitable only for small, low-performance LANs, it is largely a historical relic: most modern Apple LANs are based on EtherTalk, which uses Ethernet as the transmission method.

NuBus

NuBus is found on older Macintosh systems. It was never widely adopted as an industry standard. Consequently, the range af cards available for NuBus is rather limited.

NuBus is structured as a set of identical **slots**, implemented as 96-pin sockets on the computer motherboard. Each slot is identified by a slot number in the range $1 through $E. (Slot $0 corresponds to the main logic board; slot $F is reserved for NuBus address translation.)

In Macintosh computers, the processor bus (which connects the CPU to RAM, ROM, and the FPU) and the NuBus (which connects the NuBus slots) are connected by a **bus interface**, as shown below.

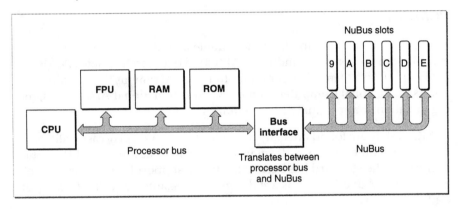

Note: NuBus is owned by Texas Instruments (`www.ti.com`). Contact them before attempting to market any products based on NuBus technology.

PCI Bus

PCI (**Peripheral Component Interconnect**) bus is a processor-independent system bus found on many current desktop computer systems, including recent Power Macintosh systems, Intel-based PCs, and DEC Alpha systems. It supports speeds up to 66 MHz and up to 32 physical PCI packages, each of which may contain up to eight separate PCI functions.

Because of its wide and growing industry acceptance, PCI is making a large number of add-in cards available to Power Mac owners. Unfortunately, not all PCI cards have driver software for Mac OS, let alone MkLinux. Be careful to find out about hardware compatibility and driver availability before you buy anything.

Note: The initial PCI bus specification (version 1.0) was developed by Intel Corporation. The specification is now managed by the PCI Special Interest Group. Contact the PCI SIG for current technical and legal information:

PCI Special Interest Group	+1 503 797-4207
P.O. Box 14070	+1 800 433-5177
Portland, OR	+1 503 234-6762 (fax)
97214 USA	

PCMCIA

PCMCIA is the longest and least memorable acronym you are likely to encounter in the computer industry. Although one wag translates PCMCIA as "People Can't Memorize Computer Industry Acronyms", it actually stands for **Personal Computer Memory Card International Association**, the organization that originated the standard.

PCMCIA slots are found on many portable computers and occasionally on desktop machines. Initially developed as a way of adding RAM to portable computers, the standard has been extended to support I/O devices, as well. Both the RAM and I/O cards are designed to be automatically detected and configured into running systems.

PCMCIA cards (commonly known as **PC cards**) use a standardized 68-pin connector. They have 26 address lines (providing 64 MB of address space) and 16 data lines. The remaining lines are used for power, control, and signalling. For instance, the SPKR# line allows I/O cards to send audio to the computer's built-in speaker.

Because of its wide and growing industry acceptance, PCMCIA is making a large number of add-in cards available for PowerBooks. Unfortunately, not all PC cards have driver software for Mac OS, let alone MkLinux. Be careful to find out about hardware compatibility and driver availability before you buy anything.

SCSI Bus

The SCSI (**Small Computer System Interface**) bus is a widely-adopted computer industry standard for connecting computers to peripheral devices. The specification provides support for hard disk drives, CD-ROM drives, printers, scanners, magnetic tape drives, and other devices that need to transfer large amounts of data.

The SCSI standard specifies the hardware and software interfaces at an abstract level, minimizing implementation dependencies. In fact, from a programming point of view, SCSI devices are pleasantly "object-oriented", conversing with the driver software by means of a message-based protocol.

A **SCSI bus** is a bus that conforms to the physical and electrical specifications of the SCSI standard. A **SCSI device** refers to any unit connected to the SCSI bus, either a peripheral device or a computer. Each SCSI device on the bus is assigned a **SCSI ID**, an integer value from 0 to 7 that uniquely identifies the device during **SCSI transactions**.

The Macintosh computer is always assigned the SCSI ID value (address) of 7, and its internal hard disk drive is normally assigned the SCSI ID value of 0. In general, only one Macintosh computer can be connected to a SCSI bus at a given time, and most Macintosh models support only a single SCSI bus.

When two SCSI devices communicate, one device acts as the **initiator** and the other as the **target**. The initiator begins a transaction by selecting a target device. The target responds to the selection and requests a command. The initiator then sends a SCSI command, and the target carries out the action. After acknowledging the command, the target controls the remainder of the transaction. The role of initiator and target is fixed for each device, and does not usually change. In general, the computer acts as initiator, with peripheral devices acting as targets.

SCSI transactions involve interaction between bus signals, bus phases, SCSI commands, and SCSI messages. The following sections briefly summarize the elements of a SCSI transaction.

The SCSI specification defines 50 bus signals, half of which are tied to ground. The table below describes the 18 SCSI bus signals that are relevant to SCSI transactions. Nine of these signals are used to initiate and control transactions; the other nine are used for data transfer (eight data bits plus a parity bit).

Signal	Name	Description
/BSY	Busy	Indicates that the bus is in use.

/SEL	Select	The initiator uses this signal to select a target.
/C/D	Control/Data	The target uses this signal to indicate whether the information being transferred is control information (signal asserted) or data (signal negated).
/I/O	Input/Output	The target uses this signal to specify the direction of the data movement with respect to the initiator. When the signal is asserted, data flows to the initiator; when negated, data flows to the target.
/MSG	Message	This signal is used by the target during the message phase.
/REQ	Request	The target uses this signal to start a request/acknowledge handshake.
/ACK	Acknowledge	This signal is used by the initiator to end a request/acknowledge handshake.
/ATN	Attention	The initiator uses this signal to inform the target that the initiator has a message ready. The target retrieves the message, at its convenience, by transitioning to a message-out bus phase.
/RST	Reset	This signal is used to clear all devices and operations from the bus, and force the bus into the bus free phase. The computer asserts this signal at startup. SCSI peripheral devices should never assert this signal.
/DB[0–7P]	Data	Eight data signals, numbered 0 to 7, and the parity signal. Macintosh computers generate SCSI parity, but may not detect parity errors.

Most Power Macintosh computers use a 50-pin **BERG** connector for internal SCSI devices and a **DB-25** connector to attach to external cabling. Some newer Macintosh computers use the **Micro-D** (SCSI-2 **external**) connector.

External devices themselves typically use either DB-25 or Amphenol Blue Ribbon (Centronics-style, with a different pin count) connectors. The table below shows the pin assignments on the internal, external, and Blue Ribbon SCSI connectors.

Int. Pin	Ext. Pin	B.R. Pin	Micro-D Pin	Signal Name	Signal Description
2	8	26	6	/DB0	Bit 0 of SCSI data bus
4	21	27	8	/DB1	Bit 1 of SCSI data bus
6	22	28	10	/DB2	Bit 2 of SCSI data bus
8	10	29	12	/DB3	Bit 3 of SCSI data bus
10	23	30	14	/DB4	Bit 4 of SCSI data bus
12	11	31	16	/DB5	Bit 5 of SCSI data bus
14	12	32	18	/DB6	Bit 6 of SCSI data bus
16	13	33	20	/DB7	Bit 7 of SCSI data bus
18	20	34	22	/DBP	Parity bit of SCSI data bus
26	25	38	24	TPWR	+5 V terminator power
32	17	41	25	/ATN	Attention
36	6	43	26	/BSY	Bus busy
38	5	44	28	/ACK	Handshake acknowledge
40	4	45	29	/RST	Bus reset
42	2	46	30	/MSG	Message phase
44	19	47	32	/SEL	Select
46	15	48	34	/C/D	Control or data
48	1	49	36	/REQ	Handshake request
50	3	50	33	/I/O	Input or output
-	-	-	1, 2	LOG5	+5 V for drive logic
-	-	-	39, 40	DSK5	+5 V for drive motor

Int. Pin	Ext. Pin	B.R. Pin	Micro-D Pin	Signal Name	Signal Description
-	-	-	1, 2, 37, 38	RTN5	GND for +5 V
25	-	-	17	n.c.	no connection
*	*	*	*	GND	Ground

Note: Unless otherwise specified, all non-signal pins are used for Ground.

A SCSI **bus phase** is an interval in time during which, by convention, certain control signals are allowed or expected, and others are not. The SCSI bus can never be in more than one phase at any given time.

For each of the bus phases, there is a set of allowable phases that can follow. For example, the bus free phase can only be followed by the arbitration phase or by another bus free phase. A data phase can be followed by a command, status, message, or bus free phase.

Control signals direct the transition from one phase to another. For example, the reset signal invokes the bus free phase, while the attention signal invokes the message phase.

The SCSI standard specifies eight distinct phases for the SCSI bus:

- **Bus free**. This phase means that no SCSI devices are using the bus and that the bus is available for another SCSI operation.

- **Arbitration**. This phase is preceded by the bus free phase and permits a SCSI device to gain control of the SCSI bus. During this phase, all devices wishing to use the bus assert the /BSY signal and put their SCSI ID onto the bus (using the data signals). The device with highest SCSI ID wins the arbitration.

- **Selection**. This phase follows the arbitration phase. The device that won arbitration uses this phase to select another device to communicate with.

- **Reselection**. This optional phase is used by systems that allow peripheral devices to disconnect and reconnect from the bus during lengthy operations.

- **Command**. During this phase, the target requests a command from the initiator.

- **Data**. The data phase occurs when the target requests a transfer of data to or from the initiator.

- **Status**. This phase occurs when the target requests that status information be sent to the initiator.

- **Message**. The message phase occurs when the target requests the transfer of a message. Messages are small blocks of data that carry information or requests between the initiator and a target. Multiple messages can be sent during this phase.

Together, the last four phases (command, data, status, and message) are known as the information transfer phases. The figure below shows the relationship of the SCSI bus phases.

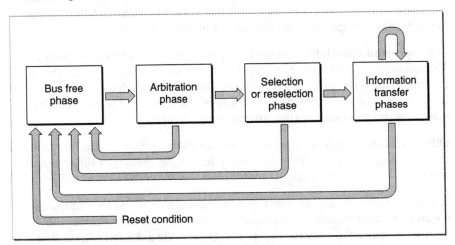

A **SCSI command** is an instruction from an initiator to a target to conduct an operation, such as reading or writing a block of data. Commands are read by the target when it is ready to do so, as opposed to being sent unrequested by the initiator.

SCSI commands are contained in a **command descriptor block (CDB)**, a data structure which can be 6, 10, or 12 bytes in size. The first byte specifies the desired operation; remaining bytes hold parameters used by the operation.

A single SCSI command may cause a peripheral device to undertake a relatively large amount of work. For example, the read command can specify multiple blocks of data rather than just one.

The primary difference between the SCSI protocol and other interfaces typically used for storage devices is that SCSI commands address a device as a series of logical blocks rather than in terms of heads, tracks, and sectors. It is this abstraction from the physical characteristics of the device that allows the SCSI protocol to be used with a wide variety of devices.

The SCSI standard specifies a number of possible messages between initiator and target. **SCSI messages** are small blocks of data, often just one byte in size, that indicate the successful completion of an operation (the command complete message), or a variety of other events, requests, and status information. All messages are sent during the message phase.

The **command complete** message is required in all SCSI implementations. This message is sent from the target to the initiator and indicates that a command (or series of linked commands) has been completed, either successfully or unsuccessfully. Success or failure of the command is indicated by status information sent earlier during the status phase.

Other SCSI messages are optional. During the selection phase, the initiator and target each specify their ability to handle messages other than the command complete message.

The SCSI standard defines the required sequence of transitions of the control and data signals to ensure reliable communication between SCSI devices. Because the **request signal (/REQ)** and the **acknowledge signal** (/ACK) both play a major role, this part of the SCSI protocol is often referred to as request/acknowledge handshaking (usually abbreviated as REQ/ACK handshaking).

The SCSI information transfer phases use REQ/ACK handshaking to transfer data or control information between the initiator and target, in either direction. The direction of the transfer depends on the particular bus phase.

The handshaking occurs on every byte transferred, and constitutes the lowest level of the SCSI protocol.

For example, during the data phase, when a target sends data to the initiator, the target places the data on the SCSI bus data lines and then asserts the /REQ signal. The initiator senses the /REQ signal, reads the data lines, then asserts the /ACK signal. When the target senses the /ACK signal, it releases the data lines and negates the /REQ signal. The initiator then senses that the /REQ signal has been negated, and negates the /ACK signal. After the target senses that the /ACK signal has been negated, it can repeat the whole process again, to transfer another byte of data.

Unless you are designing a SCSI device or writing a SCSI device driver, you do not need any special knowledge of SCSI handshaking. However, a general understanding of SCSI handshaking can be helpful when debugging. Refer to the SCSI specification for complete information about SCSI handshaking, bus phases, commands, and messages.

SCSI is an evolving standard; there are quite a few variations having to do with connector choice, electrical interfacing, number of lines, termination methods, and transmission protocols. Power Macintosh users can ignore most of these variations, however, until Apple gets involved with them.

SCSI cabling considerations

SCSI has an amazing number of cabling variations. We have seen more than a half-dozen different connectors used for SCSI:

- **DB-25** connector, used by some portable Apple peripherals and by desktop Apple system units

- **HDI-30** connector, used by some portable Apple systems

- **RJ-21 TelCo** (also known as **Amphenol blue ribbon** or **Centronics-style**) connector, defined as the SCSI-1 **external** connector

- SCSI-1 **internal** (also known as **BERG**) connector

- 50-pin **D-sub** connector (also known as **DB-50**), used by early Sun systems

- 50-pin **Micro-D** connector, defined as the SCSI-2 **external** connector

- 68-pin **P-type** connector, used with **wide** SCSI-2

- assorted miniature connectors found on miniscule internal SCSI devices

Our own preferences lie with the DB-50 (for sturdiness, etc.) and the 50-pin Micro-D (for convenience). Unfortunately, neither of these will typically be found on an Apple SCSI bus. Instead, you should expect to see mostly DB-25 and RJ-21 connectors, with an occasional Micro-D (e.g., on Zip drives).

Most Apple peripherals use the RJ-21 connector. This is convenient, because most external SCSI peripherals use this connector, as well. Some smaller peripherals, such as portable CD-ROM and disk drives, use the Apple **system** connector, which is a DB-25. This connector is *only* found on SCSI devices manufactured for the Apple marketplace. Consequently, these devices can be a bit difficult to attach to other (e.g., Sun) systems.

The DB-25 is actually a better connector than the blue-ribbon, in terms of electrical connections and strain relief. Its functionality is compromised in this application, however, by the fact that it has fewer pins than the SCSI standard specifies. To get around this deficiency, Apple wires the ground lines together. This is not ideal from an electrical standpoint and may cause unreliability in extended SCSI busses.

Note: Use of the DB-25 connector is deprecated for external devices because it eliminates the advantage of separate ground paths for each signal pin. They should be connected together in one place only: the computer.

SCSI on the Power Macintosh

Most Power Macintosh computers support **SCSI-1**, using **single-ended** wiring. (**Differential** wiring, which allows much longer cables to be used, is seldom seen in use. Apple's use of the DB-25 connector completely disallows the use of differential wiring, in any case, because there are no separate signal return lines. Sigh.)

Some recent Apple machines support **SCSI-2**, which uses the same set of lines, but has more stringent wiring and termination requirements. SCSI-2 devices generally work well in concert with SCSI-1 devices; they simply negotiate a mutually acceptable communication protocol and proceed.

SCSI-1 has a transfer rate of 2 Mbps when operating in **asynchronous mode**. Some SCSI-1 devices can handle **synchronous mode**, in which streams of bytes are sent in a single packet. This raises the transfer rate to 5 Mbps. By combining synchronous transfers with tighter cabling and termination rules, SCSI-2 raises this to 10 Mbps. Finally, there are two forms of **wide** SCSI-2 (16- and 32-bit), which achieve 20 and 40 Mbps, respectively.

Older SCSI terminators are **passive**, using only a resistor network. **Active** terminators, in contrast, use integrated circuits. If you have any SCSI-2 (i.e., recently manufactured) devices in use on your bus, you should be using an active terminator.

Note: The asynchronous and synchronous SCSI modes have essentially nothing to do with the asynchronous and synchronous communication protocols found on serial interfaces and computer system busses.

Serial Port

Power Macintosh systems typically have two **serial ports**, used for low-speed devices (e.g., printers) and communications interfaces. The ports support a subset of **RS-422** interface standard, a largely compatible extension of the **RS-232** interface found on most modems and many printers. (Apple's subset of RS-422 is compatible with RS-232; specifically, the transmit voltages are guaranteed to go negative.)

Mac OS (and most Macintosh literature) refers to the two serial ports as **printer** and **modem** ports, respectively. MkLinux, following UNIX tradition, refers to the printer port as **/dev/cua0** and to the modem port as **/dev/cua1**. For convenience, symbolic links (e.g., **/dev/modem**) may be created, as well. Note, however, that the name **/dev/printer** is already used for another purpose!

Power Macintosh serial ports can be programmed to support either asynchronous or synchronous communication formats, including AppleTalk (see above) and the full range of Apple **GeoPort** protocols. With external modules connected to the serial ports, the computer can communicate with a variety of ISDN and other telephone transmission facilities.

Apple has used three different connectors for its Macintosh serial ports. The early Macintosh serial ports used a **DB-9** connector, as found on many PCs. Later models adopted the 8-pin **mini-DIN** connectors.

Most recently, with the advent of the GeoPort, Apple has adopted the (upward-compatible) 9-pin mini-DIN connector. The added pin provides power and prevents GeoPort devices from getting plugged into an ordinary serial port. The 9-pin mini-DIN connector is laid out and used as shown below (as seen looking into the connector on the Macintosh):

Pin	Name	Function
1	HSKo	Handshake output
2	HSKi	Handshake input or external clock (up to 920 Kbit/sec.)
3	TxD–	Transmit data negative
4	Gnd	Ground
5	RxD–	Receive data negative
6	TxD+	Transmit data positive
7	GPi	General-purpose input (wake up CPU or perform DMA handshake)
8	RxD+	Receive data positive
9	+5 V	Power to external device (100 mA maximum)

Pin 9, if present, provides +5 V power from the ADB power supply. An external device should draw no more than 100 mA from that pin. The total current available for all devices connected to the +5 V supply for the ADB and the serial ports is 500 mA. Excessive current drain causes a circuit breaker to interrupt the +5 V supply; the breaker automatically resets when the load returns to normal.

Both serial ports include the **GPi (general-purpose input)** signal on pin 7. The GPi signal for each port connects to the corresponding data carrier detect input on the SCC portion of the Curio custom IC. For more information about the serial ports, see the *Guide to the Macintosh Family Hardware,* second edition.

Note: We have seen identical-looking serial cables with *totally* different internal wiring. For best results, purchase a cable expressly designed for the purpose at hand. Alternatively, check the cable wiring with an ohmmeter or a continuity tester.

Introduction to Serial Communication. Serial Communication, like any data transfer, requires coordination between the sender and receiver. For example, when to start the transmission and when to end it, when one particular bit or byte ends and another begins, when the receiver's capacity has been exceeded, and so on. A **protocol** defines the specific methods of coordinating transmission between a sender and receiver.

The scope of serial data transmission protocols is large and complex, encompassing everything from electrical connections to data encoding methods. This section summarizes the most important protocols and standards related to programming and using the Serial ports.

Note: Apple Macintosh computers either use or emulate the **Zilog 8530** serial communication chip. The technical manual 00-2034-04 (1987) for that chip is thus a valuable reference.

Asynchronous and Synchronous Communication. Serial data transfers depend on accurate timing in order to differentiate bits in the data stream. This timing can be handled in one of two ways: asynchronously or synchronously. In asynchronous communication, the scope of the timing is a single byte. In synchronous communication, the timing scope comprises one or more blocks of bytes. The terms asynchronous and synchronous are slightly misleading, because both kinds of communication require synchronization between the sender and receiver.

Asynchronous communication is the prevailing standard in the personal computer industry, both because it is easier to implement and because it has the unique advantage that bytes can be sent whenever they are ready, as opposed to waiting for blocks of data to accumulate.

Duplex Communication. Another important characteristic of digital communication is the extent to which simultaneous two-way transfers of data can be achieved.

In a simple connection, the hardware configuration is such that only one-way communication is possible (for example, from a computer to a printer that cannot send status signals back to the computer). In a half-duplex connection, two-way transfer of data is possible, but only in one direction at a time. That is, the two parties to the connection take turns transmitting and receiving data. In a full-duplex connection, both parties can transmit and receive data simultaneously. Most modern communication links are based on full-duplex connections.

Flow Control Methods. Because a sender and receiver can't always process data at the same rate, some method of negotiating when to start and stop transmission is required. Most serial drivers support two methods of controlling serial data flow. One method relies on the serial port hardware, the other is implemented in software.

Hardware flow control uses two of the serial port signal lines to control data transmission. When the driver is ready to accept data from an external device, it asserts the **Data Terminal Ready (DTR)** signal on pin 1. The external device receives this through its **Clear to Send (CTS)** input. Likewise, the Macintosh receives the external device's DTR signal through the CTS input on pin 2. When either the Macintosh or the external device is unable to receive data, it negates its DTR signal and the sender suspends transmission until the signal is asserted again.

Flow control can also be handled in software by using an agreed-upon set of characters as start and stop signals. Most drivers support **XON/XOFF flow control**, which typically assigns the ASCII **DC1** character (also known as **Control-Q**) as the start signal and the **DC3** character (**Control-S**) as the stop signal, although you can choose different characters.

Asynchronous Serial Communication Protocol. This section provides an overview of the protocol that governs the lowest level of data transmission – how serialized bits are sent over a single electrical line. This standard rests on more than a century of evolution in teleprinter technology.

When a sender is connected to a receiver over an electrical connecting line, there is an initial state in which communication has not yet begun, called the idle or mark state. Because older electromechanical devices operate more reliably with current continually passing through them, the mark state employs a positive voltage level. Changing the state of the line by shifting the voltage to a negative value is called a space. Once this change has occurred, the receiver interprets a negative voltage level as a 0 bit, and a positive voltage level as a 1 bit. These transitions are shown below.

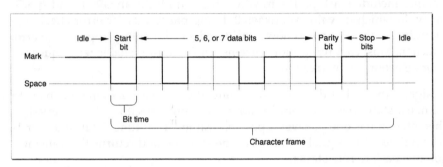

The change from mark to space is known as the **start bit**; this triggers the synchronization necessary for asynchronous serial transmission. The start bit delineates the beginning of the transmission unit defined as a character frame. The receiver then samples the voltage level at periodic intervals known as the bit time, to determine whether a 0-bit or a 1-bit is present on the line.

The bit time is expressed in samples per second, known as **baud** (in honor of telecommunication pioneer Emile Baudot). This sampling rate must be agreed upon by sender and receiver prior to start of transmission in order for a successful transfer to occur. Common values for the sampling rate are 1200 baud and 2400 baud. In the case where one sampling interval can signal a single bit, a baud rate of 1200 results in a transfer rate of 1200 bits per second (bps). Note that because modern protocols can express more than one bit value within the sampling interval, the baud rate and the **data rate** in **bits per second (bps)** are not always identical.

Prior to transmission, the sender and receiver agree on a serial data format; that is, how many bits of data constitute a character frame, and what happens after those bits are sent. The Power Macintosh supports frames of 5, 6, 7, or 8 bits in length. Character frames of 7 or 8 data bits are commonly used for transmitting ASCII characters.

After the data bits in the frame are sent, the sender can optionally transmit a parity bit for error-checking. There are various parity schemes, which the sender and receiver must agree upon prior to transmission. In odd parity, a bit is sent so that the entire frame always contains an odd number of 1 bits. Conversely, in even parity, the parity bit results in an even number of 1 bits. No parity means that no additional bit is sent. Other less-used parity schemes include mark parity, in which the extra bit is always 1, and space parity, in which its value is always 0. Using parity bits for error checking, regardless of the scheme, is now considered a rudimentary approach to error detection. Most communication systems employ more reliable techniques for error detection and correction.

To signify the end of the **character frame**, the sender places the line back to the **mark state** (positive voltage) for a minimum specified time interval. This interval has one of several possible values: 1 bit time, 2 bit times, or 1-1/2 bit times. This signal is known as the **stop bit**, and returns the transmission line back to **idle status**.

Electrical lines are always subject to environmental perturbations known as noise. This noise can cause errors in transmission, by altering voltage levels so that a bit is reversed (flipped), shortened (dropped), or lengthened (added). When this occurs, the ability of the receiver to distinguish a character frame may be affected, resulting in a framing error.

The **break signal** is a special signal that falls outside the character frame. The break signal occurs when the line is switched from mark (positive voltage) to space (negative voltage) and held there for longer than a character frame. The break signal resembles an ASCII NUL character (a string of 0-bits), but exists at a lower level than the ASCII encoding scheme (which governs the encoding of information *within* the character frame).

The RS-422 Serial Interface. The electrical characteristics of a serial communication connection are specified by various interfacing standards, one of which is the RS-422 standard used in all Macintosh computers. This standard is an enhancement of the RS-232 standard, with electrical characteristics modified to allow higher transmission rates over longer lines. Specifically, RS-422 uses differential wiring, requiring a pair of conductors for each direction.

Although the electrical voltage differences can be critical at times and should therefore not be ignored, most of the terminology and concepts remain the same across these two standards. For purposes of this discussion, it is convenient to treat these two standards as a single entity.

The specifications of the RS-422 and RS-232 standards are contained in documents available from the **Electronic Industries Associations (EIA)**. The specifications cover several aspects of the connection between data terminal equipment and data communication equipment. These aspects include the electrical signal characteristics, the mechanical description of the interface circuits, and the functional description of the circuits.

The principal interface signals specified by the EIA are described in the following list. The term **data terminal equipment (DTE)** is used to describe the initiator or controller of the serial connection, typically a computer or a printer. The term **data communication equipment (DCE)** describes a device that is connected to a DTE, such as a modem. For convenience, however, serial devices may not be wired according to this standard.

The RS-422/RS-232 signals are described below. For specific information about how these signals are used in Macintosh computers, see the *Guide to the Macintosh Family Hardware*, second edition.

- **Data Terminal Ready (DTR).** The DTR signal indicates that the DTE (that is, your computer) is ready to communicate. Deasserting this signal causes the DCE to suspend transmission. The DTR signal is the most important control line for a modem, because when it is deasserted, most modem functions cease and the modem disconnects from the telephone line. In Macintosh computers, the DTR signal is connected to the CTS signal, discussed next.

- **Request to Send (RTS)** and **Clear to Send (CTS).** The RTS signal was originally intended to switch a half-duplex modem from transmit to receive mode. The computer would send an RTS signal to the modem and wait for the modem to respond by asserting CTS. Since most communications between microcomputers are full-duplex nowadays, RTS/CTS handshaking is not often used in its original form. Rather, in most full-duplex modems, the CTS signal is permanently asserted, and the RTS signal is not used. In Macintosh computers, the CTS signal is connected to the DTR signal.

- **Data Set Ready (DSR).** The DSR signal is not used by Macintosh computers and is usually permanently asserted on microcomputer modems. It was intended to signal the computer that the modem had made a proper connection to the telephone line and received an answer tone from the modem on the other end. Modern modems communicate this information by sending messages to the computer.

- **Transmitted Data (TD).** The TD signal carries the serial data stream from the DTE to the DCE. The EIA specifications dictate that the DTR, RTS, CTS, and DSR signals must be asserted before data can be transmitted, but this requirement is not strictly followed in the computer industry.

- **Received Data (RD).** The RD signal is the counterpart of the TD signal, and carries data from the DCE to the DTE. Although the EIA specifies that this signal be in the mark state when no carrier is present, this requirement is rarely adhered to.

- **Data Carrier Detect (DCD).** The DCD signal is not used by Macintosh computers. In systems that use the signal, it is asserted by the DCE when a carrier signal is received.

- **Ring Indicator (RI).** The RI signal is not used by Macintosh computers. In systems that use the signal, it is asserted by the DCE when the telephone line is ringing.

As you can see, implementations of the RS-422/RS-232 interface do not always correspond to the specifications set forth by the EIA. This is especially true when the DCE is not a modem.

Chapter 15

- *Introduction*
- *Architecture*
- *Performance*
- *Business Issues*
- *Conclusion*

PowerPC CPU

The following report was published by Apple Computer in late 1993. Some of the information is dated, but most of it is not. In any event, it is interesting to note which of the projections have come to pass.

Note: Far too many treatments of RISC (including the one below) ignore the pioneering work of the late Seymour Cray. His design of the CDC 6600, over three decades ago, included many features found in today's RISC CPUs.

Comparing PowerPC with Pentium: A Competitive Analysis

Apple Computer, Inc.
L0608LL/A, 12/93

Introduction

The emergence of PowerPC, a new microprocessor architecture based on RISC technology, has raised questions about how it compares with Intel's CISC-based 80x86 architecture, most recently implemented in their Pentium chip. The purpose of this paper is to compare the two microprocessors by architecture, to evaluate their advantages and disadvantages, and to consider how such factors affect systems built on Pentium and PowerPC.

Architecture

A microprocessor embodies the underlying design philosophy and capabilities of its architecture. The architecture includes such design decisions as the number and size of the instruction registers, the manner in which instructions and data are moved to and from memory, whether floating-point numbers are a standard data type, and so on. The architecture is the ultimate determinant of the microprocessor's capabilities – and how fast it performs those capabilities. CISC and RISC represent two different micro-processor architectures, and thus two different sets of capabilities.

CISC versus RISC microprocessor architecture

The history of these architectures provides a foundation on which we can examine the pros and cons of Pentium and PowerPC.

Defining CISC

CISC stands for Complex Instruction Set Computing. All of today's personal computers are built on CISC microprocessors. To understand why CISC ar-chitectures rose to prominence in the 1970s, we need to look at the market conditions that prevailed then. Current CISC architectures were originally developed in the 1960s and 1970s, when a typical computer's available random-access memory was both limited and expensive. Many of the pro-cessor design decisions made at the time were based on minimizing program memory requirements. One way to reduce program memory requirements was to simplify software as much as possible by building more complexity into the processor. Though increasing the complexity of the processor had a neg-ative impact on processor performance, this trade-off was reasonable at the time. After all, it didn't matter how fast a processor could run if there wasn't enough memory left to load data and run programs.

As the price and availability of random-access memory improved dramati-cally during the 1980s and into the 1990s, processor designers reexamined performance and complexity trade-offs. An architecture that made sense in the 1970s, when a computer might have only 16 or 32 kilobytes of memory, is not necessarily an optimal architecture in the 1990s. An optimal archi-tecture today is RISC, which takes advantage of the 4 to 8 megabytes of memory that's now standard in most personal computers.

Defining RISC

RISC stands for Reduced Instruction Set Computing. The goal of a RISC architecture is to enable instructions to be executed as fast as possible. One way to accomplish this goal is to simplify the type of instructions the pro-cessor executes. The shorter and simpler "reduced" instructions of a RISC processor can run faster than the longer and more complex instructions of a CISC processor. RISC architectures enable higher performance through the use of pipelining and superscalar execution, techniques that allow more than one instruction to be executed at a time. This design requires more memory and more advanced compiler technology.

By the mid-1980s, RISC processors were commonly used in high performance workstations, in which the cost of memory was not an important issue. And now in the 1990s, memory is very affordable and advanced compilers are common, so high-performance RISC processors make sense for personal computers.

The largest computer manufacturers in the world (including Cray, IBM, Digital Equipment, Hewlett-Packard, Apple, and Sun), in all categories of computing – supercomputers, mainframes, minicomputers, workstations, and personal computers – have made a commitment to RISC, despite the fact that they have all risen to their current positions by selling CISC-based computers.

Comparing processors built on the CISC and RISC architectures

When comparing CISC and RISC chips, two key features illustrate their differences:

Speed. In general, RISC chips use pipelines to execute instructions that have been broken into segments of equal length. The pipelines process these instructions in stages, which allows RISC chips to process information at a faster rate than CISC chips. Although some recent CISC processors include pipelines, a RISC architecture is better suited to pipelining techniques because of its simpler, fixed-length instructions. This faster processing speed is one of the main reasons why RISC chips are used in most servers and workstations, where computation rates are of primary importance.

Number of transistors. For a given level of performance, CISC microprocessors typically have a higher transistor count than RISC processors. A higher number of transistors will generally translate to a larger die size and higher thermal output. Die size directly affects the cost of producing a microprocessor. And higher thermal output can necessitate special additions to the computer. Systems based on large chips, such as Pentium, may require complex heat sinks or cooling fans, leading to increased costs.

Pentium versus PowerPC

The architectures of the Pentium and PowerPC microprocessors are fundamentally different – Pentium is based on a CISC architecture, while PowerPC is a RISC architecture. A comparison of these two implementations of CISC and RISC technology tells us more about their specific advantages and disadvantages.

Pentium as a CISC processor

Pentium is the most recent implementation of Intel's 80x86 CISC-based processors, which evolved indirectly from the simple 4004 calculator chip in the early 1970s. The foundation for the Intel 80x86 architecture was set in place by the 8080 chip more than 20 years ago, in 1972. And the follow-on 8086 chip provided the blueprint for the 80x86 architecture. The architecture has expanded since then, but for Intel to maintain complete backward compatibility with older 80x86 software, the basic 80x86 architecture must remain unchanged.

80x86 compatibility

Paradoxically, the feature that would seem to give Pentium an advantage in the market is also the key to many of its weaknesses. Because Pentium must maintain complete register-level compatibility with all previous 80x86 processors, Intel must work within the restrictions of this older design. While current and future-generation RISC processors can incorporate the many architectural and design advances made over the last 15 years, Intel – because it must continue to support the 80x86 architecture – may be limited in the number of advances it can incorporate into Pentium and follow-on processors. Though this has not yet been a significant competitive weakness, the compatibility requirement may make it difficult for Intel to keep up with the performance of current and future RISC competitors.

PowerPC as a RISC processor

PowerPC, a RISC architecture, incorporates technology developed in the 1980s and 1990s. The IBM POWER (Performance Optimization with Enhanced RISC) architecture that forms the basis for the PowerPC chip takes advantage of modern implementation techniques, such as superscalar execution and deep pipelining, to increase performance. And it uses such

RISC architectural features as fixed-length instructions, large register sets, and a minimal number of memory addressing modes.

The POWER architecture was specifically designed for use in high-performance computers, such as high-end workstations and servers. PowerPC is a cost-reduced adoption of this architecture, developed jointly by Apple, IBM, and Motorola. PowerPC was designed for use in desktop computers, servers, and notebook computers.

Comparisons based on architecture

"The current Pentium chips are not the kind of parts that will make an engineer proud. Many run at only 48 megahertz to 50 megahertz, not 60 megahertz as promised. In addition, they are hot: not figuratively, literally. Some system manufacturers report that more than half the allotments actually have little fans epoxied to them, and others still bear a massive heat sink. In addition, the compiler to optimize for Pentium is not yet fully released to all software companies. Added to this are less-than-stellar benchmarks for the first generation of Pentium systems that have been tested by publications such as PC Week."

– PC Week, April 19, 1993, page 122

By comparing the architectural features of CISC and RISC, we can see how these features uncover advantages and disadvantages of Pentium and PowerPC:

Transistor count. The Pentium chip uses more than 3.1 million transistors to achieve integer performance similar to that of the PowerPC 601 chip, which uses 2.8 million transistors (see the "PowerPC 601 versus Pentium" chart). It's important to note that nearly half of the PowerPC 601 transistors are used by the on-chip cache, while only one-fourth of the Pentium transistors are used by the cache. Comparing the core logic (the total number of transistors minus the number of those devoted to cache) of the two processors shows that Pentium uses nearly twice the number of transistors (2.3 million) than the PowerPC 601 uses (1.2 million) to achieve roughly the same level of integer performance and substantially lower floating-point performance.

Pentium requires far more transistors devoted to core logic in order to implement its CISC architecture. The considerably higher core-logic transistor count increases the cost of Pentium, imposes barriers to easily achieving higher clock speeds (the PowerPC 601 has already been demonstrated in an Apple Macintosh computer running at 80 megahertz, while most Pentium processor-based computers are currently limited to 66 megahertz), and contributes to higher heat output ("X86 Sequels Increase Power But Complicate Choices", PC Week, June 28,1993, page 104).

To maintain their architectural heritage, future chips in the 80x86 architecture will likely be afflicted with high transistor counts. Thus, future chips of this architecture will probably be at size, cost, heat, and clock speed disadvantages when compared with PowerPC.

Die size. The PowerPC 601 chip is less than half the size of the Pentium chip (see the "PowerPC 601 versus Pentium" chart). The smaller die size helps to reduce the cost of manufacturing the PowerPC 601. If a manufacturer must pay more to produce a part, the company will likely have to charge more for the part. And over the long term it will be increasingly difficult for the more expensive processor architecture to maintain its place in the market.

Heat. The higher thermal output of Pentium will in all likelihood lead to higher computer costs because of the need for heat dissipation devices such as special heat sinks or fans. While the additional cost of these fans and heat sinks in a new Pentium-based system may not be high, the cost could be significant to those users who intend to upgrade their current 80486-based systems to a Pentium-based system. Most 80486-based units have neither the room nor the internal design to accommodate such cooling systems. Users with 80486-based systems may find they're unable to upgrade, because the significantly increased cooling requirements of Pentium processors were not considered by the manufacturers of the 80486-based systems.

Manufacturing cost. MicroDesign Resources recently looked at cost factors for both PowerPC and Pentium (Microprocessor Report, August 2, 1993). By examining a number of variables, including die size, wafer size, estimated yield, packaging, and testing, they estimated that Intel currently spends approximately $480 to produce a single Pentium chip. The cost of manufacturing a PowerPC 601 chip was estimated at $76. Both Pentium and PowerPC are subject to the same cost dynamics, so the cost of manufacturing both processors may be expected to decline at approximately the same rate. It follows that future generations of both processors will likely have a large cost differential as well.

Pentium and PowerPC upgrades

Many manufacturers of 80486-based personal computers include a socket on their logic boards to accommodate a future Pentium upgrade processor; called Pentium OverDrive. The high thermal output of Pentium, and the reduced performance a user can expect when installing a 66-megahertz, 64-bit processor on a 33-megahertz board designed for a 32-bit processor, has made it necessary for Intel to redefine the socket specifications for the processor, possibly delaying the availability of upgrades for 80486-based systems (PC Week, September 13, 1993, page 22).

Apple has announced that low-cost PowerPC logic board upgrades (starting under $1,000) will be available for many current Macintosh computers, and third-party manufacturers are developing PowerPC upgrades for other Macintosh models. Because the PowerPC 601 chip has a thermal output not significantly higher than current high-end 68040 processors, heat dissipation should not be an issue.

PowerPC 601 versus Pentium

Feature	PowerPC 601	Pentium
Architecture	64-bit RISC	32-bit CISC
Age of architecture	3 years	15 to 20 years[1]
Primary operating system	32 bit[2]	16 bit[3]
Transistor count	2.8 million	3.1 million
Core logic transistor count	~1.2 million	~2.3 million[4]
On-chip cache size	32 KB	16 KB
Die size	118.8 sq. mm.	262.4 sq. mm.
Heat dissipation at 66 MHz	9 Watts	16 Watts
Perf.-integer at 66 MHz	>60 SPECint92	64.5 SPECint92
Perf.-floating point at 66 MHz	>80 SPECfp92	56.9 SPECfp92
Estimated manufacturing cost[5]	$76	$483
Maximum instructions per cycle[6]	3	2
General-purpose registers	32@32-bit	8@32-bit
Floating-point registers	32@64-bit	8@80-bit
Follow-on processors	603, 604, 620	Not announced[7]

[1] Number of years depends on whether the 8080 or the 8086 is used as the starting point.

[2] System 7

[3] MS-DOS and Windows 3.1

[4] Total transistor count minus the number of transistors devoted to on-chip cache.

[5] Based on MicroDesign Research estimates published in Microprocessor Report, August 2, 1993.

[6] BYTE, August 1993, page 84.

[7] Intel has not announced additional 80x86 or Pentium processors.

Performance

Comparing Pentium performance with PowerPC performance

> "Early benchmark tests show the PowerPC running ahout 1.5 to nearly 5 times faster than a Pentium, depending on the operation."

> BYTE, August 1993, page 64

Though Pentium was originally touted as the fastest mainstream microprocessor for personal computers, PowerPC is challenging that position with equal or superior performance ratings when running identical applications. Especially notable is the fact that PowerPC outperforms Pentium by as much as 30 percent when running floating-point calculations in applications such as computer-aided design, publishing, and other computation-intensive programs. (See the "PowerPC 601 versus Pentium" chart). Pentium is faster than the 80486 in floating-point calculations, but significantly slower than the PowerPC 601.

It's true that floating-point performance is not critical for some of today's typical desktop computing programs, such as word processing or basic spreadsheet applications, so the Pentium disadvantage in floating-point performance is not critical for these applications (or at least for the versions of these applications that have been written thus far). But the many professionals who use sophisticated applications, such as complex spreadsheets, high-end graphics programs, or digital imaging software, will require fast floating-point performance to stay competitive.

In the future, fast floating-point performance will likely prompt the development of new versions of existing applications, as well as new classes of applications. These new applications will enable advanced telecommunications, video, and speech capabilities. Examples of this type of software include Apple's PlainTalk speech-recognition software and Geoport telecommunications software, which are part of Apple AV Technologies. As users adopt these new applications, fast floating-point performance will become essential.

The market research firm InfoCorp looked at the various factors likely to influence the performance of Pentium and PowerPC over the next few years. The chart below shows the performance levels, as measured by SPEC-marks (a general-purpose performance metric), of both Pentium and announced versions of PowerPC. Both Pentium and PowerPC start out with approximately equal performance in their current generations, and both improve considerably over time. But as the chart shows, InfoCorp expects that future generations of PowerPC will outperform Pentium by a significant margin.

Comparing future performance of Pentium and PowerPC

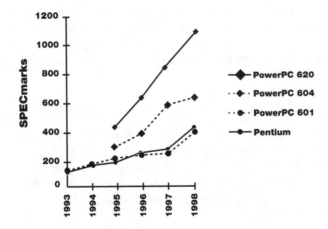

Source: InfoCorp, Motorola, and industry sources, as published in PC Week, August 9, 1993.

Business issues

Pentium and PowerPC will impact the personal computer industry in different ways, because the companies that manufacture the chips have different business strategies. Intel, as the sole source provider of Pentium and the PowerPC alliance (Apple, IBM, and Motorola), as a joint collaboration, have different resources and development strategies for their microprocessors.

Resources

We can compare the resources behind Pentium and PowerPC in the following two important areas.

Budget

Published annual reports show that Apple, IBM, and Motorola had a combined 1992 research and development (R&D) budget of more than $8 billion, while Intel's 1992 R&D budget was approximately $780 million. Though only a portion of each budget is devoted to advancing these microprocessors, it's clear that the Apple, IBM, and Motorola alliance has combined R&D resources that exceed Intel's.

Market opportunities

A larger R&D budget doesn't necessarily ensure a more successful processor. The difference between a sole-source provider and an alliance in terms of resources can have more to do with channels and market opportunities than R&D dollars. Intel has only its own resources to concentrate on development of its products.

On the other hand, the combined resources of Apple, IBM, and Motorola make advances possible that could be too costly or too risky for one company to undertake – such as developing other implementations of the PowerPC microprocessor. The PowerPC processor is being considered for use in cars, household appliances, and several other applications. The desire to address these high-volume markets allows Apple, Motorola, and IBM to justify high levels of spending to advance the architecture and to drive down the cost of PowerPC even further.

"Pentium will immediately benefit from Intel's enormous market inertia", says Michael Slater, principal of MicroDesign Resources, a California market researcher. But as software tailored specifically for RISC PCs becomes available, "and as people start to buy strictly on performance, it's the beginning of the end for the x86", he says, referring to the standard Intel chip design.

–Wall Street Journal, April 29, 1993, page B1

The benefits of multiple-source manufacturing

Sole-source manufacturing can be compared with multiple-source manufacturing by looking at the price of the product and the possibilities for future product improvement.

Pricing and future products

Customers benefit from competition between producers in the market – it drives down prices and speeds up product improvement cycles. Intel, as the sole-source provider of Pentium, will likely have little incentive to lower prices. On the other hand, Motorola and IBM will offer competitive versions of PowerPC processors, which tends to drive down prices. In the case of PowerPC and Pentium, the next generation of the PowerPC processor is expected to ship in 1994, while the next generation of Pentium processors from Intel are not expected to ship until 1995 at the earliest (PC Week, September 13, 1993, page 22). Motorola and IBM have already shown samples of the next version of PowerPC – the PowerPC 603 chip – and announced the PowerPC 604 and 620.

Process technologies

The combined technology and production resources of two of the largest semi-conductor manufacturers in the world – IBM and Motorola – suggest that PowerPC customers will benefit from the most advanced process technology. The PowerPC 601 chip is available from both Motorola and IBM, using state-of-the-art process technology. Motorola and IBM are continuing work to improve their process technology even further to produce the next generation of PowerPC chips.

Conclusion

After comparing the architectures, performance ratings, and business issues of Pentium and PowerPC, PowerPC emerges with the distinct advantage for the following reasons

- PowerPC is a high-performance RISC architecture that is poised for future growth.

- The PowerPC 601 chip is less expensive to manufacture than Pentium.

- The PowerPC 601 outperforms Pentium by a wide margin in floating-point tasks, and has comparable performance for integer tasks.

- PowerPC offers the benefits of being provided by multiple sources – giving it the support of more resource dollars, lower manufacturing costs, faster product development, and advanced process technologies.

Apple, IBM, and Motorola have invested in the future of RISC technology to develop and market PowerPC. This commitment is based on their confidence that the superiority of the PowerPC processor in the areas of price, performance, time to market, multiple sourcing, and scalability to higher performance levels will dramatically change the personal computer industry. Customers cannot afford to be constrained by the outdated CISC architecture when newer, higher-performance, and more cost-effective solutions will be adopted by their competitors. PowerPC is the first RISC processor to enter the mainstream personal computer market, and its endorsement by these three leading-edge companies attests to its promise as the new standard for desktop computers.

Suggested reading

RISC Drives PowerPC, BYTE, August 1993, pages 79-90.

PowerPC Performs for Less, BYTE, August 1993, pages 56-74.

CISCs Are Not RISCs and Not Converging Either, Microprocessor Report, March 25, 1992.

PowerPC 601 RISC Microprocessor User's Manual, available from Motorola.

Pentium Processor User's Manual, available from Intel.

PowerPC Technology: The Power Behind the Next Generation of Macintosh Systems, available from Apple.

Chapter 16:

- *Power Macintosh Product Families*
- *CPU And Bus Usage By System*
- *Chip Usage By System*
- *Chip Descriptions*

Power Mac Systems

The PTF Reference disc contains extended descriptions of selected systems. These descriptions were written early in the development of each line of systems. Consequently, new systems may have been introduced (e.g., with faster clocks) that do not fit the exact specifications given in the text.

Note: Any given Power Macintosh systems may or may not be supported by a given version of MkLinux. Check the online documentation and the MkLinux Web site (`www.mklinux.apple.com`) for definitive information.

Power Macintosh Product Families

Apple recognizes several families of Power Macintosh systems, defined largely in terms of their packaging and manner of use:

- The **Power Macintosh** system is typically found in an institutional (e.g., office and/or academic) environment. It consists of a processor chassis with several bus (e.g., NuBus or PCI bus) slots, a keyboard, and a mouse. Some Power Mac systems have built-in monitors. Anything else, including extra disk drives or application software, is optional.

- Each **WorkGroup Server** configuration is based on a Power Macintosh system. It may include a tape drive, different complements of disk and/or RAM, etc. It may also include some network-specific software.

- The **Network Server** is not really a Maciontosh, in the usual sense. It is a highly redundant system designed for high availability and ease of maintenance. It is normally used with **AIX** (IBM's version of UNIX) and a small amount of network-specific software.

- The **Performa** is packaged (and sometimes specially engineered) to be an end-user system. It is bundled with a large amount of application software and typically has strong support for Audio-Visual features such as television or video I/O.

- The **PowerBook** is a laptop Power Macintosh. It includes an integrated screen, a touchpad (in place of the mouse), etc.

Because of different I/O needs, each of these families has its own specific complement of support chips and subsystems. In addition, several types of PowerPC processors are used by Apple. This adds up to dozens of variants, from the perspective of the system software.

Note: A number of chip upgrades are available to turn Motorola 68XXX-based Macintosh systems into Power Macintosh systems. Apple has not indicated any plans to support these under MkLinux, so we do not discuss them to any significant degree. Should Apple (or some enthusiastic crew of MkLinux users) begin a serious porting effort, we will be happy to cover it. For pointers on Mac-based UNIX (and clone) systems other than MkLinux, see the MkLinux Web site (`www.mklinux.apple.com`).

CPU And Bus Usage By System

The tables below summarize CPU and system bus usage for a large number of Power Macintosh systems. This information is typically a strong indication of compatibility (or lack thereof) with a given release of MkLinux.

Performa Models	CPU	Bus
5200CD, 5210CD, 5215CD, 5220CD	603	LC
5260CD, 5260/120, 5270CD, 5280, 5300CD, 5320CD	603e	LC
5400CD, 5400/160, 5400/180, 5410CD, 5420CD 5430, 5440	603e	PCI
6110CD, 6112CD, 6115CD, 6116CD, 6117CD, 6118CD	601	NuBus/PDS
6200CD, 6205CD, 6210CD, 6214CD, 6216CD, 6218CD, 6220CD, 6230CD	603	LC
6260CD, 6290CD, 6300CD, 6310CD, 6320CD	603e	LC
6360, 6400/180, 6400/200, 6410, 6420	603e	PCI

Power Macintosh Models	CPU	Bus
5200/75 LC	603	LC
5260/100, 5260/120, 5300/100 LC	603e	LC

Power Macintosh Models	CPU	Bus
5400/120, 5400/180	603e	PCI
6100/60(AV), 6100/66(AV, D.C.)	601	NuBus/PDS
6200/75, 6300/120	603e	LC
6400/200	603e	PCI
7100/66(AV), 7100/80(AV)	601	NuBus/PDS
7200/75, 7200/90, 7200/120 (P.C.), 7215/90, 7500/100	601	PCI
7600/120, 7600/132	604	PCI
8100/80(AV), 8100/100(AV)	601	NuBus, PDS
8100/110	601+	PCI
8115/110	601+	NuBus, PDS
8200/100, 8200/120	601	PCI
8500/120, 8500/132, 8500/150	604	PCI
8500/180	604e	PCI
8515/120	604	PCI
9500/120, 9500/132, 9500/150	604	PCI
9500/180MP, 9500/200	604e	PCI
9515/132	604	PCI

PowerBook Models	CPU	Bus
1400c/117, 1400c/133, 1400cs/117	603e	PC
Duo 2300c/100	603e	dock
5300/100, 5300c/100, 5300ce/100, 5300cs/100	603e	PC

Network Server Models	CPU	Bus
500/132, 700/150	604	PCI
700/200	604e	PCI

Workgroup Server Models	CPU	Bus
6150, 6150/66	601	NuBus/PDS
7250/120	601	PCI

Workgroup Server Models	CPU	Bus
8150	601	NuBus, PDS
8150/110	601+	NuBus, PDS
8550/132, 8550/200	604	PCI
9150, 9150/120	601	NuBus, PDS

Chip Usage By System

Power Macintosh systems use a mixture of standard and custom integrated circuits. The table below summarizes custom chip usage for some representative PowerBook and Power Macintosh systems.

Chip	2300	5300	5400	6100	7200	7500	8500	9500
AMIC	○	○	○	●	○	○	○	○
Ariel	○	●	○	○	○	○	○	○
Ariel II	○	○	○	●	○	○	○	○
AWAC	○	○	○	●	○	○	○	○
AWACS	○	○	●	○	●	●	●	●
Baboon	●	●	○	○	○	○	○	○
Bandit	○	○	○	○	●	●	●	●
BART	○	○	○	●	○	○	○	○
Chaos	○	○	○	○	○	●	●	○
CIVIC	○	○	○	●	○	○	○	○
Combo	●	●	○	○	○	○	○	○
Control	○	○	○	○	○	●	●	○
CSC	●	○	○	○	○	○	○	○
Cuda	○	○	●	●	●	●	○	●
Curio	○	○	○	●	●	●	●	●
Cyclone	see CIVIC							
ECSC	○	●	○	○	○	○	○	○
Grand Central	○	○	○	●	●	●	●	●
Hammerhead	○	○	○	○	○	●	●	●

Chip	2300	5300	5400	6100	7200	7500	8500	9500
HMC	○	○	○	●	○	○	○	○
Iridium	○	○	○	○	●	○	○	○
Keystone	○	●	○	○	○	○	○	○
MESH	○	○	○	○	○	●	●	●
Mickey	○	○	○	●	○	○	○	○
O'Hare	○	○	●	○	○	○	○	○
PBX	●	●	○	○	○	○	○	○
Plan B	○	○	○	○	○	●	●	○
Platinum	○	○	○	○	●	○	○	○
Power Manager	●	○	○	○	○	○	○	○
PPC 601	○	○	○	●	●	●	○	○
PPC 603	●	●	○	○	○	○	○	○
PPC 603e	○	○	●	○	○	○	○	○
PPC 604	○	○	○	○	○	○	●	●
PSX	○	○	●	○	○	○	○	○
RaDACal	○	○	○	○	○	●	●	○
SAA7194	○	○	○	●	○	○	○	○
Sebastian	○	○	○	●	○	○	○	○
Singer	●	●	○	○	○	○	○	○
Sixty6	○	○	○	○	○	○	●	○
Squidlet	○	○	○	●	○	○	○	○
SWIM III	○	○	○	●	○	○	○	○
TREX	○	●	○	○	○	○	○	○
Valkyrie-AR	○	○	●	○	○	○	○	○
Whitney	●	●	○	○	○	○	○	○

Chip Descriptions

The text below is an alphabetically-sorted list of brief chip descriptions, covering some of the more notable chips used in Power Macintosh computers.

AMIC

The Apple Memory-Mapped I/O Controller (AMIC) is a 160-pin gate array chip that performs most I/O logic and control for Power Macintosh computers. It supports the following functions:

- handling interrupts received through Versatile Interface Adapter (VIA) channels

- DMA for Ethernet I/O

- DMA for the SWIM III floppy disk drive controller

- DMA for the Serial Communications Controller (SCC) I/O

- DMA for Small Computer System Interface (SCSI) device support

- DMA for sound I/O

- monitor support

The AMIC does not support the extended transfer protocols of the PowerPC 601 processor; using these protocols will cause a transfer error exception.

Ariel

The Ariel custom Video Output IC contains the video CLUT (color lookup table) and DAC. The Ariel IC takes the serial video data from the VRAM and generates the actual RGB signals for the external video monitor. The Ariel is pin and software compatible with the AC843 but does not support 24 bits per pixel.

Ariel II

The Ariel II custom Video IC provides a color lookup table (CLUT) and digital-to-analog converter (DAC) for driving an AudioVision monitor.

AWAC

See AWACS.

AWACS

The audio waveform amplifier and converter (AWACS) is a custom IC that combines a waveform amplifier with a 16-bit digital sound encoder and decoder (codec). It conforms to the IT&T *ASCO 2300 Audio-Stereo Codec Specification* and furnishes high-quality sound input and output. For information about the operation of the AWACS IC, see Chapter 3 of *Developer Note: Power Macintosh Computers,* available on the developer CD-ROM and as part of *Macintosh Developer Note Number 8.*

Baboon

The Baboon custom Disk Drive IC provides the interface to the expansion bay. The IC performs four functions:

- controls the expansion bay

- controls the IDE interfaces, both internal and in the expansion bay

- buffers the floppy-disk signals to the expansion bay

- decodes addresses for the PCMCIA slots and the IDE controller

The Baboon IC controls the power to the expansion bay and the signals that allow the user to insert a device into the expansion bay while the computer is operating.

The Baboon IC controls the interface for both the internal IDE hard disk drive and a possible second IDE drive in the expansion bay. The IC also handles the signals to a floppy disk drive installed in the expansion bay.

The address decode portion of the Baboon IC provides address decoding for the IDE controller portion of the IC. It also provides the chip select decode for the TREX custom IC and address decoding for the two PCMCIA slots.

Bandit

The Bandit custom PCI Bridge IC is the interface between the the PCI bus and the main processor and memory subsystem. The Bandit IC provides buffering and address translation between the processor bus and the PCI bus. The Bandit IC supports burst transfers, in both directions, of up to 32 bytes in length – the size of a cache block.

A separate logic device (gate array) provides the priorities for bus arbitration as follows:

1.   Grand Central IC (I/O device controller; highest priority)

2.   PCI slots and Bandit master, in round-robin sequence: that is, each in turn, with equal priority

The PCI expansion slots are connected directly to the PCI bus.

BART

The BART custom NuBus controller chip provides the data gateway between NuBus and the CPU bus. It acts as a CPU bus master, transferring one- or four-cycle transactions. It is compliant with IEEE Standard 1196.

Chaos

The Chaos custom IC provides data bus buffering between the video subsystem and the processor bus.

CIVIC

The Cyclone Integrated Video Interfaces Controller (CIVIC), used in the AV card, is a custom CMOS chip in a 144-pin package. The CIVIC

- manages from 1 MB to 4 MB of video RAM (VRAM)

- controls data transfers between VRAM and the SAA7194 chip and between VRAM and the Sebastian video color palette chip

- provides 32-bit or 64-bit data paths between VRAM and the main processor; supports data bursts from the main processor in all transfer modes

- controls convolution of graphics data for line-interlaced displays

- provides NTSC and PAL timing signals

- generates vertical blanking and video-in interrupt signals

Combo

The Combo custom IC combines the functions of the SCC IC (85C30 Serial Communications Controller) and the SCSI controller IC (53C80). The SCC portion supports the serial I/O port. The SCSI portion supports an internal SCSI hard drive; it is needed for upgrades to older PowerBook Duo models.

Control

The Control custom IC provides addressing and control for the video subsystem.

CSC

The CSC (color support chip) custom IC is a display controller, providing the data and control interface to the LCD panel. It contains a 256-entry CLUT, RAMDAC, display buffer controller, and flat panel control circuitry.

Cuda

The Cuda IC is a custom version of the Motorola MC68HC05 microcontroller. It provides several system functions, including

- management of the Apple Desktop Bus (ADB)

- management of system resets

- maintenance of parameter RAM

- management of the real-time clock

- on/off control of the power supply (soft power), possibly from an external signal from either Apple GeoPort serial port

- the programming interface to devices on the IIC (interintegrated circuit) bus

The devices on the IIC bus include the AWACS sound IC, the digital video decoder and scaler (DESC) on the video input module, and the Cyclops IC, which is the controller for the remote control receiver. The computer reads and writes status and control information to those devices by commands to the Cuda IC.

Curio

The Curio is a custom multipurpose I/O chip that contains a Media Access Controller for Ethernet (MACE), a SCSI controller, and a Serial Communications Controller (SCC). The SCC section of the Curio includes 8-byte FIFO buffers for both transmit and receive data streams. The Curio IC supports DMA transfers between its I/O ports and the computer's main memory.

ECSC

The ECSC (enhanced color support chip) is a custom Display Controller IC that provides the data and control interface to the LCD panel. The ECSC IC is similar to the CSC used in the PowerBook 520 and 540 models except that it can address 1 MB of video RAM. The ECSC IC contains a 256-entry CLUT, RAMDAC, display buffer controller, and flat panel control circuitry.

Grand Central

The Grand Central I/O System custom IC provides an interface between the standard Macintosh I/O devices and the PCI bus. The Grand Central IC performs the following functions:

- support for the Cuda IC (the VIA registers)

- central system interrupt collection

- support for descriptor-based DMA for I/O devices

- floppy disk interface (SWIM III)

The Grand Central IC contains a DMA controller. It provides DBDMA support for all I/O transfers, including transfers through its internal I/O controllers as well as transfers through the Curio IC for other I/O devices.

The SWIM III floppy disk drive controller in the Grand Central IC is an extension of the SWIM II design used in earlier Macintosh models. The SWIM III controller supports DMA data transfers and does not require disabling of interrupts during floppy disk accesses.

The Grand Central IC provides bus interfaces for the following I/O devices:

- Cuda microcontroller IC

- AWACS sound input and output IC

- Curio multipurpose I/O IC

- MESH controller IC for fast internal SCSI devices

The Grand Central IC also provides a 16-bit bus to other devices, including the nonvolatile parameter RAM and the Sixty6 IC. The Grand Central IC is connected to the PCI bus and uses the 33 MHz PCI bus clock.

Hammerhead

The Hammerhead custom Memory Controller IC controls the memory and cache subsystem, which includes the system bus, the main memory (a 128-bit-wide DRAM memory array), the ROM, and the L2 cache. The main memory provides low-latency memory accesses and improved memory bandwidth. The Hammerhead IC supports main memory sizes up to 2 GB.

The components of the Hammerhead IC are

- the system bus controller

- the DRAM controller

- the ROM controller

- the second-level (L2) cache controller

Data Interleaving. Even though the system data bus is only 64 bits wide, the memory controller in the Hammerhead IC can support data read operations 128 bits wide by interleaving the data from two DIMM slots. When the startup software detects two DIMMs that are the same size in adjacent banks (Bank 0–Bank 1), it enables interleaving for that pair of DIMMs.

For an interleaved transfer, the memory controller cycles both banks at the same time into a 128-bit buffer, then transfers data 64 bits at a time to the system data bus. The memory controller determines which bank's data to transfer first on the basis of address signals that carry the critical word-first information. The controller supports both the critical quad-word first behavior of the PowerPC 601 and the critical double-word first behavior of the PowerPC 603 and PowerPC 604.

Bank Base Registers. The Hammerhead IC contains a bank base register for each bank of main RAM. Each bank base register has space for a base address and control bits. The control bits set the address multiplexing mode and enable or disable data bus interleaving.

The bank base address is used to make memory banks contiguous. The system software calculates the base addresses based on the amount of memory in each of the SIMMs. The base address for each bank is based on the sum of the sizes of all the lower numbered banks.

HMC

The High-Speed Memory Controller (HMC) is a custom chip that controls all memory operations in Power Macintosh computers. The HMC has the following features that support data transfers to and from the PowerPC 601 processor:

- support for all basic transfer protocols, including all single-cycle accesses

- support for four-cycle 32-byte cache accesses

- translation of misaligned read actions into double-word read actions

- implementation of address-only transactions

- bus arbitration (of the address bus only)

The HMC does not support the following features:

- pipelining of memory bus transactions

- cache snooping

- recovery from transfer error acknowledge signals

- little-endian transfer mode

Iridium

The Iridium custom IC works with the Platinum memory controller IC to optimize data throughput during ROM, DRAM, and VRAM data transactions. It also works with the Platinum IC to accelerate some QuickDraw display operations.

Keystone

The Keystone Video Controller custom IC contains the timing and control circuits for the external video circuitry. The Keystone IC has internal registers that the video driver uses to set horizontal and vertical timing parameters. The Keystone IC also generates video refresh addresses for VRAM.

MESH

The MESH custom High-Speed SCSI Interface IC controls the SCSI bus for the internal SCSI devices. Because this bus does not have to drive a long external bus, it can operate at higher transfer rates than the external SCSI bus. The internal SCSI bus supports data transfers at up to 10 MB per second; the external SCSI bus operates at up to 5 MB per second.

Mickey

The Mickey is a composite video encoder in a 28-pin advanced bipolar CMOS chip. It is used in the AV card. The Mickey

- accepts analog RGB video signals from the Sebastian video color palette chip

- encodes to NTSC or PAL format

- produces S-video, composite, or RGB video outputs

O'Hare

The O'Hare custom IC is based on the Grand Central IC present in the Power Macintosh 7500 computer. It is a an I/O controller and DMA engine for Power Macintosh computers using the PCI bus architecture. It provides power-management control functions for Energy Star–compliant features included in the Power Macintosh 5400 computer. The O'Hare IC is connected to the PCI bus and uses the 32 MHz PCI bus clock.

The O'Hare IC includes circuitry equivalent to the IDE, SCC, SCSI, sound, SWIM3, and VIA controller ICs. The functional blocks in the O'Hare IC include the following:

- support for descriptor-based DMA for I/O devices

- system-wide interrupt handling

- a SWIM3 floppy drive controller

- SCSI controller (MESH based)

- SCC serial I/O controller

- IDE hard disk interface controller

- sound control logic and buffers

The O'Hare IC provides bus interfaces for the following I/O devices:

- Cuda ADB controller IC (VIA1 and VIA2 registers)

- AWACS sound input and output IC

- 8 KB non-volatile RAM control

- PWM outputs for brightness and contrast control on the Power
  Macintosh 5400

The SCSI controller in the O'Hare IC is a MESH controller. DMA channels
in the O'Hare IC are used to support data transfers. In the Power Macintosh
5400 computer, the clock signal to the SCSI controller is 45 MHz.

The O'Hare IC also contains the sound control logic and the sound input and
output buffers. There are two DMA data buffers—one for sound input and
one for sound output—so the computer can record sound input and process
sound output simultaneously. The data buffer contains interleaved right
and left channel data for support of stereo sound.

The SCC circuitry in the O'Hare IC is an 8-bit device. The PCLK signal to
the SCC is an 16 MHz clock. The SCC circuitry supports GeoPort and
LocalTalk protocols.

PBX

The PBX Memory Controller custom IC provides RAM and ROM memory
control and also acts as the bridge between the processor bus on the processor
and memory subsystem and the 68030-type I/O bus on the main logic board.
The PBX IC also provides bus cycle decoding for the SWIM floppy-disk
controller.

Memory Control. The PBX IC controls the system RAM and ROM and provides address multiplexing and refresh signals for the DRAM devices.

The PBX IC has a memory bank decoder in the form of an indexed register file. Each nibble in the register file represents a 2 MB page in the memory address space (64 MB). The value in each nibble maps the corresponding page to one of the eight banks of physical RAM. By writing the appropriate values into the register file at startup time, the system software makes the memory addresses contiguous.

Bus Bridge. The PBX IC acts as a bridge between the processor bus and the I/O bus, converting signals on one bus to the equivalent signals on the other. The bridge functions are performed by two converters. One accepts requests from the processor bus and presents them to the I/O bus in a manner consistent with a 68030 microprocessor. The other converter accepts requests from the I/O bus and provides access to the RAM and ROM on the processor bus.

The bus bridge in the PBX IC runs asynchronously so that the processor bus and the I/O bus can operate at different clock rates. The processor bus operates at a clock rate of 33.33 MHz; the I/O bus operates at 25.00 MHz.

Plan B

The Plan B IC provides two DBDMA channels for the 7196 DESC IC. The write channel takes data from the pixel FIFO buffer in the 7196 IC, attaches an appropriate DMA address, and performs a PCI write operation. The read channel reads the 1-bit-per-pixel clip mask from main memory.

Platinum

The Platinum custom Memory and Video Controller IC controls the memory and cache subsystem, which includes the system bus, the main memory, the ROM, the VRAM video frame buffer, and the L2 cache. The Platinum IC supports memory subsystem sizes up to 1 GB.

Data Interleaving. The Platinum memory controller IC, unlike the Hammerhead memory controller IC in the Power Macintosh 7500, 8500, and 9500 computers, supports linear memory organization only. It does not support data interleaving when like pairs of DIMM modules are installed in the RAM expansion slots.

Bank Base Registers. The Platinum IC contains a bank base register for each bank of main RAM. Each bank base register has space for a base address and control bits. The control bits set the address multiplexing mode.

The bank base address is used to make memory banks contiguous. The system software calculates the base addresses based on the amount of memory in each of the DIMMs. The base address for each bank is based on the sum of the sizes of all the lower-numbered banks.

Power Manager

The Power Manager IC is a 68HC05 microprocessor that operates with its own RAM and ROM. The IC performs the following functions:

- controlling sleep, shutdown, and on/off modes

- controlling power to the other ICs

- controlling clock signals to the other ICs

- supporting the ADB

- scanning the keyboard

- controlling display brightness

- monitoring battery charge level

- controlling battery charging

PPC 601

The principal features of the PowerPC 601 microprocessor include

- full RISC processing architecture

- parallel integer and floating-point processing units

- a branch manager that can usually implement branches by reloading the incoming instruction queue without using any processing time

- an internal memory management unit (MMU)

- 32 Kbit of on-chip cache memory

For complete technical details, see the Motorola *PowerPC 601 RISC Microprocessor User's Manual.*

PPC 603e

The PowerPC 603e microprocessor is an enhanced version of the PowerPC 603. Its principal features include

- full RISC processing architecture

- parallel processing units: one integer and one floating-point

- a load-and-store unit that operates in parallel with the processing units

- a branch manager that can usually implement branches by reloading the incoming instruction queue without using any processing time

- two internal memory management units (MMUs), one for instructions and one for data

- two separate on-chip caches (16 KB each) for data and instructions

For complete technical details, see *PowerPC 603 Microprocessor Implementation Definition Book IV.*

PPC 604

The PowerPC 604 microprocessor's principal features include

- full RISC processing architecture

- parallel processing units: load-store unit, two integer units, one complex integer unit, and one floating-point unit

- a branch manager that can usually implement branches by reloading the incoming instruction queue without using any processing time

- an internal memory management unit (MMU)

- separate caches for data and instructions, 16 KB each, four-way set associative

For complete technical details, see *PowerPC 604 Microprocessor Implementation Definition Book IV*.

PSX

The PSX custom IC provides burst mode control to the cache and ROM. It functions as the bridge between the PowerPC 603e and the PCI bus. It provides buffering and address translation from one bus to the other.

The PSX IC also provides control and timing signals for system cache, ROM, and RAM. The memory control logic supports byte, word, long word, and burst accesses to the system memory. If an access is not aligned to the appropriate address boundary, PSX generates multiple data transfers on the bus.

RaDACal

RaDACal is a high-performance digital-to-analog converter (DAC), used for the video stream to the monitor.

SAA7194

The SAA7194 is a Philips CMOS chip that decodes the color information in NTSC, PAL, and SECAM video formats using a clock synchronized to their line frequency. It is used in the AV card. The SAA7194 also

- performs input video window scaling with horizontal and vertical filtering

- produces 16-bit 1:5:5:5 RGB, 8-bit grayscale, or YUV 4:2:2 output

Sebastian

The Sebastian chip is a video color palette and video digital-to-analog converter (DAC) in a 100-pin CMOS configuration, used in the AV card. The Sebastian

- accepts digital data up to 64 bits wide, either as one 64-bit port or as one or two 32-bit ports

- lets one 32-bit port handle digital video while the other processes graphics (including QuickTime), using the same or different color lookup tables

- supports mixing video with still graphics, even with different color depths

- supports both Truecolor and pseudocolor with alpha color lookup

- supports a transparency effect when blending video with still graphics under the control of alpha channel bits at 1 to 8 bits per pixel

- uses a convolution filter to minimize flicker in line-interlaced displays

- supports displays with dot clocks up to 100 MHz

Singer

The Singer custom IC is a 16-bit digital sound codec (coder-decoder). It conforms to the IT&T *ASCO 2300 Audio-Stereo Code Specification*. Sound samples are transferred in or out through the Singer IC from sound I/O buffers maintained in main memory by the Whitney IC.

Sixty6

Sixty6 is an RGB-to-YUV converter and convolver for the second video output stream (on the Power Macintosh 8500 computer only). The Sixty6 IC converts the video data from RGB color space to YUV color space and then performs the convolution on the data in YUV color space. The 7187 DENC IC takes square pixels in YUV format from the Sixty6 IC and encodes them into composite video in either NTSC or PAL format.

Squidlet

The Squidlet is a 28-pin chip that provides a set of synchronized system clocks for Power Macintosh computers.

SWIM III

The SWIM III custom Floppy Disk Drive Controller is an extension of the SWIM II circuitry used in models such as the Macintosh Quadra 800 and Macintosh Centris 650. It includes the following new features:

- support for DMA data transfers, which minimize use of the main processor

- no requirement that interrupts be disabled during floppy disk accesses

- support for GCR and MFM formats on 1.44 MB disks

- compatibility with the manual-inject floppy disk drive

  Floppy disk drives designed to be compatible with the New Age controller used in the Macintosh Quadra 840AV and Macintosh Centris 660AV computers can easily be adapted for compatibility with the SWIM III controller.

TREX

The TREX custom IC provides the interface and control signals for the PCMCIA slots. The main features of the TREX IC are

- the interrupt structure for the PCMCIA slots

- transfers of single-byte and word data to and from the PCMCIA slots

- power management for the PCMCIA slots, including

- sleep mode

- control of power to individual sockets

- support of insertion and removal of PC cards while the computer is operating

- support for software control of card ejection

- support for time-division multiplexing (TDM), Apple Computer's technique for implementing PC cards for telecommunications

Valkyrie-AR

The Valkyrie-AR is a custom IC containing the logic for the video display. It includes the following functions:

- display memory controller

- video CLUT (color lookup table)

- video DAC (digital-to-analog converter)

A separate data bus handles data transfers between the Valkyrie-AR IC and the display memory. The display memory data bus is 32 bits wide, and all data transfers consist of 32 bits at a time. The Valkyrie-AR IC breaks each 32-bit data transfer into several pixels of the appropriate size for the current display mode—4, 8, or 16 bits per pixel. The Valkyrie-AR IC does not support 24 bits per pixel.

To keep up with the large amount of data that must be transferred into and out of the display memory, the Valkyrie-AR IC has several internal buffers. Besides input and output buffers for display data, the Valkyrie-AR IC also has a buffer for both addresses and data being sent from the main processor to the display. That buffer can hold up to four transactions, allowing the main processor to complete a write instruction to the display memory and continue processing without waiting for some other transaction that might be taking place on the display memory bus.

The CLUT in the Valkyrie-AR custom IC provides color palettes for 4-bit and 8-bit display modes. In 16-bit display mode, the CLUT is used to provide gamma correction for the stored color values. In black-and-white or monochrome mode, all three color components (R, G, and B) are the same.

The Valkyrie-AR IC uses several clocks. Its transactions with the CPU are synchronized to the system bus clock. Data transfers from the frame-buffer DRAM are clocked by the MEM_CLK signal, which runs at 60 MHz. Data transfers to the CLUT and the video output are clocked by the dot clock, which has a different rate for different display monitors.

Whitney

The Whitney custom Peripheral Support IC provides the interface between the system bus and the I/O bus that supports peripheral device controllers. The Whitney IC incorporates the following circuitry:

- VIA1 like that in other Macintosh computers

- SWIM II floppy disk controller

- CPU ID register

The Whitney IC also performs the following functions:

- bus error timing for the I/O bus

- bus arbitration for the I/O bus

- interrupt prioritization

- VIA2 functions

- sound data buffering

- clock generation

- power control signals

The Whitney IC contains interfaces for the following peripheral ICs:

- Combo, which is a combination of SCC and SCSI ICs

- Singer, the sound codec IC

The Whitney IC provides device select signals for the following ICs:

- the external video controller

- the flat panel display controller

The Whitney IC also provides the power off and reset signals to the peripheral device ICs.

Chapter 17:

- *Overview Of The PowerPC Platform Specification*

PowerPC Platform

The "white paper" below (available on www.chrp.apple.com) sets out the goals and basic approach of the major partners (Apple, IBM, and Motorola) in the PowerPC effort.

PowerPC Platform: A System Architecture

Steve Bunch
Motorola, Inc.

Steve MacKenzie
Apple Computer

Dave Tjon
IBM Corporation

Overview

The PowerPC Platform (formerly known as the Common Hardware Reference Platform) specification defines a family of computer systems on which Macintosh, PC, and UNIX-based Operating Systems (OSs) can run without platform-specific tailoring. This makes it easy to build a system based on the PPC microprocessor that can run a variety of OS but can still be optimized for price, and have additional value-added features. This paper gives an informal overview of the specification.

Introduction

A major goal of the PowerPC Platform architecture is to permit hardware platform vendors to build platforms which will run multiple operating systems, such as AIX, Mac OS, NetWare, OS/2, Solaris, and Windows NT, without requiring the OS vendors to tailor the OS to each new platform. The PowerPC Platform specification defines an architecture which melds the Macintosh and PowerPC Reference Platform [1] environments. It provides an architecture for both OS and platform designers, letting hardware and software work together by design, rather than by continual porting and integration. The PowerPC Platform architecture makes it easy to design PowerPC microprocessor based systems which run multiple OSs. The specification allows freedom in some areas of the architecture, with differences in implementation being handled by firmware which provides a consistent interface to the operating systems, or by new device drivers. Thus, it will be easier for OS writers to support a new hardware design which meets the specification.

The PowerPC Platform architecture benefits users because they can choose software solutions independently from choosing a hardware platform. It also minimizes hardware support requirements for groups who support a multiple operating system environment, since a single type of platform can handle multiple operating system environments. The architecture benefits designers by giving them direction for the basic system features, but not constraining them in ways which keep them from adding unique customer value.

Constructively Directing Designers

Desktop and low-end computer platform designers today have to choose among many building-block chips which contain bewilderingly high functionality and complexity. What guidelines do they have? What constraints guide them? In the IBM PC-derived desktop world, these have always been straightforward questions to answer: as long as the hardware still runs MS-DOS/Windows and hits the cost target, you can do almost anything you want. These issues cause most PC-class hardware designs to be essentially indistinguishable by anyone who isn't an expert, since all systems tend to use parts which perform the same functions at very nearly the same cost. This approach also permits system software development costs for platform vendors to be nearly zero.

There has never been a set of constraints so compelling as MS-DOS/Windows outside the realm of desktop PCs. Hardware designers building platforms to run UNIX, for example, have exercised their freedom to use higher-performance, easier-to-program, or just plain different, chips and interfaces from the PC realm. A major impact of this is that software development costs in producing OSs and platform-dependent software have been very high, especially compared to the PC world, due to the high cost of producing hardware-specific system software. A major purpose of the PowerPC Platform architecture is to give direction to system designers, while still enabling differentiation in areas where real value can be added, thus allowing the PowerPC microprocessor industry to build a reusable body of OS and application software that is even more compelling than the PC world has had. In the future of platforms based on the PowerPC micro-processor, we want hardware designers to be able to use whatever chips, whatever interfaces, and whatever design features they want to use, as long as the OSs run on the resulting platform without change. To make the software writer's job in this vision possible, the PowerPC Platform defines hardware facilities and interfaces that system software can count on. This encourages the development of OSs and other software for PowerPC Plat-form compatible platforms. In turn, this will encourage more hardware ven-dors to create PowerPC Platforms and subsystems, which will encourage software vendors to develop even more applications, and so on.

Overview Of The PowerPC Platform Specification

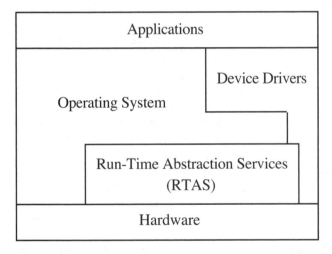

Figure 1 - Layering of Hardware and Software

Introduction

This section contains some basic information and rationale to help orient the reader to the basic features of the specification. This is only intended as an overview and the reader is referred to the actual specification [2] for details. (Note that some of the rationale in this section does not appear in the actual document.)

Platform Components

The basic PowerPC compatible platform consists of a hardware implementation containing a PowerPC processor, memory, PCI bridge, a set of mandatory non-I/O components often placed on the system board (e.g., non-volatile memory), a set of mandatory I/O devices and connectors, a set of optional I/O devices and connectors, and firmware which provides platform-independent services to OSs and device drivers. The platform layering is shown in Figure 1.

The hardware is at the base, with a layer of software known as Run-Time Abstraction Services (RTAS) on top of it. The Operating System depends on RTAS to access certain basic platform hardware. The OS accesses this hardware directly only if it is "platform-aware", that is, has knowledge of some specific hardware component(s) of the platform and has specific code to handle it. The Device Drivers will use OS and RTAS services to access basic platform features, and will directly address added-on I/O interface hardware. Applications sit on top of this layer of system software, never seeing anything but standard programming interfaces. Platforms can be constructed in a wide variety of ways. See [3] for an example which shows a sample platform. It is common for people to confuse such block diagrams with the PowerPC Platform specification. The actual specification is not a block diagram or specific platform design, and in fact does not mandate this block diagram or any other. It mandates specific software-visible interfaces and user-visible features, and leaves remaining details of implementation which are not software-visible to the hardware/platform designers. Thus, multiple busses, additional I/O, multiple processors and caches, and other system features are accommodated. This gives the hardware designers a great deal of freedom to exploit better component pricing, trade off features for cost, or optimize performance for a particular end use.

Abstraction

One of the critical differences between the PowerPC Reference Platform Specification and PowerPC Platform is that in the PowerPC Reference Platform model, all hardware abstraction to reduce OS platform porting effort was the responsibility of the OS. Some operating systems are adopting layered approaches which provide this abstraction, though in the past some OSs have not. In the PowerPC Platform architecture, an "assist" is given to the OSs. This is done by providing firmware interfaces which can make the platform independence goal easier to reach by significantly reducing the number of cases where operating systems are forced to access hardware. This eases the porting job for traditionally-structured operating systems, and may sharply reduce the number of distinct Abstraction Layer implementations needed for a broad range of PowerPC platform implementations.

It is an inescapable property of today's variety in silicon suppliers and chips that many software-visible differences exist between components that serve the same purpose.(For example, different time-of-day clock chips can require software to access them in different ways, all of which achieve the same end result.) The impact of this is to force multiple versions of software to exist within all OSs to handle every one of these more-or-less functionally equivalent devices. A better solution is to abstract the chip's function, providing platform firmware which the OS can call, rather than force each OS to know how to do it. This way, one firmware routine exists for each chip, and every OS knows how to talk to one (firm-ware) provider of the service on every platform. In the PowerPC Platform environment, the layer of abstraction firmware is usually provided by hardware platform providers. It consists of boot software based on Open Firmware [OpenFW94], and on run-time firmware called Run-Time Abstraction Services. Both RTAS and Open Firmware must be present in a compatible platform. Operating systems are required to use Open Firmware interfaces, and to use RTAS interfaces (when not platform aware), in order to be compatible. The most important aspect of the PowerPC Platform specification is that all compatible platforms present a known, fixed set of interfaces to an operating system. The OS can count on a given set of features being implemented in the same way on all platforms (e.g., interrupts), can allow another set to be implemented in an arbitrary way in hardware but to always be accessible via firmware calls (e.g., power management), and finally, can count on getting a complete description of the rest of the platform (e.g., I/ O devices) in a known format. This knowledge permits an OS not only to be ported to the PowerPC Platform "least common denominator" platform, but also to flexibly support optional and added-value platform features. In essence, an OS treats all PowerPC Platforms as being identical, up to a point. Beyond that point, the description of the machine guides the OS in loading additional software components to deal with additional hardware it finds.

Booting

Compatible platforms use Open Firmware [4], [5] to provide basic booting services. Open Firmware is capable of loading a little- or big-endian boot image (typically an OS or diagnostics) into memory from a variety of disk partitioning formats (Mac OS, FAT 41, AIX, and ISO 9660 are presently supported). Once the boot image is in memory, the image can call back to Open Firmware to obtain I/O services to boot devices, perform platform-dependent services, and if desired, to free up Open Firmware's memory resources. After the image is fully in control, it typically will free up Open Firmware and take full ownership of the platform. RTAS firmware is initialized prior to this act, and remains available to call after Open Firmware is gone. One of the most important functions Open Firmware performs is to provide an inventory of the platform hardware, in the form of the Open Firmware Device Tree, to the boot image. OSs typically use this to dynamically load device drivers for any hardware they recognize on the platform. Open Firmware also participates in some power management related functions, provides some platform management functions, and offers a low-level user interface if desired.

Platform System Board Devices

Some devices which typically appear on a platform system board are abstracted by RTAS calls. Such devices are then available in a "least common denominator" fashion to all OSs. Because the programming details of these devices are hidden from the OS, the hardware implementation is not dictated by the PowerPC Platform specification. So long as the hardware is capable of implementing the specified requirements, and firmware can implement the necessary functions using it, the designer can use any devices he or she wants.

Specific devices supported in this fashion include NVRAM, Time-Of-Day Clock (TODC), switches, lights, audible-beep device, power management hardware, simple number and text output, and PCI bridge and memory controller error status registers. These are described in the RTAS section of the specification.

In the event that an OS has a custom driver for a particular system board device, it may choose to access the device directly and never call the RTAS routine(s) which abstract it. This approach is a very useful feature of the specification, as it keeps the "least common denominator" functionality smaller while giving vendors freedom to put sophisticated functions in their platforms for use with platform-aware OSs.

Basic I/O Devices

There are many traditional "PC" and Macintosh I/O devices which are de-facto industry standards. These include asynchronous serial I/O, parallel port I/O, basic timers, sound generation, and third-party ISA DMA. Little if any innovation occurs in these devices, little is to be gained by modifying them, and OS drivers generally exist which support all of them. Several such devices are mandated by the specification. These are simply defined at the register level in the specification, providing a defined programming model for software. Note that the hardware implementor is not constrained to use a particular chip, or bus, to implement these functions. The specification only defines the programming model. Thus, platform designers are free to combine functions into different ASICs or packages in any way which makes their product design easier or cheaper, providing they maintain the programming models.

Other I/O Devices

I/O devices are described in the Open Firmware device tree. Operating systems use the information in the device tree to determine the hardware configuration, then locate OS-specific device drivers for devices which it intends to use. These drivers are generally loaded dynamically by modern OSs. The PowerPC Platform specification does not attempt to provide a BIOS with device drivers for platform I/O, as has been done historically in PC platforms. In a multi-OS standard like PowerPC Platform, there is presently no single device driver standard which would work for all OSs. Past experience has also shown that device drivers in BIOS ROMs tend to quickly become out-dated, and are generally replaced by dynamically loaded drivers anyway for production use. This topic is discussed further in a later section.

In a few cases, the specification does define certain types of I/O as being optionally present, or even required to be present, but does not define a programming model. Such requirements are not to simplify OS developers' jobs, but were put into the specification for the benefit of users. Note that Open Firmware must have a device driver for any device from which the platform is to boot. For system board bootable devices, the system firmware will provide such a driver. For plug-in cards, the required approach is to put an Open Firmware driver into the Plug-and-Play ROM on the card. The Plug and Play standard provides for this capability. If a complete driver is not provided in ROM, most Open Firmware implementations will provide alternate ways to load the necessary driver (e.g., floppy disk). However, no specific method is mandated by the PowerPC Platform specification itself.

Minimum System Requirements And System Classes

The specification defines three classes of platforms: portables, desktops, and servers. The commercially interesting configurations, and in fact the space available for connectors and other I/O attachments, is usually vastly different for platforms of these different classes. The specification recognizes this, and provides different definitions of the minimum hardware that must be present in a platform of each class.

For example, a portable machine does not have space for a large number of connectors, so the minimum requirement for external ports is reduced below that of a desktop. Similarly, a server may have no directly-attached users, so its minimum requirements for I/O devices need not include a graphics display or keyboard. The specification includes a table which relates the key platform features described in the document to the minimum hardware requirements for each class of platform. Note that there is no difference in firmware requirements for different platform classes.

Infrastructure-Induced Requirements

A major purpose of the PowerPC Platform specification was to allow the coexistence of the Macintosh and PC worlds in a single PowerPC microprocessor based platform. The desktop and portable machines which are built to the specification must be able to live in either world. I/O devices exist today with specific PC or Macintosh interfaces: Mice and keyboards may use PS/2 or Macintosh ADB connectors, asynchronous serial I/O uses 9-pin D-shell connectors on a PC, but uses a mini-DIN 9 pin connector on a Macintosh. The PC world uses almost exclusively IDE disks, the Macintosh world uses almost exclusively SCSI disks. Such differences in interface reach deeply into the infrastructure supporting both families of machines, and in fact, all the way into the homes of owners of each type of computer. All the user experience, dealer knowledge, stock on shelves, and factories putting out PC peripheral hardware or Macintosh peripheral hardware will not stop overnight. Acknowledging the presence of these two infrastructures, and the fact that they will not go away quickly, was necessary for the specification to be effective. Much thought went into how to make it economical to implement.

The PowerPC Platform specification did not adopt a "converged" I/O model in which only one way was present to do any given I/O function because the necessities of infrastructure dictate multiple approaches. The specification permits some freedom of choice of specific hardware ports by hardware implementors, but ensures that users will find the support they need in their operating system and applications. In general, the approach taken is that OSs will support both the Macintosh and PC ways of doing key external interfaces, such as keyboards and mice, so that when the hardware is present it will perform as expected. The Minimum System Requirements section of the specification details the platform requirements, taking into account the different uses to which laptop, desktop, and server computers are put.

Although the specification does not require it, platform vendors who choose to provide ports to connect both Macintosh and PC peripherals to a system may add some cost to the platform. However, the actual amount of cost added is likely to be quite small. This cost also generates genuine benefit to end users, as it increases the variety and number of external ports they have available to use to connect to external peripherals. This gives them greater freedom of choice in peripheral purchases, which can translate to a lower total system cost.

OS-Influenced Requirements

Each of the OSs targeted for PowerPC Platforms has a legacy of past hardware platforms, and places certain requirements onto any platform it runs upon. These include Mac OS, which has always run on Apple-designed platforms, the PC-compatible OSs such as Netware, OS/2, Solaris x86, and Windows NT, which run on systems built with commodity PC-based chips, and server operating systems such as AIX and Solaris, which have typically run on customized hardware. To keep potential costs low, the specification sometimes adopted existing interfaces that were supported by most of the operating systems, forcing a few OSs to adapt. For example, the specification defines a traditional PC programming model for the floppy disk controller. In a few cases, the specification describes new interfaces, where no existing mechanism fulfilled most of the requirements. In this latter case, most or all of the operating systems must adapt. An example of this is the use of a new memory map.

An example of adopting both new and old interfaces is the interrupt controller. Since the traditional PC-based interrupt scheme does not work efficiently for multiprocessor systems and does not efficiently provide a large number of interrupts for larger desktop and server configurations, the PowerPC Platform specification adopted the OpenPIC interrupt controller [6] as its primary interrupt mechanism. This permits efficient multiprocessor interrupt systems to be built, and is extensible to very large server configurations. Because almost all of the operating systems already had implementations in place for the PC-style cascaded-8259 interrupt scheme, it was included in the specification. This was included mainly as a legacy item and is not used for future I/O expansion. While this was technically unnecessary, the 8259 functionality is usually buried inside already-present chips, and therefore adds negligible cost.

System States

The PowerPC Platform specification implicitly and explicitly defines a few of the behaviors which buyers of platforms can expect. Since many user-visible details of system operation are defined by each operating system, some of these behaviors are described as being possible, but are not mandated, by the specification.

Time-Related States

The platform goes through several important stages in the process of being powered-up from an initially reset and powered-off state. This is depicted in Figure 2. As shown there, from the initial powered-off state, a system typically enters a power-on self test (POST) phase, then boots an operating system into memory, then discards Open Firmware and enters a fully OS-controlled state in which it runs for an indefinite time, and finally enters either a low-power state ready for a rapid resumption later, or powers off into a fully reset state. Variations permitted within the specification to these simple states include such enhancements as automatically running diagnostics after a failure, more complex power management states, or multi-boot (i.e., running different OSs) without power-down. Note that RTAS Firmware is available during the period that the OS is running, unlike Open Firmware, which may or may not be present.

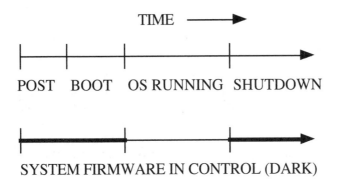

Figure 2 - Time Line of OS/System Firmware Control

Power-Related States

In addition to the time-related states described above, a platform may also implement a set of power management related states. In practice, all operating systems have their own power management concepts and implementation. The PowerPC Platform philosophy is that power management policy is strictly the province of the operating system and its utility programs.

Interface to the power management mechanism, that is, the way the policy decisions are carried out in hardware, is the job of either I/O device drivers (for some devices), or the RTAS abstraction firmware. Hardware is not expected to autonomously make power management decisions and carry them out without OS knowledge.

Direction For The Next PowerPC Platform Revision

The PowerPC Platform specification was produced by a multi-company group of system architects, with significant input from industry partners. All the participants were interested in protecting their engineering and customer bases from unwarranted change and from loss of functionality. This is a major strength of the specification. Many portability or adoption problems that might be faced by OS and application writers, hardware engineers, and end users were considered and solved for the PowerPC Platform specification. However, it is a goal of the current and future PowerPC Platform specification work that new technologies be introduced and embraced. The PowerPC Platform specification will evolve with time to include new technologies; this section describes some of the issues which may drive this change.

Some of the things we would have liked to do in the first version of the PowerPC Platform specification were simply not reasonable for a first issue. Not only did the specification itself have to be produced in a reasonable time, but the platforms have to be implemented, OSs have to be ported, and some new infrastructure needed has to be created. We chose to start with a straightforward but extensible first version. With the benefit of user feedback and open discussion, the specification will evolve to meet future market needs. When adding new functionality, the transition from prior to new approach will be smooth, permitting vendors and customers to adopt the new features at their own pace.

An example of a change that might be considered is the simplification to the architecture is to simplify the interrupt structure by completely eliminating the traditional 8259 interface, and using the OpenPIC controller for all interrupts. This will be difficult to do quickly, as it requires all the OSs to change, and requires all I/O chips to make their interrupt sources accessible to connect to an OpenPIC controller. Some ISA bridge chips available today contain the 8259 controller as well as some interrupt sources which are not brought out of the chip. As an optimization, eliminating the 8259 interface would improve OS performance, reduce the number of I/O pins and gates required, and give vendors more freedom in chip partitioning, helping them in their quest to build very-low-chip-count platforms.

New Technology

As new and important developments arise in the industry, such as online teleconferencing, embedded video, and new I/O interfaces, we must constantly decide if a technology is yet at the point where it is a de-facto or de-jure standard (and therefore no longer an "added-value" product differentiator). If it is, we will consider adopting it into the PowerPC Platform specification to reduce the variety of implementations and consolidate software implementations. This is an on-going activity.

Conclusions

The PowerPC Platform specification allows the PowerPC industry to migrate to a set of platforms that all present a common set of software programming models to all OSs. This permits shrink-wrap OSs to be ported to the specification, and to run on compatible platforms, without having to do further platform-specific ports.

The first release of the specification satisfies its objectives, and is well-suited to the marketplace. Future additions and changes to the specification will be made in order to both lead and to follow the industry, in order to reduce the complexity and cost of building platforms to an absolute minimum while increasing their functionality.

References

[1] *The PowerPC Reference Platform*, Version 1.1, available from IBM or Motorola, 1994.

[2] Apple, IBM, Motorola, *The PowerPC Microprocessor Common Hardware Reference Platform: A System Architecture*, Morgan-Kaufman Press, San Francisco, CA, Version 1.0, November 1995. Will also be made available on the World Wide Web sites of Apple, IBM, and Motorola.

[3] MacKenzie, Steve; Tjon, Dave; Steele, Allan; Bunch, Steve; *The PowerPC[TM] Hardware Reference Platform*, white paper distributed at Macintosh Developers' Conference, May 1995. Available from Apple, IBM, or Motorola public relations departments, or via their World Wide Web sites.

[4] IEEE, *Standard for Boot (Initialization Configuration) Firmware, Core Requirements and Practices*, document IEEE-P1275, available from IEEE.

[5] *The PowerPC Reference Platform binding to: IEEE Std 1275-1994*, and *PowerPC Processor binding to: IEEE Std 1275-1994*, in progress, available via anonymous ftp from playground.sun.com, in /pub/ p1275/bindings/postscript/*.ps.

[6] *Open PIC Multiprocessor Interrupt Register Interface Specification,* Rev. 1.2d, Mar. 17, 1995, available from AMD.

Chapter 18:

- *General*
- *Internals*
- *PowerPC*

Hardware Bibliography

The following listings are sorted into rough categories. Please be aware, however, that no such categorization scheme is perfect. In particular, please note that many of these "Hardware" references may contain information on Mac OS, which is very definitely a piece of software.

Within the topical categories, the entries are coded and sorted by type, as:

B	Book
B/C	Book with one or more CD-ROMs
C	one or more CD-ROMs
F	FTP archive
P	Periodical (e.g., magazine)
W	World Wide Web site

General

B   *Advanced Digital Audio*
Ken C. Pohlmann, Ed.
Sams, 1991, 0-672-22768-1

B   *The Art of Electronics*, 2nd. ed.
Paul Horowitz, Winfield Hill
Cambridge, 1990, ISBN 0-521-37095-7

B   *Handbook for Sound Engineers*, 2nd. ed.
Glen Ballou, Ed.
Sams, 1991, 0-672-22752-5

B   *Principles of Digital Audio*, 2nd. ed.
Ken C. Pohlmann
Sams, 1992, 0-672-22634-0

B/C   *The Power Mac Book!*, 2nd. ed.
Ron Pronk
Coriolis, 1996, ISBN 1-883577-67-5

P   *MacUser*

letters@macuser.ziff.com
http://www.macuser.com/

MacUser
P.O. Box 56986
Boulder, CO 80322-6986 USA

+1 303 665-8930
+1 303 604 7455 (fax)

P   *MacWEEK*

letters@macweek.com
http://www.macweek.com/

Customer Service Department
MacWEEK, c/o JCI
P.O. Box 10634
Riverton, NJ 08076-0634 USA

+1 609 786 8230
+1 609 786 2081 (fax "To: MacWEEK")

P   *Macworld*

subhelp.macworld@neodata.com

Macworld
P.O. Box 54529
Boulder, CO 80322-4529 USA

+1 800 288-6848 (USA only)
+1 303 604 1465
+1 303 604 7644 (fax)

P   *MacTech*

info@xplain.com
http://www.mactech.com/

MacTech Magazine
Xplain Corporation
1617 Pontius Avenue, 2nd Floor
Los Angeles, CA 90025-9555 USA

+1 310 575 4343
+1 310 575 0925 (fax)

P/W *Develop*

adc@applelink.apple.com
ftp://ftpdev.info.apple.com/Developer_Services/Periodicals/
develop/
http://devworld.apple.com/apda.html

Apple Developer Catalog
Apple Computer, Inc.
P.O. Box 319
Buffalo, NY 14207-0319 USA

W *Misc. Apple Developer Resources*

http://devworld.apple.com/mkt/adtop.shtml
http://www.apple.com/
http://www.info.apple.com/

Internals

B *Designing Cards and Drivers for the Macintosh Family,*
3rd ed.
Apple Computer
Addison-Wesley, 1992, ISBN 0-201-60855-3
Also on 9512 Dev. CD

B *Guide to the Macintosh Family Hardware,* 2nd ed.
Apple Computer
Addison-Wesley, 1990, ISBN 0-201-52405-8

B *How Macs Work*

John Rizzo, K. Danial Clark
Ziff-Davis, 1996, ISBN 1-56276-401-2

B   *Inside Appletalk*, 2nd ed.
Gursharan S. Sidhu, et al.
Addison-Wesley, 1990, ISBN 0-201-55021-0

B   *Macintosh Family Hardware Reference*
Apple Computer
Addison-Wesley, 1988, ISBN 0-201-19255-1

B   *Macintosh Technology in the Common Hardware Reference Platform*
Apple Computer
Morgan Kaufmann, 1995, ISBN 1-55860-393-X

B   *NuBus Data Book*
Texas Instruments
Texas Instruments, 1991, Part # SDID001B

B   *NuBus Line Card*
Texas Instruments
Texas Instruments, 1991, Part # SDIB001

B   *PCI System Architecture*, 3rd. Ed.
Mindshare
Addison-Wesley, 1995, ISBN 0-201-40993-3

B   *PCMCIA*, 2nd. Ed.
Mindshare
Addison-Wesley, 1995, ISBN 0-201-40991-7

B   *The PowerPC Macintosh Book*
Stephan Somogyi
Addison-Wesley, 1994, ISBN 0-201-55021-0

B   *PowerPC Microprocessor Common Hardware Reference Platform: A System Architecture*
Apple Computer, IBM, Motorola
Morgan Kaufman, 1995, ISBN 1-55860-394-8

B   *Technical Introduction to the Macintosh Family*, 2nd Ed.

Apple Computer
Addison-Wesley, 1992, ISBN 0-201-62215-7

C   Developer CD (Reference Library)

C   *Inside Macintosh*: CD-ROM
Apple Computer
Addison-Wesley, 1995, ISBN 0-201-40674-8

W   Common Hardware Reference Platform

http://chrp.apple.com/
http://www.austin.ibm.com/resource/technology/chrp/index.html

W   Developer Services and Products

devsupport@apple.com
http://dev.info.apple.com/reference.html

PowerPC

B   IBM/Motorola:

PowerPC Microprocessor Family:
The Programming Environments

PowerPC 601 RISC Microprocessor Technical Summary

PowerPC 601 RISC Microprocessor User's Manual

PowerPC 603e RISC Microprocessor Hardware Specifications

PowerPC 603 RISC Microprocessor Technical Summary

PowerPC 603 RISC Microprocessor User's Manual

PowerPC 603e RISC Microprocessor Hardware Specifications

PowerPC 603e RISC Microprocessor Technical Summary

PowerPC 603e RISC Microprocessor User's Manual

PowerPC 604 RISC Microprocessor User's Manual

PowerPC 604 RISC Microprocessor Technical Summary

PowerPC 620 RISC Microprocessor Technical Summary

PowerPC Tools

B   *Computer Architecture:*
        A Quantitative Approach, 2nd. Ed.
        John L. Hennessy, David A. Patterson
        Morgan Kaufman, 1995, ISBN 1-55860-329-8

B   *POWER and PowerPC*
        Shlomo Weiss, James E. Smith
        Morgan Kaufman, 1994, ISBN 1-55860-279-8

B   *The PowerPC Architecture:*
        A Specification for a New Family of RISC Processors, 2nd Ed.
        IBM Corporation
        Morgan Kaufman, 1994, ISBN 1-55860-316-6

Chapter 19:

Software Bibliography

The following listings are sorted into rough categories. Please be aware, however, that no such categorization scheme is perfect. In particular, please note that many of the "Hardware" references may contain information on Mac OS, which is very definitely a piece of software.

Within the topical categories, the entries are coded and sorted by type, as:

B	Book
B/C	Book with one or more CD-ROMs
C	one or more CD-ROMs
F	FTP archive
P	Periodical (e.g., magazine)
W	World Wide Web site

Linux & UNIX

Administration

Network Administration

B   *!%@::*
         A Directory of Electronic Mail Addressing & Networks,
         4th Ed.

Donnalyn Frey, Rick Adams
O'Reilly, 1994, ISBN 1-56592-046-5 (discontinued)

B   *DNS & BIND*
Paul Albitz, Cricket Liu
O'Reilly, 1992, ISBN 1-56592-010-4

B   *Getting Connected:*
The Internet at 56K and Up
Kevin Dowd
O'Reilly, 1996, ISBN 1-56592-154-2

B   *Linux Network Administrator's Guide*
Olaf Kirch
O'Reilly, 1995, ISBN 1-56592-087-2

B   *Linux Network Administrator's Guide*
Olaf Kirch
SSC, 1994, ISBN 0-916151-75-1

B   *Managing Internet Information Services:*
World Wide Web, Gopher, FTP, and more
Cricket Liu, et al
O'Reilly, 1994, ISBN 1-56592-062-7

B   *Managing NFS and NIS*
Hal Stern
O'Reilly, 1991, ISBN 0-937175-75-7

B   *sendmail*
Bryan Costales, et al
O'Reilly, 1993, ISBN 1-56592-056-2

B   *TCP/IP Network Administration*
Craig Hunt
O'Reilly, 1992, ISBN 0-937175-82-X

B   *Using & Managing uucp,* 2nd Ed.
Ed Ravin, et al
O'Reilly, 1996, ISBN 1-56592-153-4

B/C   *Building a Linux Internet Server*

George Eckel, Chris Hare
New Riders, 1995, ISBN 1-56205-525-9

B/C *Running a Perfect Internet Site with Linux*
Dee-Ann LeBlanc
QUE, 1996, ISBN 0-7897-0514-1

Security & Privacy

B *Actually Useful Internet Security Techniques*
Larry J. Hughes, Jr.
New Riders, 1996, ISBN 1-56205-508-9

B *Applied Cryptography:*
Protocols, Algorithms, and Source Code in C, 2nd ed.
Bruce Schneier
Wiley, 1996, ISBN 0-471-11709-9

B *Bandits on the Information Superhighway*
Daniel J. Barrett
O'Reilly, 1996, ISBN 1-56592-156-9

B *Building Internet Firewalls*
D. Brent Chapman, Elizabeth D. Zwicky
O'Reilly, 1995, ISBN 1-56592-124-0

B *Computer Crime:*
A Crimefighter's Handbook
David Icove, et al
O'Reilly, 1995, ISBN 1-56592-086-4

B *Computer Security Basics*
Deborah Russell, G.T. Gangemi, Sr.
O'Reilly, 1991, ISBN 0-937175-71-4

B *Computers Under Attack:*
Intruders, Worms, and Viruses
Peter J. Denning, Ed.
Addison-Wesley, 1990, ISB650-0*ood Privacy*
Simson Garfinkel
O'Reilly, 1994, ISBN 1-56592-098-8

B   *Practical UNIX & Internet Security*, 2nd ed.
Simson Garfinkel, Gene Spafford
O'Reilly, 1996, ISBN 1-56592-148-8

B   *UNIX System Security*
David A. Curry
Addison-Wesley, 1992, ISBN 0-201-56327-4

System Administration

B   *Essential System Administration*, 2nd Ed.
Æleen Frisch
O'Reilly, 1995, ISBN 1-56592-127-5

B   *Linux - Installation and Beyond* (VHS video)
Yggdrasil
Yggdrasil, 1996, ISBN 1-883601-16-9

B   *System Performance Tuning*
Mike Loukides
O'Reilly, 1990, ISBN 0-937175-60-9

B   *UNIX System Administration Handbook*, 2nd Ed.
Evi Nemeth, et al
Prentice Hall, 1995, ISBN 0-13-151051-7

B   *When You Can't Find Your UNIX System Administrator*
Linda Mui
O'Reilly, 1995, ISBN 1-56592-104-6

B/C   *Linux Configuration and Installation*, 2nd Ed.
Patrick Volkerding, et al
MIS: Press, 1996, ISBN 1-55828-492-3

General

B   *A Quarter Century of UNIX*
Peter H. Salus
Addison-Wesley, 1994, ISBN 0-201-54777-5

B   *Berkeley Software Distribution* (set)
CSRG, UC Berkeley

USENIX and O'Reilly, 1994, ISBN 1-56592-082-1

B   *Harley Hahn's Student Guide to UNIX,* 2nd. Ed.
Harley Hahn
Osborne/MGH, 1996, ISBN 0-07-025492-3

B   *Learning the UNIX Operating System*
Grace Todino, et al
O'Reilly, 1993, ISBN 1-56592-060-0

B   *Linux (1)*
(Linux: Users Reference Manual)
John Purcell, Ed.
Just Computers!, 1995, ISBN 1-885329-07-5

B   *The Linux A-Z*
Phil Cornes
Prentice Hall, 1997, ISBN 0-13-234709-1

B   *The Linux Bible,* 4th ed.
Yggdrasil, 1996
ISBN 1-883601-20-7

B   *Linux Companion*
Mark F. Komarinski
Prentice Hall, 1996, ISBN 0-13-231838-5

B   *Linux Encyclopedia*
Trans-Ameritech

B   *Linux in a Nutshell*
Jessica Perry Hekman
O'Reilly, 1996, ISBN 1-56592-167-4

B   *Linux Installation & Getting Started*
Matt Welsh
SSC, 1995, ISBN 0-916151-77-8

B   *Linux Man:*
The Essential Man Pages for Linux
Linux Systems Labs, 199?, ISBN 1-885329-07-5

B   *Linux Multimedia Guide*
Jeff Tranter
O'Reilly, 1996, ISBN 1-56592-219-0

B   *The Linux Sampler*
Belinda Frazier, Editor
SSC, 1995, ISBN 0-916151-74-3

B   *Linux Universe*
Stefan Strobel, Thomas Uhl
Springer-Verlag, 1995, ISBN 0-387-94506-7

B   *The New Hacker's Dictionary*, 3rd. Ed.
Eric S. Raymond
MIT Press, 1996, ISBN 0-262-68092-0

B   *Proceedings of the First Conference on Freely Redistributable Software*
Free Software Foundation
FSF, 1996, ISBN 1-882114-47-7

B   *Running Linux*, 2nd ed.
Matt Welsh, Lar Kaufman
O'Reilly, 1996, ISBN 1-56592-151-8

B   *The UNIX Companion*
Harley Hahn
Osborne/MGH, 1995, ISBN 0-07-882149-5

B   *The UNIX Desk Reference:*
The hu.man Pages
Peter Dyson
Sybex, 1996, ISBN 0-7821-1658-2

B   *UNIX in a Nutshell:*
System V Edition, 2nd. ed.
Daniel Gilly, et al
O'Reilly, 1992, ISBN 1-56592-001-5

B   *The UNIX Programming Environment*
Brian W. Kernighan, Rob Pike
Prentice Hall, 1984, ISBN 0-13-937681-X

B/C   *The Complete Linux Kit,* 2nd ed.
Stefan Strobel, Thomas Uhl
Springer-Verlag, 1996, ISBN 0-387-14227-4

B/C   *The Complete Linux Kit*
Daniel A. Tauber
Sybex, 1995, ISBN 0-7821-1669-8

B/C   *Linux:*
The Complete Reference
Richard Peterson
Osborne, 1996, ISBN 0-07-882189-4

B/C   *Linux:*
The Complete Reference, 4th ed.
John Purcell and Amanda Robinson, Eds.
Linux Systems Labs, 1996, ISBN 1-885329-11-3

B/C   *Linux:*
Unleashing the Workstation in your PC, 2nd ed.
Stefan Strobel, Thomas Uhl
Springer-Verlag, 1996, ISBN 0-387-94601-2

B/C   *Linux Secrets*
Naba Barkakati
IDG Books, 1996, ISBN 1-56884-798-X

B/C   *Plug and Play Linux*
Yggdrasil

B/C   *Prime Time Freeware for UNIX*
Prime Time Freeware

B/C   *Red Hat Linux Unleashed*
Kamran Husain, et al
SAMS, 1996, ISBN 0-672-30962-9

B/C   *Running Linux Companion CD-ROM*
O'Reilly, Red Hat
O'Reilly, 1996, ISBN 1-56592-212-3

C   *Caldera Network Desktop*

Caldera

C   *Caldera Network Desktop Application Bundle*
Caldera

C   *Craftworks Linux*
Craftwork Solutions

C   *Linux Archive Monthly*
Pacific HiTech

C   *Linux Developer's Resource 6 CD Set*
InfoMagic

C   *Linux Games++*
Pacific HiTech

C   *Linux Hacker's 10*
Pacific HiTech

C   *Linux Internet Archives*
Yggdrasil

C   *Linux Quarterly CDROM*
Morse Telecommunication

C   *Linux Runtime System*
Pacific HiTech

C   *Linux Toolbox*
InfoMagic

C   *Linux-FT*
Lasermoon

C   *Linux-Ware*
Trans-Ameritech

C   *Red Hat Linux*
Red Hat Software

C   *Official Slackware*
Walnut Creek CDROM

C   *Turbo Linux*
         Pacific HiTech

C   *WGS Linux Pro*
         WorkGroup Solutions

F   MINI-LINUX (French)
         ftp://ftp.loria.fr/pub/linux/minilinux.fr/

P   *Linux Journal*

         Specialized Systems Consultants

P   *UNIX Review*

         http://www.unixreview.com/

         UNIX Review
         Miller Freeman
         411 Borel Ace., #100
         San Mateo, CA 94402 USA

         +1 800 829-5475 (US only)
         +1 904 445-4662
         +1 904 446-2774 (fax)

W   Debian Linux
         http://www.debian.org/

W   DLD - Deutsche Linux Distribution (German)
         http://www.delix.de/Linux/

W   GUUG (German UNIX User Group)
         http://www.guug.de/GUUG/

W   Hallow's Slackware 3.0 Upgrade Page
         http://www.cris.com/~hallow/linux/

W   International Linux Congress
         http://www.linux-kongress.de/

W   Linux Documentation Project
         http://sunsite.unc.edu/mdw/

W   Linux for PowerPC
           http://www.linuxppc.org/linuxppc/

W   Linux-FT
           http://ftp.lasermoon.co.uk/linux-ft/linux-ft.html

W   Linux Gazette
           http://www.redhat.com/lg/

W   Linux Information
           http://www.linux.org/

W   Linux Plug-and-Play Hardware Support
           http://www.redhat.com/pnp/

W   UK.LINUX.ORG
           http://www.linux.org.uk/

W   UniForum
           http://www.uniforum.org/

W   UnixWorld online
           http://www.wcmh.com/uworld/

W   USENIX
           http://www.usenix.org/

Internals

B   *Advanced Topics in UNIX:*
           Processes, Files, & Systems
           Ronald J. Leach
           Wiley, 1996, ISBN 1-57176-159-4

B   *The Design and Implementation of the 4.3BSD UNIX*
           Operating System
           Samuel J. Leffler, et al
           Addison-Wesley, 1989, ISBN 0-201-06196-1

B   *The Design and Implementation of the 4.3BSD UNIX*
           Operating System Answer Book
           Samuel J. Leffler, Marshall Kirk McKusick
           Addison-Wesley, 1991, ISBN 0-201-54629-9

B   *The Design and Implementation of the 4.4BSD UNIX*
Operating System
Marshall Kirk McKusick, et al
Addison-Wesley, 1996, ISBN 0-201-54979-4

B   *The Design of the UNIX Operating System*
Maurice J. Bach
Prentice Hall, 1986, ISBN 0-13-201799-7

B   *Inside Linux:*
A Look at Operating System Development
Randolph Bentson
SSC, 1996, ISBN 0-916151-89-1

B   *Lions' Commentary on UNIX 6th Edition with Source Code*
John Lions
Peer-to-Peer, 1996, ISBN 1-57398-013-7

B   *UNIX Internals:*
The New Frontiers
Uresh Vahalia
Prentice-Hall, 1995, ISBN 0-13-101908-2

B   *UNIX Systems for Modern Architectures:*
Symmetric Multiprocessing and Caching for Kernel
Programmers
Curt Schimmel
Addison-Wesley, 1994, ISBN 0-201-63338-8

B/C   *Linux Kernel Internals*
Michael Beck, et al
Addison-Wesley, 1996, ISBN 0-201-87741-4

B/C   *Panic!:*
UNIX System Crash Dump Analysis
Chris Drake, Kimberly Brown
Prentice Hall, 1995, ISBN 0-13-149386-8

Programming

B   *Applying RCS and SCCS:*
From Source Control to Project Control

Don Bolinger, Tan Bronson
O'Reilly, 1995, ISBN 1-56592-117-8

B   *The Bison Manual:*
Using the YACC-compatible Parser Generator, for Version 1.25
Chris Donnelly, Richard Stallman
FSF, 1993, ISBN 1-882114-45-0

B   *The C Programming Language,* 2nd Ed.
Brian W. Kernighan, Dennis M. Ritchie
Prentice Hall, 1988, ISBN 0-13-110362-8

B   *C*
A Reference Manual, 4th Ed.
Samuel P. Harbison, Guy L. Steele
Prentice Hall, 1995, ISBN 0-13-326224-3

B   *CGI Programming in C & Perl*
Thomas Boutell
Addison-Wesley, 1996, ISBN 0-201-42219-0

B   *Debugging with GDBVersion 4.16*
Richard Stallman, Cygnus Support
FSF, 1996, ISBN 1-882114-09-4

B   *Exploring Expect:*
A Tcl-based Toolkit for Automating Interactive Programs
Don Libes
O'Reilly, 1994, ISBN 1-56592-090-2

B   *Flex:*
The Lexical Scanner Generator, Version 2.3.7
G. T. Nicol
FSF, 1993, ISBN 1-882114-21-3

B   *The GNU C Library Reference Manual for Version 1.09*
Sandra Loosemore, et al
FSF, 1996, ISBN 1-882114-53-1

B   *GNU Make, Version 3.75 Beta*
Richard Stallman, Roland McGrath
FSF, 1996, ISBN 1-882114-79-5

B   *Learning Perl*
             Randal L. Schwartz
             O'Reilly, 1993, ISBN 1-56592-042-2

B   *Mastering Regular Expressions*
             Jeffrey E. F. Friedl
             O'Reilly, 1997, ISBN 1-56592-257-3

B   *Perl 5 Desktop Reference*
             Johan Vromans
             O'Reilly, 1996, ISBN 1-56592-187-9

B   *Porting UNIX Software:*
             From Download to Debug
             Greg Lehey
             O'Reilly, 1995, ISBN 1-56592-126-7

B   *Programming perl,* 2nd Ed.
             Larry Wall, et al
             O'Reilly, 1996, ISBN 1-56592-149-6

B   *sed & awk*
             Dale Dougherty
             O'Reilly, 1990, ISBN 0-937175-59-5

B   *Software Portability with imake,* 2nd Ed.
             Paul DuBois
             O'Reilly, 1996, ISBN 1-56592-226-3

B   *The Standard C Library*
             P.J. Plauger
             Prentice Hall, 1992, ISBN 0-13-131509-9

B   *termcap & terminfo*
             John Strang, et al
             O'Reilly, 1988, ISBN 0-937175-22-6

B   *The Termcap Manual:*
             The Termcap Library and Data Base
             Richard Stallman
             FSF, 1996, ISBN 1-882114-87-6

B   *Using and Porting GNU CC for Version 2.7.2*
Richard Stallman
FSF, 1996, ISBN 1-882114-36-1

P   *The Perl Journal*

http://work.media.mit.edu/tpj/
perl-journal-subscriptions@perl.com

The Perl Journal
P.O. Box 54
Boston, MA 02101 USA

W   Comprehensive Perl Archive Network (CPAN)
http://www.perl.com/

W   The Perl Institute
http://www.perl.org/

The Perl Institute
2850 SW Cedar Hills Blvd., #62
Beaverton, OR 97005-1354 USA

Utilities

B   *Calc Manual:*
GNU Emacs Calc Version 2.02
Dave Gillespie
FSF, 1992, ISBN 1-882114-18-3

B   *The GNU Awk User's Guide*
Arnold Robbins
FSF, 1996, ISBN 1-882114-26-4

B   *GNU Emacs Lisp Reference Manual for Emacs Version*
19.29
Bil Lewis, et al
FSF, 1995, ISBN 1-882114-71-X

B   *GNU Emacs Manual for Version 19.33*
Richard Stallman
FSF, 1996, ISBN 1-882114-05-1

B   *Learning the bash Shell*
Cameron Newham, Bill Rosenblatt
O'Reilly, 1995, ISBN 1-56592-147-X

B   *Learning GNU Emacs*, 2nd ed.
Debra Cameron, et al
O'Reilly, 1996, ISBN 1-56592-152-6

B   *Learning the Korn Shell*
Bill Rosenblatt
O'Reilly, 1993, ISBN 1-56592-054-6

B   *Learning the vi Editor*
Linda Lamb
O'Reilly, 1990, ISBN 0-937175-67-6

B   *Making TeX Work*
Norman Walsh
O'Reilly, 1994, ISBN 1-56592-051-1

B   *MH & xmh:*
Email for Users & Programmers
Jerry Peek
O'Reilly, 1995, ISBN 1-56592-093-7

B   *Programming in Emacs Lisp:*
An Introduction
Robert Chassell
FSF, 1995, ISBN 1-882114-41-8

B   *Texinfo:*
The GNU Documentation Format
Robert Chassell, Richard Stallman
FSF, 1995, ISBN 1-882114-63-9

B   *UNIX Power Tools*
Jerry Peek, et al.
O'Reilly, 1993, ISBN 0-553-33402-2

B   *Using csh and tcsh*
Paul DuBois
O'Reilly, 1995, ISBN 1-56592-132-1

Mach

B *Advanced Computer Architecture:*
Parallelism, Scalability, Programmability
Kai Hwang
McGraw-Hill, 1993, ISBN 0-07-031622-8

B *CMU Computer Science:*
A 25th Aniversary Commemorative
Richard F. Rashid, Ed.
ACM Press, 1991, ISBN 0-201-52899-1

B *Concurrent Systems:*
An Integrated Approach to Operating Systems, Database, and
Distributed Systems
Jean Bacon
Addison-Wesley, 1993, ISBN 0-201-41677-8

B *The Design of OS/2*, 2nd Ed.
Michael S. Kogan, Harvey M. Deitel
Addison-Wesley, 1995, ISBN 0-201-52886-X

B *Distributed Operating Systems*
Andrew S. Tanenbaum
Prentice Hall, 1995, ISBN 0-13-219908-4

B *Distributed Operating Systems:*
The Logical Design
A. Goscinski
Addison-Wesley, 1991, ISBN 0-201-41704-9

B *Distributed Systems, Concepts, and Designs*
G. Coulouris, et al
Addison-Wesley, 1994, ISBN 0-201-62433-8

B *Load Distribution:*
the Implementation of the Mach Microkernal
Dejan S. Milojicic
Vieweg, 1994, ISBN 3-528-05424-7

B *Mach:*

Konzepte und Programmierung
Christoph Zimmermann, Albrecht W. Kraas
Springer-Verlag, 1993 (in German)

B *Operating System Concepts,* 4th Ed.
Abraham Silberschatz, Peter Galvin
Addison-Wesley, 1994, ISBN 0-201-50480-4

B *Programming under Mach*
Boykin, et al
Addison-Wesley, 1993, ISBN 0-201-52739-1

B Mach Workshop and Symposium Proceedings
USENIX

   Mach Workshop Proceedings
   USENIX, October 1990, no ISBN

   Mach Symposium Proceedings
   USENIX, November 1991, no ISBN

   Mach III Symposium Proceedings
   USENIX, April 1993, ISBN 1-880446-49-9

B Mach 3 Documentation Series
Open Group Research Institute (RI)

   Final Draft Specifications OSF/1 1.3 Engineering Release
   RI, May 1993

   OSF Mach Final Draft Kernel Principles
   RI, May 1993

   OSF Mach Final Draft Kernel Interfaces
   RI, May 1993

   OSF Mach Final Draft Server Writer's Guide
   RI, May 1993

   OSF Mach Final Draft Server Library Interfaces
   RI, May 1993

B MK++ Kernel Series

Open Group Research Institute (RI)

MK++ Kernel Executive Summary
RI, May 1995

MK++ Kernel High Level Design
RI, July 1995

MK++ Kernel Interface
RI, May 1995

B   Research Institute Microkernel Series
Open Group Research Institute (RI)

Operating Systems Collected Papers, Volume I
RI, March 1993

Operating Systems Collected Papers, Volume II
RI, October 1993

Operating Systems Collected Papers, Volume III
RI, April 1994

Operating Systems Collected Papers, Volume IV
RI, October 1995

F   Papers included with the Mach 3.0 distribution
ftp://riftp.osf.org/pub/snapshot/osfmach3/

mk_papers (1.4 MB, PostScript)

Mach Scheduling Framework

Microkernel Modularity with Integrated Kernel Performance

New Synchronization Services for OSF Mach: Synchronizers

NORMA IPC Version Two: Architecture and Design

OSF Microkernel Performance Suite (MKPS)

OSF-RI MK6.1 Real-Time Threads Library: Rthreads Interface Guide

Real-Time Local and Remote MACH IPC: Architecture and Design

RPC Design for Real-Time Mach

release_notes/ (0.4 MB, PostScript)

OSF-RI Unencumbered Mach Microkernel: Release Notes

spec93/ (5.6 MB, PostScript)

OSF Mach (Approved) Kernel Interfaces

OSF Mach (Approved) Kernel Principles

OSF Mach (Approved) Server Writer's Guide

OSF Mach (Approved) Server Library Functions

asst. kernel interface papers

W   Open Group Research Institute
http://www.osf.org/RI/

X Window System

B   *The X Window System in a Nutshell*
Ellie Cutler, et al
O'Reilly, 1992, ISBN 1-56592-017-1

B/C   *X User Tools*
Linda Mui, Valerie Quercia
O'Reilly, 1994, ISBN 0-56592-019-8

P   *The X Journal*

The X Journal
P.O. Box 5050
Brentwood, TN 37024-5050 USA

+1 800 361-1279 (USA only)
+1 615 370-4845 (USA fax)

+44(0) 1858 435 302
+44(0) 1858 434 958 (fax)

W   X Consortium
ftp://ftp.x.org/
http://www.x.org/

Chapter 20:
Contact Information

Addison-Wesley

Addison-Wesley
Route 128
Reading, MA 01867
USA

http://www.aw.com/
+1 800 822-6339 (USA only)
+1 617 944-3700

Apple Computer

Apple Computer, Inc.
1 Infinite Loop
Cupertino, CA 95014
USA

http://www.apple.com/
+1 408 996-1010

Caldera

Caldera, Inc.
633 South 550 East
Provo, UT 84606
USA

info@caldera.com
http://www.caldera.com/
+1 800 850-7779 (USA only)
+1 801 377-7687
+1 801 377-8752 Fax

Cambridge

Cambridge University Press
40 West 20th Street
New York, NY 10011-4211
USA

information@cup.org
http://www.cup.org/
+1 212 924-3900
+1 212 691-3239 Fax

Coriolis

Coriolis Group Books
7339 E. Acoma Dr., #7
Scottsdale, AZ 85260
USA

http://www.coriolis.com/
+1 800 410-0192 (USA only)
+1 602 483-0192

Craftwork Solutions

Craftwork Solutions, Inc.
4320 Stevens Creek Blvd., #170
San Jose, CA 95129
USA

support@craftwork.com
info@craftwork.com
http://craftwork.com/
+1 408 985-1878
+1 408 985-1880 Fax

Free Software Foundation

See GNU Project

GNU Project

The GNU Project
59 Temple Place, Suite 330
Boston, MA 02111-1307
USA

gnu@prep.ai.mit.edu
ftp://prep.ai.mit.edu/pub/gnu/
http://www.gnu.ai.mit.edu/
+1 617 542-5942
+1 617 542-2652 Fax

IBM Microelectronics

USA:

IBM Microelectronics
Mail Stop A25/862-1
PowerPC Marketing
1000 River Street
Essex Junction, VT 05452-4299
USA

http://www.ibm.com/
+1 800 769-3772
+1 800 769-3732 Fax

Europe:

IBM Microelectronics
PowerPC Marketing
Department 1045
224 Boulevard J. F. Kennedy
91105 Corbeil-Essonnes CEDEX
France

(33) 1-60-88 4920

Japan:

IBM Microelectronics

(81) 775-87-4745

PowerPC Marketing
Department R0260
800 Ichimiyake
Yasu-cho, Yasu-gun
Shinga-ken
Japan 520-23

(81) 775-87-4735 Fax

IDG Books

IDG Books Worldwide, Inc.
919 E. Hillsdale Blvd., Suite 400
Foster City, CA 94404
USA

feedback@www.idgbooks.com
http://www.idgbooks.com/
+1 800 762-2974 (USA only)
+1 415 655-3000

InfoMagic

InfoMagic
11950 N. Hwy. 89
Flagstaff, AZ 86004
USA

info@infomagic.com
http://www.infomagic.com/
+1 800 800-6613 (USA/Canada)
+1 520 526-9565
+1 520 526-9573 Fax

International Data Group

See IDG Books

John Wiley & Sons

See Wiley

Just Computers!

Just Computers!
607 Martin Ave., Suite 100A
Rohnert Park, CA 94928
USA

sales@justcomp.com
http://www.justcomp.com/
+1 707 586-5600
+1 707 586-5606 Fax

Lasermoon

Lasermoon Ltd.
The Forge, Fareham Road,
Wickham, Hants. PO17 5DE,

info@lasermoon.co.uk
ftp://ftp.lasermoon.co.uk/
http://ftp.lasermoon.co.uk/

England

+44 (0) 1329 834944
+44 (0) 1329 834955 Fax

Linux International

Linux International
Patrick D'Cruze, Secretary
P.O. Box 80
Hamilton Hill, WA
Australia, 6163

li@li.org
http://www.li.org/

Linux Systems Labs

Linux Systems Labs
615 N. Campbell
Royal Oak, MI 48067-2122
USA

sales@lsl.com
http://www.lsl.com/
+1 800 954-2829 (USA only)
+1 810 716-1700
+1 810 399-5354 Fax

MIS Press

MIS Press
115 West 18th Street
New York, NY 10011
USA

misspress@interport.com
http://www.mispress.com/

MIT Press

MIT Press
55 Hayward Street
Cambridge, MA 02142
USA

mitpress-orders@mit.edu
http://mitpress.mit.edu/
+1 800 356-0343 (USA only)
+1 617 625-8569

Morgan Kaufman

Morgan Kaufmann Publishers Inc.
340 Pine St, 6th floor
San Francisco, CA 94104
USA

orders@mkp.com
http://www.mkp.com/
+1 415 392-2665
+1 415 982-2665 Fax

Morse Telecommunication

Morse Telecommunication

info@morse.net

26 East Park Avenue, #240   http://www.morse.net/
Long Beach, NY 11561   +1 800 GO MORSE (USA only)
USA   +1 516 889-9500
                                   +1 516 889-9665 Fax

Motorola

USA:

Motorola Literature Distribution   http://www.mot.com/
P.O. Box 20912
Phoenix, AZ 85036
USA

Europe:

Motorola Ltd.
European Literature Center
88 Tanners Drive
Blakelands
Milton Keynes
MK14 5BP, England

Japan:

Nippon Motorola Ltd.
4-32-1, Nishi-Gotanda
Shinagawa-ku
Tokyo 141, Japan

Asia-Pacific:

Motorola Semiconductors H.K. Ltd.
Silicon Harbour Centre
No. 2 Dai King Street
Tai Po Industrial Estate
Tai Po, N.T., Hong Kong

New Riders

New Riders Publishing   info@mcp.com
201 West 103rd St.   http://www.mcp.com/newriders/

Indianapolis, IN 46290
USA

O'Reilly

O'Reilly & Associates
103A Morris Street
Sebastopol, CA 95472
USA

nuts@ora.com
ftp://ftp.ora.com/
http://www.ora.com/
+1 800 998-9938 (USA only)
+1 707 829-0515
+1 707 829-0104 Fax

The Open Group Research Institute

The Open Group
11 Cambridge Center
Cambridge, MA 02142
USA

ftp://riftp.osf.org/
http://www.osf.org/
http://www.osf.org/RI/
+1 617 621-8700

Osborne/McGraw-Hill

Osborne/McGraw-Hill
2600 Tenth Street, Sixth Floor
Berkeley, CA 94710
USA

http://www.osborne.com/
+1 800 227-0900

Pacific HiTech

Pacific HiTech
3855 South 500 West, Suite M
Salt Lake City, UT 84115
USA

http://www.pht.com/
+1 801 261-1024
+1 801 261-0310 Fax

Peer-to-Peer

Peer-to-Peer Communications, Inc.
P.O. Box 640218
San Jose, CA 95164-0218
USA

info@peer-to-peer.com
http://www.peer-to-peer.com/
+1 408 435-2677
+1 408 435-0895 Fax

Prentice Hall

Prentice Hall

orders@prenhall.com

113 Sylvan Avenue, Rt. 9W
Englewood Cliffs, NJ 07632
USA

http://www.prenhall.com/
+1 800 947-7700 (USA only)
+1 201 592-2000

Prime Time Freeware

Prime Time Freeware
370 Altair Way, Suite 150
Sunnyvale, CA 94086
USA

info@ptf.com
http://www.ptf.com/
+1 408 433-9662
+1 408 433-0727 Fax

QUE

QUE Corporation
11711 N. College Ave.
Carmel, IN 46032
USA

info@mcp.com
http://www.mcp.com/que/
+1 317 573-2500
+1 800 428-5331
+1 317 573-2583 Fax

Red Hat Software

Red Hat Software
P.O. Box 4325
Chapel Hill, NC 27515
USA

info@redhat.com
ftp://ftp.redhat.com/
http://www.redhat.com/
+1 919 309-9560

SAMS

Sams Publishing
201 West 103rd St.
Indianapolis, IN 46290
USA

info@mcp.com
http://www.mcp.com/sams/
+1 317 573-2500
+1 800 428-5331
+1 317 573-2583 Fax

Specialized Systems Consultants

See SSC

Springer-Verlag

Springer-Verlag
175 5th Avenue
Attn: Computer Science

custserv@spint.compuserve.com
http://www.springer.de/
+1 800 SPRINGER (USA only)

New York, NY 10010
USA

SSC

SSC, Inc.
P.O. Box 55549
Seattle, WA 98155
USA

sales@ssc.com
http://www.ssc.com/
+1 206 782-7733
+1 206 782-7191 Fax

Sybex

Sybex, Inc.
1151 Marina Village Parkway
Alameda, CA 94501
USA

info@sybex.com
http://www.sybex.com/
+1 510 523-8233
+1 510 523-6840 Fax

Texas Instruments

TI Product Information Center
Texas Instruments
8505 Forest Lane, MS 8671
Dallas, TX 75243
USA

2pic@ti.com
http://www.ti.com/
+1 972 644-5500

Trans-Ameritech

Trans-Ameritech Systems, Inc.
2342A Walsh Avenue
Santa Clara, CA 95051
USA

info@trans-am.com
http://www2.zoom.com/tae/
+1 408 727-3883
+1 408 727-3882 Fax

USENIX

The USENIX Association
2560 Ninth Street, Suite 215
Berkeley, CA 94710
USA

office@usenix.org
http://www.usenix.org/
+1 510 528-8649
+1 510 548-5738 Fax

Vieweg

Vieweg Publishing
P.O. Box 58 29

(06 11) 16 02 18
(06 11) 16 02 26 Fax

D-65048 Wiesbaden
Germany

Walnut Creek CDROM

Walnut Creek CDROM   orders@cdrom.com
4041 Pike Lane, Suite D   ftp://ftp.cdrom.com/
Concord, CA 94520   http://www.cdrom.com/
USA   +1 800 786-9907 (USA only)
                                      +1 510 674-0821 Fax

Wiley

John Wiley & Sons, Inc.   info@qm.jwiley.com
605 Third Ave.   http://www.wiley.com/
New York, NY 10158-0012   +1 212 850-6000
USA   +1 212 850-6088 Fax

WorkGroup Solutions

USA:

> WorkGroup Solutions, Inc.   wgs@gcs.com
> P.O. Box 460190   ftp://ftp.wgs.com/pub2/wgs/
> Aurora, CO 80046-0190   http://www.wgs.com/
> USA   +1 303 699-7470
>   +1 303 699-2793 Fax

Outside of the USA:

> MULTiSOFT Datentechnik GmbH   +49 89 641-7904
> Postfach 312   +49 89 641-2794 Fax
> 82827 Gruenwald/Munich
> Germany

Yggdrasil

Yggdrasil Computing   info@yggdrasil.com
4880 Stevens Creek Blvd., Suite 205   http://www.yggdrasil.com/
San Jose, CA 95129-1024   +1 800 261-6630 (USA only)
USA   +1 408 261-6630
                                      +1 408 261-6631 Fax

Ziff-Davis

Ziff-Davis Press
5903 Christie Ave.
Emeryville, CA 94608
USA

info@mcp.com
http://www.mcp.com/zdpress/
+1 800 688-0448 (USA only)

Index

Fan Mail...

Authors And Vendors:

A powerful demonstration of Linux portability.

Adam Richter, President
Yggdrasil, USA

It is a pleasant surprise to see Apple support the creation of a free operating system for the Macintosh – especially when it is a Mach- and Linux-based version of the GNU system. The only disappointment is that it is accompanied by some proprietary software and documentation. That means there is still work for you to do!

Richard Stallman, Chief GNUisance
The GNU Project
(Author of GCC, GNU Emacs, ...)

Linux has been successful both as a cultural phenomenon and as a technical design. MkLinux demonstrates yet again the strength of the Linux design and the power of the Linux phenomenon. I look forward to the innovations it enables for PowerPC-based personal computers.

Michael Tiemann, Co-founder
Cygnus Support, USA
(Author of GNU C++)

Commercial Users:

Now the two most powerful operating systems can be run on the same machine!

Gordon Bailey, Sales
FlashNet Communications, USA

MkLinux: Linux for the rest of us!

Matt Brincho, Software Engineer
Molecular Simulations, USA

I laughed, I cried, my nerd quotient rose 20 points.

David Emery, Webmaster
Macgallery Japan, Japan

MkLinux is faster and more robust than any of those emulated UNIX evironments we've tried!

Dave Johnson, System Administrator
Wind River Systems, USA

Learned so much with it that we'll be operating a Web Server in a few weeks.

Philippe Laliberté, Tech. Director
Oeil Scénique, Canada

Not since the day I got my first Mac, back in 1985, have I stayed up so long into the wee hours, playing, marveling at the wonders hidden within my computer. Hurrah to the OSF and to Apple for this admirable effort.

Max Newell, Principal
Kafka Design, USA

Yow! A workstation on *my* desktop!

Tim Voght, President
Voght Systems, USA